Deaths
Internation

Deaths in Custody:
International Perspectives

Edited by

Alison Liebling and Tony Ward

Whiting & Birch Ltd

MCMXCIV

Published on behalf of the Institute for the Study and Treatment of Delinquency by Whiting & Birch Ltd, PO Box 872, Forest Hill, London SE23 3HL, England.
USA: Paul & Co, Publishers' Consortium Inc, PO Box 442, Concord, MA 01742.

British Library Cataloguing in Publication Data.
A CIP catalogue record is available from the British Library

ISBN 1 871177 55 3 (cased)
ISBN 1 871177 42 1 (limp)

Printed by Bourne Press, Bournemouth, England

Deaths in Custody: International Perspectives

Contents

Foreword

People celebrate anniversaries in different ways. These papers record the Diamond Jubilee of the Institute for the Study and Treatment of Delinquency: an international conference on Deaths in Custody. As David Biles reminds us, the subject is a large one, including consideration of 'all cases where a person dies, of whatever cause, while in the custody of police or prison authorities, whether that custody is lawful or not, regardless of the actual location of the death'. Judicial hanging is omitted, but the subject remains considerably wider than suicide alone, although prison suicide sadly remains memorably with us.

The valuable learning on this under-researched subject emerges in contributions from Australia, Canada, the USA, Ireland, Holland and Switzerland, and even in a measure from England. It can be fairly stated to be a real indication of current knowledge. Reading the edited papers now makes me very much aware of the presumption of the *Review of Suicide and Self Help in Prison Service Establishments in England and Wales* prepared by the Inspectorate of Prisons in 1990, and published shortly before the Woolf Report. It was a very ambitious review. We set out over a hundred recommendations, mostly modest but some fairly extensive, designed to lower anxiety in prison, in particular for young inmates without much experience of custody. We compared, under the direction of Dr Malcolm Faulk, psychiatric care in prison with care in the National Health Service. We criticised the lack of occupation and lack of purpose which we found to be associated with self-harm in many establishments. Above all we said that suicide prevention should not be considered an issue solely for doctors: staff, fellow inmates, visitors and prison workers should all be required to respond.

The excellent White Paper of 1991, *Custody Care and Justice*, largely supported us, and I hope that the merits and also the failures of our *Review* spurred on the writing of papers, which you are now about to read. I hope that reading may be followed by a second conference, so that increasing knowledge of what, I repeat, is an under-researched subject, may at least be spread internationally.

His Honour Judge Stephen Tumim
HM Chief Inspector of Prisons

ACKNOWLEDGMENTS

We would like to thank Martin Farrell and Julia Braggins of ISTD. John Freeman, who chaired this conference, did not live to see the published outcome of his tremendously hard work. He was delighted to hear that publication arrangements were underway before his sudden illness in 1991.

One of the most important contributions to the conference could never be adequately reproduced in print. David and Margaret Mills and Doreen and Bill Hook courageously shared with us their experiences in the aftermath of their sons' deaths in prison.

We would like to thank David Neal, John Ditchfield and others in prison service headquarters and the research and planning unit, who gave us their support and have worked so hard in recent years to translate research and commentary into policy and practice.

Special thanks go to Maureen Brown, at the Cambridge Institute of Criminology, for patient secretarial assistance.

Finally, we would like to thank all the contributors, conference attenders and others who have waited patiently for this volume to make headway against a tide of other pressing commitments. We hope that it is still of sufficient interest and relevance to encourage a next conference on the same theme in the near future.

Introduction

Alison Liebling and Tony Ward

Deaths in custody remain one of the most urgent yet poorly researched and documented issues in criminology, sociology and the public and policy arena. Internationally, increasing concern about suicides in prison, about the future of prison health care, and about conditions and treatment in custody have resulted in many recent changes in practice, high profile pressure group action and modifications in our understanding of the nature of imprisonment. Despite this interest, few books exist on the topic (see Institute of Race Relations, 1991; Scraton and Chadwick, 1987; Hogan et al., 1988; Benn and Walpole, 1986).

This edited collection of papers brings together selected contributions to an International Conference held at Canterbury in celebration of the 60th Anniversary of the Institute for the Study and Treatment of Delinquency. The Conference was the first of its kind, aiming to bring together academic experts, practitioners and volunteer organisations from all over the world, to develop a greater practical and theoretical understanding of this field. The book organises some of the best contributions to this conference into themes, providing the first comprehensive and international overview of the nature and extent of the problem, outlining several issues of particular concern, and illustrating management and prevention techniques found to be successful in North America, Australia and in Europe. Inevitably in such a collection there are omissions. Amongst the most significant are contributions from the Samaritans, who have played such a major role in the development of suicide awareness and the provision of support

1

for prisoners. Also omitted are the questions and discussions which took place most profitably throughout the conference. These discussions included valuable contributions from countries not represented amongst the formal papers, such as Nigeria. We learned a great deal from these informal discussions and found the exchanges between countries most stimulating. We also benefitted from the contributions made by presence of the many practitioners who were not presenting formal papers: police, prison governors and officers, who so often feel on the receiving end of ill-informed and emotive criticism. That these differences were aired at all was an important first step in the resolution of some of the most crucial of these differences.

The contributors to this book examine deaths in custody from a wide range of perspectives – from those of critical campaigners (Chs.7, 9 and 10) to those of prison doctors (Ch.3). The competition between medical, political administrative and sociological knowledges reflected in the book is a relatively recent and, in our view, healthy development. The aim of this introduction is to set that development in its historical, political and theoretical contexts.

If deaths in custody have been politicised in recent years to an extent which some may find alarming, this situation is not without historical precedent. For a period in the mid-19th century, deaths in prisons, workhouses and other custodial institutions were a source of intense controversy - often fanned by a small band of populist coroners (Anderson, 1987) such as Thomas Wakley, radical MP, surgeon and founder of the Lancet (Sim and Ward, forthcoming). The bland verdicts of death by the visitation of God which standard in the eighteenth century (Forbes, 1977, 1978), gave way in some cases to verdicts by which the coroners' juries linked deaths in custody to specific aspects of institutional regimes, such as inadequate or punitive diets (Sim, 1990, pp.46-47). One notorious suicide, that of Edward Andrews in Birmingham Prison in 1851, led to the governor himself being jailed for three months for assault (Hill, 1857, p.232).

Not only deaths in custody, but deaths in general, took on heightened political significance in the early Victorian period. For statisticians like William Farr, the mortality statistics (which he compiled on behalf of the Registrar-General) were an index of the moral as well as physical health of the nation

(Cullen, 1975; Eyler, 1975). As Lindsay Prior observes, 'there are good grounds for believing that death in the 19th century was perceived rather as a social disease than as an isolated physiological event and that Victorian medicine attempted to develop a political economy of death rather than an anatomy of disease' (Prior, 1989, p.45).

Prior argues that modern medical and legal discourses about death are characterised by a 'suppression of social action and social structure, epitomised by the narrowing of the range of causes deemed relevant by coroners and their avoidance of questions of blame and liability' (Prior, 1989; see also Scraton and Chadwick, 1987, pp.34-40). Death has been medicalised and medicine has been individualised. One major exception would appear to be the vast sociological literature on suicide (McIntosh, 1985). True, however, to its origins in moral statistics (Hacking, 1990), the sociological study of suicide has remained largely a study of suicide rates; at first as a basis for the aetiological analysis (Durkheim, 1952), and more recently as social constructs which reveal more about the meaning of deaths to others than about the deaths themselves (Douglas, 1967; Atkinson, 1978).

Durkheim's *Suicide* (1952, first published 1897) includes a very brief discussion of suicide in prison (p.346). Durkheim claims that imprisonment in itself develops a very strong tendency to suicide, which he suggests arises partly from cell life and partly from 'the community-life of the prison ... The society of evil-doers and prisoners is known to be very coherent; the individual disappears completely and prison discipline has the same effacing tendency'. In this respect the suicides of prisoners are analogous to those of soldiers, which Durkheim treats as a rare example in modern western societies of altruistic suicide resulting from excessive social integration (pp.228-239). Had Durkheim further explored the significance of cell life and prison discipline he might have concluded that some prison suicides fell into the even rarer category of fatalism: 'suicides attributable to excessive physical or moral despotism ... the ineluctable and inflexible nature of a rule against which there is no appeal (p.276) - a description which perfectly fits some of the Victorian examples described by Priestly (1985, pp.180-184). Despite their superficiality, Durkheim's remarks foreshadow two of the main themes of the twentieth-century sociology of prisons: the total institution's (Goffman, 1961) assault on the inmate's sense of self, and the sometimes oppressive solidarity of the inmate subculture (Clemmer, 1940; Sykes, 1957). The relationship between the sociology of suicide and of total institutions has hitherto been little explored (but see Chs.6 and 7).

Sociological studies by Douglas (1967), Atkinson (1982) and Taylor (1982) produced a new sociology of suicide based on a critique of official statistics. These studies were not taken up by those interested in prison suicides, nor did they penetrate medico-psychiatric approaches to suicide research continuing both inside and out of prisons. Somehow prison suicide research has remained insulated from sociological critiques but has proceeded largely undisturbed by questions of definition, validity, comparability or reliability. It was not just the question of (prison) suicide rates which remained insulated from such probing. The equally significant problem of explanation was unhampered by sociological study. Inquests tended to 'produce' the sort of knowledge about suicide that coroners, other officials and families 'looked for'. Explanation focused on individuals and individual pathology rather than upon social institutions, despite Durkheim's pronouncements in sociology that:

Society, the collective experience of humanity, 'lives in' the subjective experience of individuals (Taylor, on Durkheim, 1982, p.18).

Both the epidemiological study of suicide rates and the psychiatric study of individual pathology have contributed to what Jack (1992) calls the *neglect of meaning* in suicide research. As Taylor argued, fact-gathering is not the same as knowledge-gathering. The empirical world may be directly observable but these 'facts' do not in themselves constitute explanation ('interpretative empiricism'). This type of understanding should be supplemented by a more refined ('verstehen') form of explanation, with figures as a cautious guide. The gap between these medical and sociological approaches has only very recently begun to close (see the excellent treatment of this failure of sociology to 'take root' in England and Wales, thus leaving the suicide field freely the preserve of clinical studies by medical men, in Anderson, 1987). Our combination of speakers sought to contribute to the opening of such a dialogue.

So far as deaths in custody are concerned, the medical

approach has predominated until recently. The major source of information for such studies (Topp, 1979, Dooley, 1990) has been the inmates' prison files, and much of the research has been done by prison medical officers and others associated with prison administration. As Jean-Claude Bernheim's review of French and Canadian literature (Ch.7) shows, the dominance of prison suicide research by prison medicine is by no means confined to Britain.

Deaths in psychiatric hospitals have similarly been studied mainly from a psychiatric perspective - although psychiatrists are not necessarily blind to the social processes occurring with institutions (see Kobler and Stotland, 1964). (One notable study which adopts a different perspective is Reynolds and Farberow, 1976). Deaths in police custody have only recently become a subject for sociological attention (Box, 1983; Warwick Inquest Group, 1985; Scraton and Chadwick, 1986, 1987; Biles, this volume), although a number of North American scholars have addressed the issue of fatal police shootings (e.g. Takagi, 1974; Sherman and Langworthy, 1979; Chappell and Graham, 1985).

THE RE-POLITICISATION OF DEATHS IN CUSTODY

It was the academically neglected topic of deaths in police custody, and other deaths connected with policing, that was at the forefront of political controversy in the late 1970s and early 1980s. The cases of Liddle Towers (1978), Jimmy Kelly (1979), Blair Peach (1979), Winston Rose (1981), Colin Roach (1983) and James Davey (1983) - to name only the most publicised - have been well documented elsewhere (Benn and Worpole, 1986; Scraton and Chadwick, 1987; Independent Committee of Inquiry, 1988), as have the deaths in prison in the same period (Coggan and Walker, 1982). The concern felt in some quarters about these cases was a product not only of their individual circumstances but of a sense that they were symptomatic of an ominous drift towards a more coercive form of state control (Hall et al., 1978; Benn and Worpole, 1986).

Political concern about the cases of Peach, Kelly and others led to the publication in 1980 of the first statistics on deaths in police custody. The figures appeared to show a sharply rising rate of deaths throughout the 1970s, and a disproportionate number of deaths in the Metropolitan Police District

(INQUEST, 1983). Though it remains unclear how far these phenomena were the product of inconsistent recording practices (INQUEST, 1989), they did nothing to allay the anxieties of those who feared that the police in general, and the Met. in particular, were increasingly out of control (Bundred, 1982, pp.63-64). The Select Committee on Home Affairs published a report on Deaths in Police Custody (House of Commons, 1980). While declining to look at individual cases and dismissing generalised allegations of police brutality (para.289), which none of its witnesses had made, the report usefully drew attention to the plight of those arrested from drunkenness, who continue to make a major contribution to deaths in police cells (Schmidt, 1989).

The organisation INQUEST, launched in 1981, grew out of a number of campaigns about individual causes célèbres, including those of Towers, Peach and Kelly and the prison deaths of Barry Prosser and Richard Cartoon Campbell. It originated largely as a left-wing response to the perceived growth of state violence, but also drew on a tradition of campaigning about standards of medical care in prisons, originating in the Prison Medical Reform council of the 1960s and continued by RAP (Radical Alternatives to Prison) and PROP, the National Prisoners' Movement (Ryan, 1977; Fitzgerald, 1977). With funding from the Greater London Council, INQUEST was able to observe coroners' inquests and advise bereaved relatives in a wide range of cases. One consequence was that an increasing proportion of its energies were drawn into dealing with comparatively routine custodial deaths which had previously aroused relatively little public concern, including prison suicides and the accidental or natural deaths of alleged drunkenness offenders whose need for medical treatment was overlooked (Benn and Worpole, 1986, pp.19-35, 78-94). As its interests broadened, its political stance became harder to define. A worker for the organisation - which Tony Ward was from 1982 to 1990 - could spend the morning sitting alongside representative of the Police Federation to plan the next move in the campaign for better provisions for drunkenness offenders, and the evening marching in protest at the latest controversial death in an inner-city police station.

Some of the most controversial deaths in police custody have involved black or ethnic minority suspects, and these have been discussed by the Institute of Race Relations (1991), among others, as illustrative of wider causes for concern about police conduct toward black citizens. The IRR, as well as MIND and INQUEST, have also highlighted the issue of deaths in psychiatric hospitals (see Burke, 1990). At the time of writing, official inquires are taking place into deaths at Ashworth and Broadmoor Special Hospitals, while nine nurses at the third special hospital, Rampton, have been arrested in connection with a patient's death.

In August 1992 HMSO published a Report of the Committee of Inquiry into Complaints about Ashworth Hospital (HMSO, 1992, Cm 2028 I and II). The Report, based on an Inquiry chaired by Louis Blom-Cooper, QC of the Mental Health Act Commission, called for a 'cultural change' throughout the Special Hospitals System. In fact, the role of Special Hospitals is being reviewed in the light of the Inquiry Team's Report. The investigations began in 1991 after a Channel 4 television documentary 'A Special Hospital' made a number of specific allegations of improper care and ill-treatment of patients at Ashworth. There were two deaths (one by suicide, but given an open verdict at the inquest), one case of physical maltreatment, accusations of sexual improprieties and a number of other complaints:

> *Gary Harrington, predictably and preventibly, hanged himself in his room on 1 May 1990 (HMSO, 1992, p.51).*

> *From our studies in depth of all these four cases, there is a wealth of evidence to demonstrate how, from the moment when society intervened in the lives of each of these four mentally disordered persons, there has been failure upon failure to care for and treat them properly (ibid).*

Factors found by the inquiry team to have contributed to these accusations included: inappropriate placement in special hospital; insufficient assessment on reception; inadequate nursing and medical care; under-investigation of complaints of psychological harm, criminal violence and degradation; inadequate and incomplete investigation of the circumstances of death; too little human compassion; inadequate reporting and neglect of the deceased's family.

The extensive and detailed Report is a salutary reminder that one of the major contributors to the number of deaths in custody is harsh institutions: hospitals and prisons, but also families and other social institutions. The Report itself is impressive in its scope - perhaps equal to the Woolf Report in its depth of analysis and the potential significance of its recommendations. The 90 recommendations made by the team included measures to address the oppressive sub-culture of denigration and devaluing of patients, extremist political views and abuses of power found amongst a sub-group of staff, and measures to improve poor staff-management relations. There are many lessons in the Report for the prison service. In their conclusions, the team write:

Our wider inquiry has revealed a hospital environment and culture which has given rise to numerous incidents arising from an uncaring and demeaning attitude towards patients. There has occurred a good deal of harassment of patients and some physical bullying (Home Office, 1992, p.252).

The Report contained a chapter on deaths in special hospitals (pp.211-222). This chapter points out the very natural fears and anxieties aroused by deaths in such or similar institutions and the resulting necessity for proper and open investigation. In relation to this, the team recommended the setting up of internal inquiries by hospital management to be held in every case of a death at Ashworth, in parallel with an 'improved' inquest. Its report should be made available to the deceased's next of kin (Home Office, 1992, p.215).

The team also recommended that Ashworth should be visited in the near future by the Committee for the Prevention of Torture and Inhuman or Degrading Treatment or Punishment.

PRISON SUICIDES: TOWARDS CONSENSUS?

Though deaths in police custody raise issues of great importance, it is the problem of prison suicides that has come to dominate public debate about deaths in custody, as it dominated the ISTD conference which gave rise to this book.

Concern about prison suicides has been stimulated by an alarming rise in the number of prisoners dying by their own hands (Not all such deaths are officially recorded as suicides: see Ch.2). Implicit criticism from coroners' juries through the medium of lack of care verdicts has also played a part (see Chs.9 and 10), as has pressure from the Howard League (Grindrod, 1990) and INQUEST.

The lack of care verdict reflects both the politicisation and the medicalisation of prison suicides. On the political front, the determination with which lawyers acting for prisoners' families have argued for the legal propriety of such verdicts (see the High Court decisions in *R v. Southwark Coroner* (1987) and *R v. Birmingham Coroner* (1990)), has undoubtedly been stimulated by INQUEST, and by what Prior (1989, p.65) describes as that organisation's 'struggle to choose a socially relevant cause of death drawn from a framework other than the clinical one' so much favoured in coroners' courts. Yet the recognition of culpable neglect of the prisoner's well-being as a legally relevant cause of death has been achieved largely by defining the prevention of suicide as a medical issue. Most lack of care verdicts on self-inflicted prison deaths have been returned because juries have (presumably) been convinced that had prison doctors taken note of the risk factors set out in Home Office Circular Instructions, and placed the inmate on special watch, the death might have been averted. What the inquest, with its focus on individual cases and individual responsibility, cannot address is the questionable value of the procedures themselves, or the contribution to suicide of wider aspects of the prison regime.

Fortunately the somewhat sterile preoccupation with procedure which reached its apogee in the (then) Chief Inspector of Prisons' thematic review of suicides in prison in 1984 has been left behind in more recent official and political responses. The Chiswick Report on suicides at Glenochil, a Scottish young offenders' institution (Scottish Home and Health Department, 1985) marked an important step towards a broader approach to prevention, even if it did not did not entirely break with the psychiatric emphasis on individual pathology (Scraton and Chadwick, 1985). Judge Tumim, the present English Chief Inspector of Prisons, faced with the manifest failure of the administrative changes introduced in the wake of his predecessor's recommendations, produced a report (Home Office, 1990) which stated clearly that suicide in prison was not primarily a psychiatric problem and could not be seen in isolation from the unacceptable characteristics of many prison regimes. At the same time the Home Office commissioned a long-term research project into suicide attempts in male prisons to be carried out by the Institute of Criminology in Cambridge. The research was to look in detail at prisoners' own views about motivation and it was to be set in the context of understanding prison regimes.

Judge Tumim's report was broadly welcomed both within the prison service and by the penal lobby; and many of its recommendations were repeated in the Woolf Report on prison disturbances (Home Office, 1991) which Judge Tumim partly co-authored. At the ISTD conference we had the impression of a tentative consensus that the Tumim Report was pointing in the right direction, coupled with some sharp disagreements about how well the Prison Service was following the signposts. Such disagreements have re-emerged in debates over recent cases (Ch.9). How far the chapters that follow reflect a consensus, and how far they show a continuing conflict between different political and theoretical perspectives, we leave the reader to judge.

PART ONE:

THE NATURE AND SCOPE OF THE PROBLEM

INTRODUCTION

Opinion differs as to how large and therefore how significant the problem of deaths in custody actually is. It is impossible to enter any debate without some clear picture of the nature and scope of the problem. This part of our collection opens the way: how many deaths in custody are there? How can they best be counted? What are meaningful figures and can comparisons be drawn with the general population? Inevitably, one of the omissions of (especially critical) commentary on deaths in custody is the possibility that some deaths (perhaps most notably, suicides) may be prevented in custody, thus altering the profile of those who go on to take their own lives. Staff involved in such incidents, where deaths are actually prevented, inevitably feel frustrated and betrayed by such omissions. Such prevented or averted deaths cannot be included in any meaningful way in the calculation of death rates. David Biles, the Deputy Director of the Australian Institute of Criminology in Canberra, spoke to us in his capacity of head of research to the Australian Commission into Aboriginal Deaths in Custody. Since the conference, the Royal Commission Report has been published and some of its recommendations acted upon. A volume of research papers by David Biles and David McDonald of the Criminology Unit of the Royal Commission has also been published by the Australian Institute of Criminology (Biles and McDonald, 1992). This collection comprehensively summarises a wealth of policy, practice and research information on all aspects of the Commission's work and interests.

In the paper included in this collection, David Biles quite controversially gave his overview of the scope covered by the conference theme. Having defined what can rightfully be considered to be a 'death in custody' - including those in military prisons, mental hospitals and those in transit from one penal establishment to another - Biles argued that deaths in custody are a 'problem' largely because of the secrecy which surround them rather than because of the absolute numbers alone, which remain relatively small in his view. He argued, perhaps here most controversially, that death rates in prison might actually be lower than death rates amongst populations of offenders on probation in the community. He considered the role of those 'experts' who are concerned with the problem of custodial deaths, ranging from architects and designers of custodial facilities to police and prison administrators.

Dr Enda Dooley, formerly a Senior Medical Officer at Broadmoor and now Director of Prison Medical Services in Ireland, was asked by the prison service to review all unnatural deaths occurring in prisons in England and Wales between 1972 and 1987 inclusive. This detailed study brought up to date the well-known survey by Topp (1979) adding the important dimension of motivation to the range of variables studied. A total of 422 deaths occurred. Those unnatural deaths which were considered suicide on clinical grounds but which did not receive such a legal verdict were compared to legally-defined suicides in an attempt to elucidate the legal perception of such deaths. This comparison has important implications for prevention strategies, most of which are designed and implemented with legally defined prison suicides in mind.

We were pleased to have the Director of the Prison Medical Service (now Prison Health Care) and a Senior Medical Officer at the Conference. Their presence amongst the list of main speakers was a welcome sign of their concern and commitment to the problem of deaths in custody in England and Wales. The Medical Directorate have been analysing prison suicides since 1987. This was the year of a sudden increase in such deaths. They found that 75 per cent of suicides were occurring in local prisons, about equally divided between those on remand and sentenced prisoners. The remand population is clearly at high risk. They show from their figures that other high risk factors include a history of mental illness, self-injury, drug abuse, alcohol abuse, sex offending and long sentences. The chapter presents their findings in detail and then discusses the practical difficulties of managing this group within the prison setting.

The chapter by Paul O'Mahony from the Department of Justice in Ireland provides the first comprehensively argued treatment of the relative merits of using different base rates from which to calculate prison suicide rates. He argued that the limitations and underlying assumptions of prison suicide rates have been neglected. When comparing the suicide rates of the prison population with the general population, or of different prison systems, or of one prison system over time, the choice of a rate: that is, whether it should be based on reception figures or daily average population figures, becomes crucial. His chapter examines the assumptions underpinning the various methods and illustrates the practical implications of the use of such rates. He argues, perhaps unexpectedly, that a rate based on the daily average population is the most appropriate.

Finally in this section, two contributions from the Netherlands: a paper on 'Deaths in Police Custody and Prison in Holland' by G. de Jonge and a paper on 'Deaths in Dutch Prisons' by H.R. Kleinjan and R.E. Smidt. Alarmed by a pilot study carried out by a member of the Hague bar a Dutch group of defence lawyers set out to investigate the occurrence of deaths in custody. It was found that deaths in police custody were not systematically reported or recorded. The Dutch department of Justice has since started to gather this data. Deaths in prison are registered and this data is made publicly available. They revealed that the suicide rate in custody exceeded that in the community by a factor of ten. In Holland an investigation into causes of deaths in custody is not obligatory and, when it is ordered, it is not public in the way the England and Wales inquest procedure is made public by the Coroners' Act. A Dutch working group is gathering information about deaths in custody which are reported in the press. On the basis of the data obtained a report with proposals for obligatory and public enquiries will be presented to the government.

One

Deaths in custody: The nature and scope of the problem

David Biles

I would like to offer my warm congratulations to the Institute for the Study and Treatment of Delinquency on attaining its diamond jubilee and, in particular, for deciding to celebrate this attainment by hosting an international conference on a subject of great topicality and concern in many parts of the world. I am greatly honoured to have been asked to make this contribution to the conference.

I will try to set the scene for the conference by briefly mentioning a number of different aspects of the theme of deaths in custody. This is then to be a 'tour of the horizon' of the subject rather than an attempt to be comprehensive. I hope to show that the problem of deaths in custody is multifaceted and complex and therefore is not likely to be resolved by simple solutions. My aim is to highlight the complexity and the dilemmas inherent in the subject.

I have spent the last three years of my working life being totally immersed in this subject while attached to the Australian Royal Commission into Aboriginal Deaths in Custody. I will not in this address present in any systematic way the findings from the research that my colleagues and I undertook for that Royal Commission, but I will briefly mention some aspects, and I must also hasten to point out that nothing I will say should be interpreted as indicating the possible contents or recommendations of the final report of the Royal Commission which is yet to be presented to the governments of the Commonwealth of Australia and of the six States and the Northern Territory. Any views that I express are my own and are not to be attributed to either the Australian Institute of Criminology or the Royal Commission.

DEFINITIONS

Before embarking on the substance of my paper I would like to say just a few words about the definition of deaths in custody. It is really quite an arbitrary matter but I would suggest that the definition should include all cases where a person dies, of whatever cause, while in the custody of police or prison authorities, whether that custody is lawful or not, regardless of the actual location of the death. Thus, cases where the person dies in a hospital but is still technically in custody at the time of death would definitely be included, and my personal inclination would be to also include cases where the deceased was out of custody at the time of death but where the death may have resulted from injuries sustained during the period of custody.

There is a problem about whether to include or exclude cases where a prisoner was terminally ill and was released, possibly by the royal prerogative of mercy, a few days before the death occurred. I suggest that the way to solve this problem is to pose the hypothetical question: would the person have been free to leave were it not for the illness or injury that resulted in death? In this case, the answer is clearly 'no', and therefore it should be listed as a death in custody.

A further difficulty arises where a person dies who has escaped from prison or police custody. If such a person were killed while in the act of escaping it would clearly be a death in custody, but it would be more difficult to classify the case if the person had been an escapee for a long period of time. It would seem to be nonsensical to describe the death of old man who had escaped from a prison decades earlier as a death in custody.

I have deliberately excluded from this consideration deaths that occur in custody other than that administered by police or prison authorities. I do recognise, however, that the principles that may be established in this area should apply with equal force to deaths that occur in juvenile detention facilities, in the closed wards of mental hospitals, in military prisons and lockups, and in detention centres for illegal immigrants. But what of boarding schools, normal army barracks, even university halls of residence? It really is difficult to know where to draw the line, and I will leave that for others to resolve. As I said, the definition of deaths in custody is really quite arbitrary.

What Is the Problem?

Perhaps by way of introduction some attempt should be made to establish whether or not deaths in custody are really a problem. Is this an issue which is a matter of serious concern to the general public in this country and elsewhere? That is not an easy question to answer, but there can be no doubt that the suicides of prisoners have been extensively reported in the newspapers of England, and there is certainly concern about suicides in prisons and in county jails in the United States as many civil legal actions have claimed that the deaths were caused by either poor physical design of facilities or by poor management. Deaths in custody have also been the subject of significant public concern in Australia, and anyone who has seen the film 'Cry Freedom' would agree that there is a significant concern about deaths in custody in South Africa. But none of this proves that there should be concern. After all the total numbers of people who die in prison or police custody in any country in the world are minuscule compared with the numbers of deaths resulting from homicide in the community, from suicide in the community, from traffic accidents or from industrial accidents.

There is a significant difference, however, between deaths from these other causes and deaths in custody, and that difference stems from the fact that what happens in prisons and in police stations is generally not open to public scrutiny. It is the secret nature, or what is perceived to be the secret nature, of police and prison custody that makes deaths in those situations qualitatively different from nearly all other deaths, and it is that difference that fuels the demand for the most thorough and public inquiry into every death in custody that occurs. Anything less than full and open disclosure of the facts can leave the seeds of suspicion in people's minds and these can prompt a series of increasingly sinister questions. Was he or she driven to suicide? Was it really suicide or did those guards kill the person and then make it look like suicide? Were the staff negligent in not maintaining normal surveillance? Did the receiving officer, in either a prison or police station, fail to recognise signs of ill health, injury or the possibility of suicide? Or, if the officer did recognise those signs, was he or she reckless in choosing to disregard them? In short, did the system contribute to the death of the person in police or prison custody?

It is these and similar questions which make deaths in custody a matter of concern in every civilised country ... regardless of the actual numbers that occur. Furthermore, and perhaps even more importantly, whenever the state takes a person into *its* custody then the state is responsible for the care and wellbeing of that person. If, for whatever reason, that person dies, there can hardly be more dramatic proof of the state's failure to meet that responsibility.

Let us accept then, at least for the time being, that deaths in custody are a problem, and that they are a problem of legitimate concern to the general public. One might go further and suggest that if the public do not see deaths in custody as a problem then they should, as in democratic societies we all have some collective responsibility for the failures as well as the successes of our governments. Regardless of democratic ideals, however, the harsh reality is that deaths in custody are potentially a very serious problem because of the threat of civil legal action which could be extremely costly for custodians and their political masters. At the end of the day, therefore, it is the threat of legal action that is likely to force police and prison officials to take this matter very seriously.

Who Are the Experts?

Leaving that thought aside, however, the question that I would like to pose at this point is: *whose problem is it?* It is almost too easy to say that deaths in custody is a problem for politicians, especially for ministers whose responsibilities include police or prison administration. That is undoubtedly true, but to whom should the ministers turn for advice and assistance? Who are the experts in this field? Who really knows about deaths in custody? Who owns the problem?

I suspect that the real answer is that no one is a complete expert in this field, but that a relatively large number of quite different types of people know some things about some aspects of the problem. Because of that, and because deaths in custody has been approached quite differently in different countries, if we are going to do something about it we need to start with a conference that is both multidisciplinary and international, such as this one. Let me quickly review the list of the types of people that I believe can make a contribution to the discussion of this topic.

First on the list we must place those people who are responsible for the administration of police and prison systems in which the deaths in question have occurred, or may occur in the future. Well run police and prison systems, with a sense of purpose and with high staff morale, will surely keep deaths to a minimum. Police and prison administrators therefore are obviously of central relevance, but they, like the ministers whom I mentioned earlier, are likely to seek advice and assistance from other professionals. Senior police and correctional administrators should definitely be here, but I do not believe that they have all of the answers themselves.

The second category of experts that I would add to the list of people who are obviously relevant are various representatives of the law. It is of course the law that determines the type of behaviour that may lead to custody, and sooner or later a judge or a magistrate will make a determination about custody in each individual case. Also, it is that special class of magistrates known as coroners who inquire into, and report upon, any deaths in custody that might occur.

The next group of people whose expertise is relevant to deaths in custody are psychologists and psychiatrists. They are the experts on depression and the identification of suicide proneness, and they should also be able to advise on the way to reduce stress in custodial environments. Psychological insights should also help in the handling of traumatic grief that is experienced by the relatives of those who have died in custody. Perhaps we should include sociologists on the list as well, as they should be able to contribute ideas about the way to establish harmonious interpersonal relations between people in custody. They may also be able to help us to understand why certain social classes in society are much more likely than others to be in police or prison custody in the first place. But we know from a number of different countries in the world that indigenous minorities in a population are very much more likely to be locked up than are the non-indigenous majorities. This is certainly the case with native Americans and Canadians, the Maori people of New Zealand, Australian Aborigines and the Gypsies of Central Europe. Perhaps therefore we should include an anthropologist or two to explain why this gross over-representation of indigenous people occurs. Before we leave the social sciences, I would have to suggest that criminologists be included as they are supposed to know about the operation of criminal justice systems, including custodial systems. Even if they do not really know anything relevant, criminologists will almost certainly have plenty to say!

The list of relevant experts is already becoming rather long, but medical practitioners must also be added as they are the only people who can advise on how to recognise injuries or illness which may prove to be fatal unless treated. Also the medical specialists who advise coroners, forensic pathologists, must be added as well. Finally, a place must be found for architects and designers as the evidence now seems to be conclusive that the architectural design of custodial facilities can be linked with high or low numbers of deaths in those facilities.

There are probably other professional groups and academic disciplines that can also assist, but it seems that at a minimum the types of people who are relevant to the issue are: politicians, especially relevant ministers, correctional administrators, police administrators, judges, magistrates and coroners, psychologists and psychiatrists, sociologists, anthropologists, criminologists, medical practitioners, forensic pathologists, and architectural designers. Perhaps we should add researchers as there must be someone in the group who can collect and interpret statistics, especially epidemiological statistics, but hopefully one or more of those already included can do that. The group of so called experts is certainly large enough as it is.

I would like to devote the remainder of the time available to me to a brief consideration of six or seven sub-topics which are related to each other and which seem to me to be of some importance to the general topic of the nature and scope of the problem. Some of the information that I will give stem from the research that I and my colleagues undertook in Australia, but as I pointed out at the outset I will not attempt a systematic or comprehensive review of that research programme.

CAUSES OF DEATH

The first sub topic that I would like to address is that of the causes of death in both police and prison custody. It seems to be true of most countries that slightly more people die in prisons than in police custody, but as there are nearly always many times more people in prison than in police cells, it is clear that police custody is very much more dangerous than is custody in prisons. (This finding is especially true for Australian Aborigines.) Notwithstanding this difference, however, the causes of death in police and prison custody are remarkably similar. Our findings suggest that in both custodial environments, approximately 46 per cent of deaths are attributable to suicide and 35 per cent to natural causes, the remainder being due to accidents or homicides, the latter generally between inmates. We have found that there is considerable similarity between different nations in the pattern of causes of death in custody, even though there are some interesting differences which are probably due to the conventions of coroners, particularly in relation to open findings, findings of suicide and/or misadventure.

Most of the cases that are classified as suicides in either police or prison custody are the result of hanging. This is in sharp contrast to suicides in the general community which are more likely to be due to shooting, gassing, overdosing on sleeping tablets, or jumping from high places. This striking difference is almost certainly the result of the fact that the opportunities for suicide in custody are extremely limited, and it is an unfortunate fact that hanging is much more likely to be fatal than the other methods that are more widely attempted in the community. Hanging is probably the most lethal of all of the forms of self- destructive behaviour. It is also clear that it is very difficult to eliminate all opportunities for a hanging. There is ample evidence to show that the removal of belts and neckties is insufficient as many people hang themselves with strips of blanket, singlets, underpants or socks, and it is also clear that a person does not need to be fully suspended for the act to be lethal, and therefore the removal of high hanging points in cells is not sufficient to ensure the safety of inmates. Even such mundane items as a tap on a handbasin, the frame of a bed, or the hinge on a door can be used to facilitate a suicide by hanging if the person is sufficiently determined. It is therefore extremely difficult to prevent every possibility of hanging and attempts to do so are likely to cause increased stress, misery and loss of self esteem. The more we try to prevent suicides the more we may drive people to attempt it.

THE PSYCHOLOGY OF HANGING

It seems to me that there are at least two, and probably three, quite different psychological states that are associated with hanging of people in custody. Quite apart from judicial hangings, which are not relevant to this conference, I would like to suggest that one type could be described as *aggressive hanging*. This is the type of case that most commonly occurs in police custody, often when the individual is under the influence of alcohol or drugs. In these cases, there is never a suicide note and it seems highly likely that he (it is nearly always a male) did not intend to end his life, the motive being to cause trouble for the custodial authorities. In these cases, a finding of misadventure or accident is probably more accurate than one of suicide.

Aggressive hanging is to be contrasted with what I call *depressive hanging,* which is more likely to occur in prison. This type of case occurs when the individual really does want to end his or her life, and is often foreshadowed by several days of tranquillity. During this time the person is quite likely to give away personal possessions and also to prepare suicide notes, sometimes a large number of them. Even though the actual behaviour may be virtually identical to that displayed in the aggressive cases, it is obvious that the psycho-dynamics of the two types of cases are quite different.

There is a third type of hanging which has a psychological basis which is quite different again from the two types described above. I refer here to auto-erotic strangulation, sometimes known as sexual asphyxia. This could be called *erotic hanging*. Without describing the sometimes elaborate and bizarre procedures involved, these cases are characterised by an attempt to heighten sexual satisfaction by causing a partial compression of the carotid artery. This practice is extremely dangerous as unconsciousness can occur within seconds and death within minutes. Deaths of this type should clearly be classified as accidental, but they are not always recognised as cases of sexual asphyxia and may be wrongly seen as suicidal as some officials are apparently not aware of this form of behaviour.

There is a real dilemma here, as just mentioning the practice of sexual asphyxia (even without giving the details of how it is done) may have the effect of encouraging experimentation that is extremely hazardous, but if police investigators and coroners are not aware of this form of conduct then incorrect classifications of the causes of death will inevitably occur.

The Reporting of Suicide

A similar dilemma may be identified in relation to the reporting by the media of cases of suicide, the danger being that the media reports may stimulate or provoke others to do the same thing. This is a particular danger if the method of suicide is unusual or if the person who committed suicide was well known. Very carefully designed and conducted research on this issue in the United States over the past two decades leaves me in no doubt that the number of suicides increases following the coverage of suicide stories in the newspapers. Sociologists explain this phenomenon by reference to imitation and suggestibility, while the newspapers themselves call it the 'copycat syndrome'. Whatever name is used, it must be recognised that unfettered and prominent media coverage of suicide, whether in custody or in the general community, may have extremely undesirable consequences in the form of even higher numbers of suicides.

I do not suggest that publicity has contributed to higher numbers of deaths in custody in recent years, but as far as the United Kingdom and Australia are concerned, that possibility cannot be entirely discounted. In both countries the calendar year of 1987 yielded some quite remarkable statistics. This was a disaster year in both countries. In England and Wales in 1987 there were over 40 prison suicides compared with an average of just under 30 in each of the previous seven years. In Australia the pattern was almost identical with 1987 producing extremely high numbers of suicides in both prison and police custody, but remarkably the number of deaths in custody from natural causes were also much higher in that year than the average. From all causes there were 93 deaths in police and prison custody in Australia in 1987 compared with an annual mean of just over 40 in the seven preceding years. The fact that natural causes deaths also increased in that year tends to undermine the hypothesis of suggestibility, as also does the fact that suicides in the general community were higher than usual in 1987. Even though we are left with the Scottish verdict of 'unproven', I would suggest that great care be taken to avoid unnecessary publicity about any form of suicide.

SELF INFLICTED HARM

The next topic that I would like to mention very briefly is that of self-inflicted harm or attempted suicide of persons in custody. Research in this area is bedevilled by the problems of the definition of relevant incidents and establishing adequate recording procedures, but a small study that we undertook with the co-operation of all Australian police and prisons departments found that there were at least 16 times as many incidents of self-inflicted harm which did not result in death as there were of completed suicides. This study also found a remarkably high number of females who engaged in self-laceration or, as it is commonly known, 'slashing-up'. One gained the impression that this behaviour had become endemic in some institutions while remaining virtually unknown in others. In the light of this type of evidence, the notion of suggestibility, or perhaps it should be called 'fads and fashions', again seems to be relevant.

REDUCING THE NUMBERS IN CUSTODY

Whatever the underlying causes of deaths in custody, and whether or not the suggestibility theory is valid, the action that is often proposed to reduce the numbers of deaths, if not to eliminate them entirely, is simply to reduce the numbers of people who are in custody. The argument goes: if there are fewer people locked up then fewer people will die in those circumstances, and that argument is quite persuasive. Certainly there is plenty of room for reducing prison numbers in most countries, and this can be done I believe without increasing the crime rate. We all know that imprisonment rates, or the numbers of people incarcerated per 100,000 of the population, vary between about 400 in the United States and South Africa, while in Britain and most European countries the rates are under 100. In The Netherlands the rate is under 50, and in Australia it is approximately 75. Great differences in imprisonment rates have also been demonstrated between the States in the United States and between the States and Territories of Australia.

If adequate data were available, I have no doubt that the use of police custody would also be shown to vary enormously between different nations and between different regions within nations. It is in fact much easier, I believe, to reduce the numbers in police custody than it is to reduce prison numbers. There is not likely to be a public outcry if police decide as a matter of policy to proceed wherever possible by summons rather than by arrest, to use bail more frequently, to reduce the length of stay in cells, and to take intoxicated people to sobering up shelters rather than to police stations, while on the other hand, the public may well protest if prison numbers are reduced by shortening the length of sentences imposed, by releasing more prisoners on parole, or by sentencing more serious offenders to non custodial penalties. Nevertheless there is scope for both sets of numbers to be reduced, and if that happens I have no doubt that the numbers of deaths in custody will also come down.

There is, however, a serious complication with this argument that needs to be taken into account. The central question becomes: is our aim just to reduce the numbers of deaths in custody or is it to prolong life in general by reducing the numbers of all preventable deaths? The complexity of this issue is readily shown by looking at the numbers of deaths among persons serving non-custodial correctional orders.

DEATHS IN NON-CUSTODIAL CORRECTIONS

One of the small projects that my colleagues and I undertook for the Royal Commission in Australia examined the numbers of people who died over a specified period of time while they were serving probation, parole, community service or similar non-custodial correctional orders. This study found that persons serving these orders were more than twice as likely to die than were persons of similar ages in prison. To put this rather crudely, it seems that law breakers in the community are much more likely to die than are law breakers in prison. It is obvious that custody, notwithstanding its well known dangers and shortcomings, has the effect of reducing or eliminating some of the hazards that confront young adults in the community, and the most important of these are traffic accidents. Also in prison, there is less opportunity for illegal drug use, there are fewer options for suicide, and there is also some level of surveillance and medical care, even if less than perfect. Prison clearly provides a degree of protection, as also does police custody. Therefore reducing the numbers of people in custody may well create more problems than it resolves. If, for example, it were possible to reduce the number of people in prison by 50 per cent by establishing a liberal parole or early release scheme, I would be fairly confident in predicting a reduction of about 50 per cent in the numbers of deaths in prison. At the same time, however, I would also predict higher numbers of deaths among the parolees or early releasees, with the net result being an increase rather than a decrease in the total number of deaths in that population group. A similar result would also be found if the numbers in police custody were reduced. There would certainly be fewer deaths in both prison and police custody, but whether or not that is all that matters is a different question.

Notwithstanding the dilemma associated with reducing the numbers of people in custody, I would argue that this is a worthy goal in its own right. In the interests of human dignity, as well as for economic reasons, we must always aim to keep the numbers of people in police and prison custody at the lowest level that is consistent with the maintenance of public safety.

INTERNATIONAL COMPARISONS

The last piece of empirical research that I would like to mention is a small study that I completed last year which attempted to establish whether or not there were differences between nations in the incidence of deaths in police and prison custody. Possibly the most disturbing finding of this study was the fact that very few countries were able to supply the necessary information. Many countries apparently did not keep adequate records of deaths in custody, or, if they did, they were not readily accessible.

Nevertheless, I was able to obtain some usable information from 13 different jurisdictions in relation to deaths in prison, but from only four in relation to deaths in police custody. As far as deaths in prison are concerned, I calculated for each country, or for each jurisdiction, the average number of deaths per year from all causes per 1000 of the average prison population. Thus a single figure could be used for comparative purposes. To my surprise, and perhaps to your surprise as well, the lowest prison death rate that I found was for England and Wales. Moving up the list, slightly higher rates were found for Sri Lanka, Japan and Scotland, middle level rates were found for Canada (the provincial system), the United States (for both State and Federal systems), New Zealand and South Africa, while the group of countries with the highest prison death rates were Australia, Finland, Canada (the Federal system), and Thailand, being the highest of all. The Australian rate was in fact found to be exactly twice as high as that of England and Wales. I have examined that comparison fairly closely and the results of that exercise are shortly to be published in the *Howard Journal of Criminal Justice*. I will therefore not repeat the details here.

MONITORING OF TRENDS

I would not for one moment suggest that the compilation of statistics on deaths in custody does anything to solve the problem. As I said earlier, the actual numbers may be relatively small and yet they have the capacity to cause extreme emotional anguish as well as national and international embarrassment. It is therefore important that some level of monitoring of the numbers be undertaken. While it is essential that there are thorough and public inquiries into every individual case, the monitoring process can take a broader view and alert governments to unexpected increases or changes in locations or causes that may be of particular concern. If, for example, the 1987 phenomenon were ever to recur, of if remand imprisonment is shown to continue to be a high risk area, or if particular regions or institutions report increased numbers, then governments can be quickly alerted as to the need for remedial action.

I would therefore encourage all countries to monitor all deaths in police and prison custody in a systematic manner on a permanent basis, and I would also suggest that the United Nations is the appropriate body to co-ordinate that work. As the use of custody in general, and deaths in custody in particular, are both issues of very particular relevance to the maintenance of human rights, it is perhaps a matter of some surprise that the United Nations has not yet expressed formal interest in this subject. In my view, the appropriate section of the United Nations to undertake this work would be the Crime Prevention and Criminal Justice Branch which is located in Vienna. This branch is already responsible for a major crime survey every five years and is also responsible for the Standard Minimum Rules for the Treatment of Prisoners as well as many other international instruments. It could easily take on this additional task.

CONCLUSION

I have not made any attempt to specify the types of actions that I think may be needed to reduce the number of deaths in police or prison custody, as that is a challenge to be faced by the conference as a whole rather than by just one of the participants. I do hope, however, that I have provided some sort of stimulus for the more purposeful discussions that are to take place over the next few days.

Two

Unnatural death in prison: Is there a future?

Enda Dooley

INTRODUCTION

Death in prison, especially self-inflicted death, has been a cause of increasing concern in recent years. Official concern has resulted in a number of government reports (Home Office, 1984; 1986; 1990) dealing with this subject. Public and official concern has been exacerbated by the dramatic increase in prison suicides in England and Wales in recent years. The increase in the rate of prison suicide has far outstripped the rise in the average daily population (ADP) which has occurred during the 1980s. Figures 1 and 2 illustrate graphically the rise in self-inflicted death compared to the rise in ADP. Though the ADP has levelled during the last couple of years the suicide rate has continued upwards until recently (it now appears to have stabilised at around 34-45 per year). In 1990 a total of fifty prison inmates killed themselves in England and Wales. This was the largest number for any single year to date.

In the light of this concern and the lack of descriptive data regarding the characteristics of inmates who kill themselves I undertook a review of all unnatural deaths occurring among those in prison custody in England and Wales during the years 1972 to 1987 inclusive. In addition to studying those deaths which received a coroner's verdict of suicide (Dooley, 1990a) other unnatural death verdicts were also surveyed (Dooley, 1990b). From initial discussion with prison medical officers

Unnatural Death in Prison: Is There a Future?

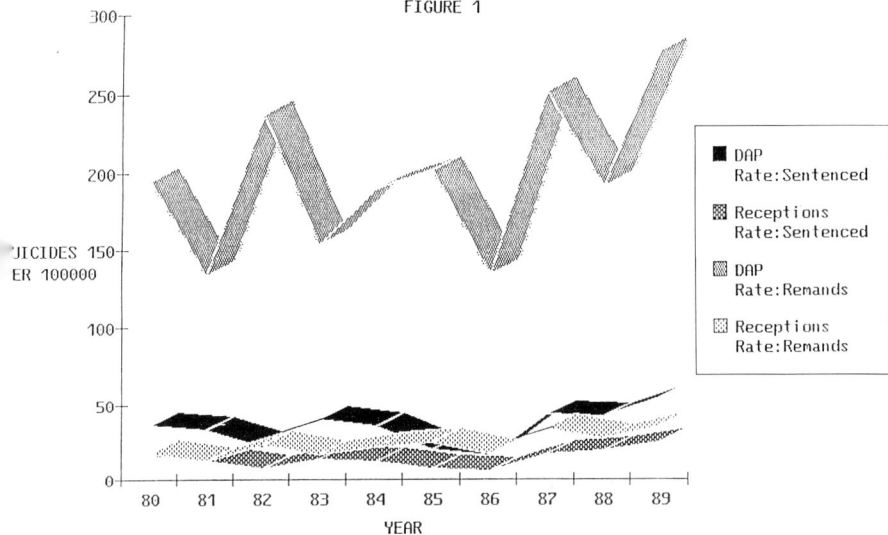

FIGURE 1

SUICIDES PER 100000 — YEAR

Legend:
- DAP Rate:Sentenced
- Receptions Rate:Sentenced
- DAP Rate:Remands
- Receptions Rate:Remands

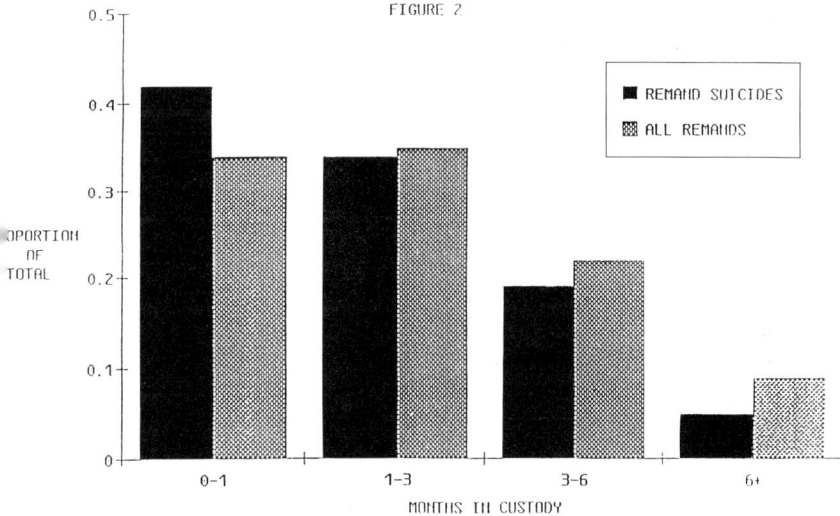

FIGURE 2

PROPORTION OF TOTAL — MONTHS IN CUSTODY

Legend:
- REMAND SUICIDES
- ALL REMANDS

and Home Office staff it was apparent that a number of deaths which were self-inflicted in prison were, for various reasons, not being recorded as suicides by coroners. The characteristics of these 'consciously self-inflicted deaths' were compared to the suicides (Dooley, 1990b). It is worth noting that HM Chief Inspector of Prisons in his latest report on prison suicide (Home Office, 1990e) has recognised this somewhat arbitrary distinction and spoken of 'self-inflicted deaths' rather than 'suicides'. This paper summarises the findings of this research and, in the light of the most recent report by the Chief Inspector of Prisons, comments on the implications for minimisation or prevention of death in prison.

UNNATURAL DEATH IN PRISON, 1972-87

During the sixteen years 1972-87 inclusive, a total of 442 verdicts of unnatural death were brought in by coroners on individuals dying in prison in England and Wales. Of these, 300 were classified as suicide and the remaining 142 received other verdicts indicating that death was not due to natural causes. Permission was obtained from the Home Office to trace the Inmate Medical Record (IMR) files in these cases. A variety of information was extracted from the files. In addition to demographic data an attempt was made to identify a possible/ probable motivation for these self-inflicted deaths on the basis of comments left by the deceased, reports by staff, etc.

PRISON SUICIDE

As mentioned above a total of 300 prison deaths during the period in question were considered to be suicides. It was possible to trace the records in 295 cases.

Five (1.7 per cent) of the suicides were female. While this is less than the proportion of females in the prison population (c.3 per cent) the difference is not significant. The mean age at death was 32.9 years and this is significantly older than the prison population mean. Thirty-one (10.3 per cent) were under 21 years of age when they died. In terms of ethnic background the suicide group did not differ significantly from the overall prison population (based on 1987 figures). There was no evidence that suicide in prison was more common in ethnic minorities.

A significant excess of suicides occurred during the months of July-September compared to the rest of the year. It has been suggested that this may be related to longer delays before appearing in court during the summer months, or even to the fact that this delay in combination with hot weather may make living in prison even more intolerable. The numbers on any particular day of the week did not differ significantly. Almost 50 per cent occurred at night (i.e. between midnight and 8 a.m.) with the rest scattered evenly throughout the day.

The previous finding that suicide was much more common during the early stages of imprisonment was supported by this study. Over a quarter killed themselves within a month of initial reception and over 50 per cent within three months. It should be noted, however, that almost a quarter had been in prison over a year when they killed themselves. Almost 50 per cent of these suicides were on remand at time of death. This was very significantly in excess of the average remand population over the period of the study which was 11 per cent of the ADP. In looking at the sentenced group those serving longer sentences (over 4 years) were significantly over-represented. Over 25 per cent of the sentenced suicides were serving a life sentence compared to a prison average of 4.4 per cent over the period of the study. The sentenced suicide group had significantly more cases convicted of violent or sexual offences compared to the sentenced prison population.

Over 90 per cent of these prison suicides killed themselves by hanging with small numbers dying from overdoes and other means.

Almost a third had a previous psychiatric history. In addition, approximately 25 per cent had a history of alcohol and/or drug abuse. 43 per cent had self-injured at some time in the past and 22 per cent had done so during the period of custody that preceded death. In was notable that previous methods of self-injury mirrored those used in the community (i.e. overdoses or wrist-cutting). While it is worrying that in only 16 per cent of cases was the risk of suicide noted prior to death it should be borne in mind that motivation or desire to self-injure is not constant and may develop rapidly in a prison situation in response to various stressors.

As outlined above an attempt was made to tentatively establish a motive for the suicidal act. In some cases a suicide note made clear the motivation. At the other extreme in 10 per cent of cases there was, in spite of investigation at the time, subsequent inquest, etc. no apparent motive for the suicide. In 40 per cent of the remainder suicide was considered due to an inability to cope with imprisonment (sentence length, regime, victimisation, etc.). A further 15 per cent were considered to have killed themselves due to outside pressures (family, legal, etc.). 13 per cent killed themselves due to guilt for the offence (60 per cent of this group had been charged or convicted of homicide and 16 per cent had killed their spouse. 30 per cent had committed offences with a sexual component). In 22 per cent of cases it was considered that suicide occurred in the context of mental disorder and that this was a direct cause of death.

Unnatural Deaths

During the period under study 142 deaths in prison received unnatural verdicts other than suicide. On further review it was considered that in 52 of these cases death had been 'consciously self-inflicted' (CSI). While in many cases the method and circumstances of these 52 deaths were identical to deaths recorded as suicide elsewhere it may be that the onus on the coroner to establish proof of intent before bringing in a suicide verdict led to an open or misadventure verdict.

When compared to the suicides described above these 52 deaths were similar in most respects. A number of significant differences did emerge, however, which merit comment. Significantly more of the CSI group were female, single, died by methods other than hanging (especially fire), and had self-injured previously during the period of custody in which death occurred. Fewer were on remand compared to the suicide group. The findings among the suicide group that death occurred most commonly at night was reversed. Over 80 per cent occurred during the day-time or evening (especially 8 a.m. to 5 p.m.).

Furthermore, significantly more of the CSI group had been prescribed major tranquillizers during the month prior to death.

What conclusions may be drawn from this comparison? It would appear that in the prison context coroners are less likely to bring in a suicide verdict where it can be implied that the victim hoped for intervention (deaths occurring during the day using less immediate methods). In addition, it would appear that a history of previous self-injury, recent psychiatric treatment, or psychotic illness may also have influenced the coroner in doubting the genuine intent or capacity to form intent. The excess of females in this group (bearing in mind that self-injury is relatively more common in females both in prison and in the community) may also have caused coroners to doubt the genuine intent of female deaths.

It was noticeable that homicide occurred relatively infrequently in English prisons during this period. Only 16 cases occurred (a mean rate of 2.4 per 100,000 of the ADP). This is less than one tenth of the homicide rate in US prisons (Lester, 1987). The rate of homicide in the general community is approximately seven times greater in the US.

LESSONS FOR FUTURE PREVENTION

The most recent report by HM Chief Inspector of Prisons on prison suicide (Home Office, 1990e) has outlined the preventive strategies employed to date by the Prison Department. These were outlined in Circular Instruction 20/1989 dealing with Suicide Prevention. This involves identifying inmates who may be suicidal, helping them, reducing opportunities for further self-injury, and ensuring education and communication between staff. Action required by various staff following the completion of a Reception Screening form (F1996) or a Referral Form (F1997) are outlined in some detail. There are, however, a number of difficulties with this type of risk monitoring. Suicide risk, especially in prison, is not a consistent factor in most cases. It depends on a number of stressors both within and without the prison. Some of these may be acute and some chronic. Using screening methods based on known risk factors will produce far more 'at risk' cases than will ever attempt to commit suicide. This, in turn, has the problem of diminishing the impact on staff of such screening. In addition, screening on observation or information will miss those cases who give very little or no indication of their intention.

While it will never be possible to prevent all prison suicides (no more than would be possible in the community) the minimisation of prison suicide should be possible given that the current rate is approximately ten times the rate for young men aged 15-34 years in the general population (McClure,

1987). I believe that successful minimisation will require an examination of the effects and stresses of imprisonment together with steps to minimise these. The process of imprisonment, especially remand, is not only accompanied by loss of liberty but also by a loss of control over various facets of one's existence. The prison regime exacerbates this helplessness by removing any vestiges of dignity (overcrowding, slopping out, etc.) and denying the individual any responsibility for himself. The prisoner does what he is told and little else. Frequent changes of staff and location exacerbate these feelings. At a time of gross overcrowding and high turnover (especially in remand prisons) changes in staff working practices have led to a situation in some cases where the level of staffing (and hence support and communication opportunities) has decreased.

Individuals vary in their ability to cope with rapidly changing stresses. What is known is that eventually coping ability is overwhelmed and the organism breaks down. The form of breakdown and degree of overt manifestation may vary. Eventually the stage of helplessness passes on to one of hopelessness where suicide may be seen as the only means to resolve an intolerable situation. In a somewhat similar way the rapid increase in the prison population in the late 1980s, along with other factors outlined above, may have overwhelmed the coping ability of the prison system as an organisation. Death in prison may have been one manifestation of this organisational breakdown. Though the population has begun to decrease the organisation may take longer to again function relatively efficiently and, therefore, any hoped for drop in suicides will lag behind the present drop in the prison population (as, indeed, appears to be happening). Various strategies involving the altering of prison regimes and the need for a culture change have been recommended (Home Office, 1990e; Smith, 1991). What is apparent is that methods reliant on observation, e.g. close supervision, video monitoring, etc., are only viable in the short term, acute situation. Isolation from contact with others is only likely to exacerbate feelings of hopelessness. Experience has indicated that to tackle this sense of helplessness and ensuing hopelessness there is a need to dramatically improve communication, both internally between staff and inmates, and externally between inmates and the outside world (families, legal advisers, etc.). Internal communication requires adequate staff (regardless of discipline) to be available to inmates on a regular basis and adequate training for staff to enable them to pick up the subtle cues which may indicate the need for further intervention. Communication with the outside could be facilitated by extending the access to telephones by prisoners (with appropriate controls) and by more liberal visiting and access procedures.

In summary, the phenomenon of suicide in prison can be seen as an indication of the personal and functional organisation of not only the prisoners contained therein, but of the prison system itself. I would argue that to effectively tackle this problem priority should be given to assessing the effect of the prison regime on individuals (with the intention of encouraging communication and lessening stress), rather than seeking to address the vulnerability of an individual at a particular time without addressing the precipitating factors within the system.

Three

Prison suicides: Theory and practice

Rosemary Wool and Robin Ilbert

History

In 1983 a lack of care verdict, following the suicide of a young man at Ashford Remand Centre, caused such public concern that the Home Secretary of the day was constrained to ask Her Majesty's Chief Inspector of Prisons to undertake a review of prison suicides. This review was followed by the setting up of a Prison Service Working Group on Suicide Prevention to take forward the Chief Inspector's Recommendations. New instructions relating to suicide prevention were issued to the Service early in 1987 as a Circular Instruction (3/87). The working group's definition of the task of the prison service in preventing suicide was:

> ... to take all reasonable steps to identify prisoners who are developing suicidal feelings; to treat and manage them in ways that are humane, and are most likely to prevent suicide; and to promote recovery from suicidal crisis.

The instructions provided for:

1. screening of every prisoner entering custody, and on transfer, for high risk suicide factors;
2. a uniform method of communicating between staff and medical officers regarding suicide risk in inmates;

3.   training in suicide prevention for all staff.

Review of prison suicides from 1976

Between 1976 and 1986 inclusive, the average number of prisoners in custody increased from 41,443 in 1976 to 46,889 in 1986. The greatest increase was in the remand population from 5,090 in 1976 to 9,962 in 1986. The number of suicides ranged from 11 (1987) to 23 (in 1984). Thus the rate of suicides in the prison population for 100,000 varied over that period from the lowest, 26.46 per 100,000 in 1977, to the highest, 53.05 per 100,000 in 1984.

It was a shock when in 1987 the number of suicides doubled, i.e. to 43 (46 prisoners killed themselves; there being a verdict of misadventure in 3 of those cases). The rate per 100,000 in 1987 was, therefore, 88.79. The hope was that 1987 was a freak year, but sadly that was not proved to be the case. In 1988 41 killed themselves; in 1989 52; and in 1990 51 apparently killed themselves. At the time of writing all inquests have not been held into the 1990 suicides.

Table 1
Inquest Verdicts - 1988 and 1989

Category		1988	1989
Killed himself		13	11
Took his own life		6	7
Suicide		14	17
Open verdict	hanging	5	8
Misadventure	overdose	1	-
	hanging	1	-
	burns[1]	-	1
	poisoning	-	2
	swallowing[2]	-	1
Lack of care	hanging	1	-
Accidental	hanging	-	5
Total		41	52

Notes:
1   *self-inflicted burns and inhalation of fumes*
2   *died some time after swallowing plastic knife/fork*

Table 2
Relationship of Population to Suicide

	1977	1987	1990
Average prison population:			
Total	41,590	48,425	44,974
Sentenced	35,659	37,530	35,535
Remanded	5,281	19,625	9,439
Rate of suicide per 100,000 population:			
	26.46	88.79	113.00

A comparison of the 1987 to 1990 suicides

An analysis of those who killed themselves in 1987 shows a disproportionate number were on remand, i.e. 30 were on remand and 16 were sentenced. The remand state has always been a high risk factor, but the gap had widened since 1984. In 1984 there were 10 sentenced prisoners who killed themselves and 13 remand prisoners; in 1985 8 sentenced and 14 remands; and in 1987 5 sentenced prisoners killed themselves and 12 prisoners on remand killed themselves. However, 1990 has reversed that trend, there being 53 per cent on remand and 47 per cent sentenced (27 and 24 cases respectively).

Type of establishment

In 1987, 33 of the 46 prisoners (i.e. 74 per cent), who killed themselves were in local prisons and remand centres. In 1990, 41 of the 51 (i.e. 80 per cent) were in local prisons and remand centres. This deteriorating situation in the local prisons and remand centres cannot be ignored.

Location

1. *Shared accommodation* CI 3/87 specifically recommended shared accommodation for prisoners in high risk categories but not considered to be in need of prison hospital admission. In fact in 1987, 22 per cent of those who killed themselves were in shared accommodation; and in 1990, 23.5 per cent were in shared accommodation. This recommendation will clearly need to be reviewed.

2. *Prison hospital* Understandably prison hospitals are common prison locations for suicides to occur as high risk

inmates will be so located. In 1987, 30 per cent of suicides occurred in prison hospitals; and in 1990, 25 per cent occurred in prison hospitals.

3. *Segregation unit* Inmates are placed in segregation either for their protection or for good order and discipline reasons. In 1987, 15 per cent of suicides occurred in segregation units; and in 1990, 9 per cent occurred in segregation units.

Table 3
Location

	1987		1990	
	no.	%	no.	%
Total	46	100	51	100
Remands and trials	30	65	27	53
Sentenced	16	35	24	46
Locals and remand centres	33	74	41	80
Prison hospitals	14	30	13	25
Segregation units	7	15	5	9
Shared accommodation	10	22	12	24

Note: 1972-1986 Lowest = 11 Highest = 23

Medical and other significant history
Mental illness and previous para-suicidal behaviour are known high risk factors. In 1987, 33 per cent of suicides had a history of mental illness; and 9 per cent were actually mentally ill at the time of the offence. In 1990, those ill at the time of the offence had increased to 21.5 per cent, whilst those with a history of mental illness had increased to 33 per cent.

The number identified as having made previous para-suicide attempts had increased from 35 per cent in 1987 to 51 per cent in 1990. Prisoners diagnosed as addicted to drugs prior to reception into prison custody had increased from 19.5 per cent in 1987 to 27 per cent in 1990; and those diagnosed as suffering from alcoholism had increased from 13 per cent in 1987 to 27 per cent in 1990. These figures seem to indicate that the population is becoming more mentally disabled.

Offences

Homicide and sex offences are well-known as high risk factors. In 1987, 16 per cent of those who killed themselves were either facing charges or serving sentences in relation to homicide. This percentage had increased to 21.5 per cent in 1990, reflecting the increasing number of life sentence prisoners in custody. The percentage of sex offenders committing suicide remained at 16 per cent over the three year period.

Table 4
Significant History

	1987		1990	
	no.	%	no.	%
Mental illness at time of offence	4	9	11	22
History of mental illness	15	33	17	33
Previous suicide attempt	16	35	26	51
Drug addiction	9	20	14	27
Alcoholism	6	13	14	27
Homicide	7	16	11	22
Sex offence	7	16	8	16

Conclusions

This part of the paper does not attempt to draw conclusions or offer solutions. It is a cause of great concern that the prison suicides have remained high since 1987, which was the year they suddenly doubled. As Director of Prison Medical Services Rosemary Wool is continuing to analyse the recent suicides, to discover avoidable factors, and to communicate these findings to the Prison Board, and to all doctors and health care staff working in the prisons. Active consideration is being given by the Prison Service to Judge Tumim's report into prison suicides. Everybody is committed to improving the record.

THE PRACTICALITIES OF SUICIDE PREVENTION IN PRISON

In this second section, I want to do just two things. One is to give you some idea of the practicalities of suicide prevention in a moderate sized local prison and the other is to offer you some observations stemming from these practical aspects.

My first practical point relates to reception. Prisoners arrive in prisons during the afternoon or evening, in batches, cold, tired, poorly clad, and with a mixed bag of hopes and fears. They must be documented, fed, bathed, dressed, and medically examined, all at the wrong end of the day and by tired staff, in order to be located on a wing before the day staff go off duty. Initial suicide screening takes place at this time: in the nature of things, it therefore follows that the process is rapid and that detailed follow up will be reserved for the next day. I want to comment on this because much emphasis is rightly currently laid on the importance of the reception process for suicide prevention and for welfare and it is we who will have to complete our part of that task within the extant time scale. I believe that effective identification of those at risk is being achieved during reception and despite the time scale. We have in prison an initial suicide prevention form (Form 1996) for use in reception and this is not only available but is engraved on the minds of every hospital officer and every doctor: he has it in front of him on the table and in his head, thus affording himself the opportunity for eye to eye contact with each and every new patient whom he sees. It takes very little training in order to develop the intuitive skills needed to spot those in need of special care, and indeed evidence from one of my senior medical officer colleagues in a London prison shows that pick up rates of those at suicide risk in reception amongst full-time medical officers new to the job approximate to rates achieved by experienced prison doctors within a very short while. And indeed (and despite the need we all perceive for more spacious, more welcoming, and better decorated reception premises with better and more discrete medical rooms), the suicide figures for the year 1990 demonstrated that only one out of 51 suicides took place on the evening of reception, and even in that case, the order for shared accommodation had not been acted upon. Therefore my own feeling is that, despite all the inherent disadvantages for staff and inmates alike of having to perform this particular task at the time and in the place it is performed, the prison service's response to the challenge of suicide prevention in this particular area is an effective one. I do not want you to think that I feel in the least complacent here but I do think that it is not a bad record when you consider that our patients, in sharp contrast with those referred by general practitioners to national health service consultants, arrive with us with no details which could help us other than the occasional police warning and perhaps a warrant for a medical report from the court.

My second point concerns medical management of those at such risk. How do you manage someone who is distressed, angry, despairing, frightened, disturbed, hostile, often confused as a result of drug abuse? Where can he go that night? Dare you prescribe simply 'shared cell' in the main prison? Is this fair on the other potential occupant of the cell? Will it prevent death anyway? (Prisoners can hang themselves while their room mates are asleep or temporarily out of the cell). Or should he come into your hospital and if so, where? Very few prison hospitals currently have a ward staffed at night - would that they did. And will your patient, in such a ward by day, be a person who might upset the fine balance of other patients in your ward - people often convalescent from psychiatric illness and/or awaiting Mental Health Act transfer to a national health service hospital, and people facing very serious charges who form an already somewhat fragile 'mutual support' group? Or, in order initially to preserve life, is the use of a suicide proof room and suicide proof clothing the only immediate stratagem?

On this second point, I put it to you that there is and will always be a need in certain instances for this initial type of seclusion, primarily and exclusively as a life preserving device. Those of you who have never been in a position of medical responsibility for such patients at this early stage of imprisonment and mental disturbance simply cannot appreciate the impracticality in certain instances of initial placement in a general ward. We have been fortunate in the small number of suicides which have taken place recently in the ward situation but it will require only a small increase in that type of prison death for there to be public pressure put on the doctor to make greater use of seclusion rather than lesser use as is currently the case. I make absolutely no apology for saying that the prison doctor must be free to use his own clinical judgement on this point: if his judgement is swayed by non medical opinion, lives will be lost.

My third point concerns rehabilitation. On this subject, may I say to start with that even if the suicide location must be initially an unfurnished room or a protective room, the rehabilitation process will start on the morning after reception, with careful and sympathetic interviewing and progress towards a furnished room or to the hospital ward. This, in contrast to reception, is the unhurried part of the process - time when coffee is drunk, cigarettes are shared, and Kleenex tissues required. We are all carers, and you will all know exactly what I mean. Rehabilitation towards the main prison is constantly being improved these days: in my prison as in the vast majority of prisons now, this involves not only daily discussion with my medical colleagues and liaison with wing principal officers, but referral to those in the probation services seconded to the prison who have special experience in counselling, free access to the Samaritan service, and free access to a local bereavement community group who visit. Also, and increasingly, rehabilitation involves the capacity for remand prisoners to have virtually free access to outside telephones.

Communications. What I have said so far relates in so many ways to the whole process of communications and human interaction. One facet of this is the facility of communication to doctors from any member of the staff of a prison if someone is found to be at perceived suicide risk. A referral form exists for this eventuality (Form 1997) which can travel from the member of staff concerned to the doctor's desk within minutes. My own response on receipt of this form is to ask where the patient is. So far as I am concerned, it is as immediate a requirement as is the requirement of any medical officer on receipt of an injury form to see the injured patient. The introduction of this particular suicide prevention measure within the prison service has not proved to be devalued by low threshold over use, and although in the nature of statistics regarding suicide one cannot tell how many lives have been saved by this communication facility, I am quite certain that many lives have been saved.

Two final points. The first I shall call the 'Fine adjustment of the microscope'. We all know that high suicide risk categories of prisoners are identifiable. But there may well be fluctuations, trends from time to time, and indeed paradigm cases which can sensitise prison doctors to particularities. For you will understand that to identify a risk group is still a far cry from identifying the man at the moment of decision. Let me give you two examples of what I mean by fine adjustments. Last year, we had six suicides amongst the under 30s in which, in the absence of any other clear indicators, failure to achieve bail appeared to be the causative factor. During the previous year, only two such cases were recorded. Is this a trend? I do not know. What I do know is that it is sufficiently telling for me to want every prison doctor to be aware of it. Lives might be saved. The second example is the depressed lifer. Lifers can slip into slow despair so imperceptibly as to make it difficult for those responsible to detect the shift in mood. We now have instances of these cases, thanks to the initiative of Dr. Wool four years ago in instituting the annual medical review of deaths in prison. These people are often the ones who *do* leave suicide notes, so we know something of their state of mind. Again, examples of such cases are now known to the prison medical service in general. Let us hope that, as we get better at scrutinising deaths in prison, more will emerge under this microscope.

And now, a final and very personal plea for those of us who work as doctors in prison. The difference between suicides in prison and suicides of those at liberty is that, in the case of the first group, responsibility has been passed from the individual to the state. It follows from this that each and every prison suicide is subject to intense scrutiny, both by the prison service itself and by the coroner. This process creates a set of circumstances in which those immediately responsible for the care of the deceased experience feelings of guilt. These feelings are frequently compounded by the apparent needs of the family or the public to find a scapegoat.

Remember therefore, in the case of each suicide, that follow up support should be built in not only for those immediately on the scene, but also for those (that is to say the doctors themselves) who had the care of the deceased.

Four

Prison suicide rates: What do they mean?

Paul O'Mahony

Any, other than the most cursory of statistical examinations of the occurrence of suicide in prison, will involve a process of interpretative comparison, for example between the prison population and the general population, or between prison systems, individual prisons or types of prisoner. Such comparisons usually require the use of incidence rates which are standardised both with respect to the number of persons and the period of time under examination. In the case of a relatively rare event such as suicide, rates are normally calculated for the period of a year and per 100,000 persons, so that the incidence rate can be defined as:

$$\frac{\text{Number of events in a year}}{\text{Number of people at risk during the year}} \times 100,000$$

Such a suicide rate refers to the number of suicides per 100,000 man-years with each at-risk individual generally observed for one man year.

However, in the prison situation it is frequently the case that only a minority of prisoners are observed for a full man-year. As the Home Office Working Party (Home Office, 1986) puts it: '... the average population figure for prisons in any one year is made up of shorter stays by many times that number of prisoners'. The picture is further complicated by the widely-held belief that the risk of suicide is by far the greatest in the first days of a period of custody. For example, Topp (1979) tells us that among Dr Gover's main observations when he first examined the problem of suicide in British prisons (Gover, 1879) was that suicide occurred most frequently during the first week. Topp's inquiry reached a similar conclusion and indeed, the Home Office Working Party report concluded that 'all studies agree that the week following reception whether on remand or sentence is a time of very high risk' (Home Office, 1986).

If risk is greater in the early period of custody, then the risk accumulated during a man-year which is shared by several prisoners will tend to be greater than the risk accruing to a man year spent by one individual. This unequal relationship has led the Home Office Working Party to question the usefulness of a suicide rate based on the daily average population and to suggest that 'a more valid measure might be the number of suicides per 100,000 receptions' (Home Office, 1986).

Such doubts about the appropriateness of prison suicide rates can lead to serious and far reaching confusion. A notable example is HM Chief Inspector of Prisons' statement on the suicide rate for remand compared with sentenced prisoners. Judge Tumim wrote:

> *Researchers to date have given us limited guidance. The figures as between remands and convicted for suicide 1980-1988 (published by Lloyd, 1990) show a rapidly changing scene, but no clear pointer as to which group most suicides belong* (Home Office, 1990).

However, Lloyd himself states that 'from the British perspective perhaps the most important finding is the high rate of suicide amongst the remand population' (Lloyd, 1990). This serious muddle is the result of equivocation between the daily average population and the receptions rate. Figure 1 shows how a very substantial differential between remand and sentenced daily average population suicide rates for England and Wales 1980-1989 almost entirely disappears if the comparison is based solely on the supposedly 'more valid' reception rates.

The present paper attempts to elucidate the general issue by examining in some detail the assumptions underlying both the daily average population rate and the receptions rate, thus

Prison Suicide Rates: What Do They Mean?

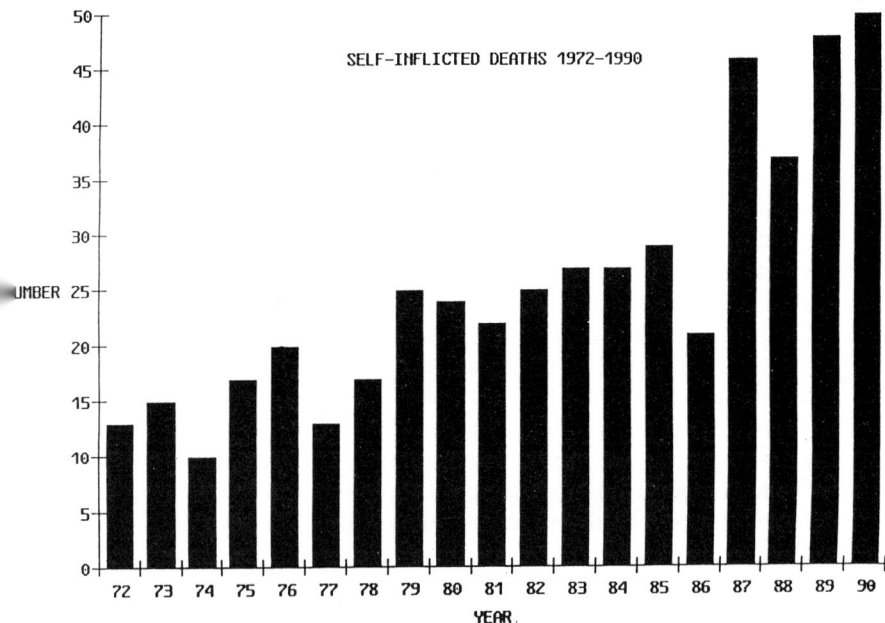

SELF-INFLICTED DEATHS 1972-1990

facilitating a more informed decision about the relative validity
of the two rates in the calculation of prison suicides.

By way of an example, it will be useful to compare a prison
with a daily average population of 1,000 and a town with a
population of 1,000. The movement into and out of the prison is
such that within one year 4,000 different people are imprisoned,
including the 1,000 already imprisoned at the beginning of the
year and the 3,000 new receptions arriving during the year.
The movement into and out of the town is so minimal as to
justify the assumption of a constant town population. The
suicide rate for the town, then, is based on the monitoring of
each of 1,000 people for a whole year. The town rate is akin to
and can stand for the general population rate. The prison rate,
on the other hand, is based on the monitoring of 4,000 people
for an average of three months each. The periods monitored for
the prisoners are, furthermore, highly variable, ranging from
perhaps a day or two to a full year. Nonetheless, the important
point is that the process of comparison presupposes an
equivalence between the prison rate (that is the daily average
population rate) and the town rate (the conventional general
population rate).

The assumed equivalence between the daily average population rate and the general population rate entails a particular model of the occurrence of suicide. This model assumes that the risk of suicide is constant over time regardless of how many individuals share the risk, that is, share each unit (man-year) of 'at-risk' time. In other words, the daily average population rate makes one person monitored over one year equivalent, in terms of assessing risk, to four people monitored over a total of one year and this operation implies that suicide is an isolated event which can befall any individual at any point in the continuum of time. From a statistical point of view this situation can be recognised as one in which the Poisson distribution is applicable, so that, if we know the average number of suicides over a number of years, using the Poisson Formula we can calculate the probability of a particular number of suicides occurring in any specific year.

Criticism of the daily average population rate by the Home Office Working Party (Home Office, 1986) and their suggestion that it be rejected in favour of the receptions rate is based on the belief that prison suicides are more likely in the early period of imprisonment. If this is in fact the case, contrary to the model underlying the daily average population rate, the risk of suicide is not constant over time. If there is an enhanced risk of suicide in the early period of imprisonment, prison suicide rates based on the daily average population can be expected to increase as the man-year is shared by an increasing number of individuals.

There is another related statistical problem with the daily average population rate. This arises from the fact that each man-year for the town population of our example can obviously sustain only one suicide, while each man-year for the prison population can sustain up to four suicides because the man year is shared by four men. Theoretically, therefore, it is possible for the prison rate to breach the maximum suicide rate of 100 per cent. For example, if every second prisoner committed suicide the suicide rate would be 200,000 per 100,000 or 200 per cent. This is of course a paradoxical and unacceptable result which highlights a serious limitation inherent in the use of the daily average population rate in the calculation of prison suicide rates. It is only necessary to apply the rate to a less rare event than suicide, such as catching a cold, to see that this kind of breach of the theoretical maximum is possible and constitutes a genuine statistical problem.

These are serious criticisms of the daily average population rate, but they do not in themselves tell us anything about the validity of the receptions rate, which must be judged on its own merits. Firstly, it should be noted that for any particular year there is an exact mathematical relationship between the daily average population rate and the receptions rate. The receptions suicide rate is the product of the daily average population rate and the ratio of the daily average population to the number of receptions. Taking the current example, if in a particular year there were ten suicides in a prison of size 1,000, then the daily average population suicide rate would be 1,000 per 100,000. The receptions rate would be this figure reduced by one third, that is, by the ratio of the daily average population to the number of new receptions in that year (1,000:3,000). Therefore, the receptions rate would be 333 per 100,000. In other words the receptions rate simply reduces the daily average population rate by the factor by which the number of new receptions exceeds the daily average population.

Clearly, the receptions rate entails entirely different assumptions to those underlying the daily average population rate. It could be argued that the receptions rate ignores the time dimension altogether, that it operates according to a model which sees suicide risk as a property either of the individual, akin to eye colour, or of the event of imprisonment. However, since the receptions rate is frequently used for comparison with other rates like the general population rate, which are invariably based on time, such conceptual approaches can be readily dismissed. Furthermore, as Mausner and Kramer point out, a receptions rate which deals with suicide in isolation from the notion of time cannot be strictly considered a rate at all, since by definition 'a rate is a special form of proportion that includes specification of time' (Mausner and Kramer, 1985).

Focusing then on the implications of the receptions rate for the time dimension, it is clear that while the daily average population rate implies that one man-year shared by several individuals is equivalent to one man-year pertaining to only one individual, the receptions rate implies that each of the various fractions of a man-year pertaining to the individual receptions into prison, are equivalent to a whole man-year. Thus, in the example, while only 1,000 man-years were actually spent in the prison, the receptions rate is implicitly based on 3,000 man-years. It is therefore, an inherent and flagrantly false claim of the receptions rate that the prisoners, who were in fact only in custody for an average of three months, were monitored for the complete year.

This crucial point also highlights a further anomaly in the receptions rate. This is the rate's exclusion from consideration of prisoners who were already in custody (for an unknown length of time) at the beginning of the year. In the example it can be assumed that 1,000 prisoners, that is, the daily average population, are excluded from the receptions rate in this way. There would appear to be no logical rationale for this exclusion, especially since the receptions rate is specifically intended to account for all the different individuals who were at risk of suicide in any one year. In the current example, ignoring the possibility of repeat admissions within the same year, 4,000 different prisoners (that is, the daily average population plus the receptions into prison), were at some risk of suicide. It appears logical, then, to expand the receptions rate to include the 1,000 prisoners in custody at the beginning of the year.

Expanding the receptions rate in this way has the added advantage of making more transparent the mathematical relationship between the daily average population rate and the receptions rate. The revised, expanded receptions rate is now precisely one quarter of the daily average population rate, that is, 250 per 100,000. It can now quite readily be seen that the revised receptions rate manages to reduce the suicide rate by a factor of four simply by making the average prison stay of three months (a quarter of a year) equivalent to a full year. The average prison stay, in fractions of a year, is calculated by dividing the daily average population by the daily average population plus all new receptions, that is, by the same process through which one arrives at the expanded receptions rate.

There is another problem with the unrevised receptions rate, which arises from the exclusive focus on receptions. This relates to the situation found in a long stay prison where the new receptions in a year are less numerous that the daily average population. In this situation the receptions rate for suicide will be greater than the daily average population rate. If, for example, there were 500 receptions in a prison of 1,000, the receptions rate would be twice the rate based on the daily average population. The receptions rate, therefore, implies that only 500 of the 1,500 prisoners who spent an average of two thirds of a year in prison, were at any risk of suicide. This is clearly untenable and constitutes an additional *reductio ad absurdum* of the receptions rate.

The various problems with the receptions rate are so serious that it is possible to dismiss the view of the Home Office Working Party that the receptions rate may be the more valid rate, particularly for comparisons with the general population rate. We can conclude that the receptions rate is so seriously flawed that it is of little or no practical value. It should be avoided because it inevitably involves false assumptions and misleading implications. However, the unacceptability of the receptions rate does not guarantee the validity or usefulness of the daily average population rate. It is, therefore, necessary to return to a consideration of the serious criticisms that have already been expressed about that rate.

Two major problems with the daily average population rate were noted: first, the possibility that the rate is overstated because the man-year is shared by several people whose risk of suicide may be greater in the early days of custody; second, the theoretical possibility that the maximum rate of 100 per cent for an event such as suicide, which is of course unrepeatable, may be breached, again because the man-year is shared by several people.

There are two important aspects to the first issue:

1. the strength of the evidence for the proposition that the risk of suicide is greatest in the early days of custody;
2. how serious a problem it is for the daily average population rate if this proposition is indeed true.

While the empirical evidence is clear that a majority of suicides do in fact occur in the early days and months of custody it is a fallacy to jump from this fact to the conclusion that the risk of suicide for any individual is greater in the early period. This question is entirely separate and proof depends on an examination of the relationship between the proportion of suicides that are early and the proportion of time spent by prisoners that can be classified as early. None of the studies referred to by the Home Office Working Party actually investigates whether or not there is an excess of suicide cases among prisoners with short durations of custody over the expected number derived from baseline estimates, that is, from a count of the actual number of early man-days served. It is clear, given the large turnover of the prison population and the low mean duration of detention that in any one year a very large proportion of the man-days served in prison will be early man-days. For example, in the prison of 1,000 with 3,000 receptions, almost all the 3,000 receptions will serve a first week of imprisonment but only a maximum of 1,000 and probably considerably less will serve days 366, 367, and so on of a sentence or remand. The excess of early man-days served may well be sufficient to account for the excess of early suicides. In this regard it is highly relevant that Philips discovered in her study of Brixton prison (Philips, 1986) that the mean duration of stay of suicide cases was in fact longer than the mean duration of stay of non-suicide cases. Two other studies, which have made adequate comparisons with the baseline, also fail to show that risk is very substantially greater in the early days of custody. Novick and Remmlinger (1978) compared the stage at which inmates committed suicide over time with the normal reduction of the prison population due to release and conclude that 'the risk of suicide remains high throughout incarceration'. Burtch and Ericson (1979) found a relatively small excess of suicides in the period of the first third of a sentence with 41 per cent of observed suicides occurring in this period compared with an expected proportion of 33 per cent.

Figure 2 compares the time of death for all remand self-inflicted deaths in England and Wales for 1980-1989 with the average period already spent in custody by the stock of remand prisoners on June 30 for the years 1980-1989. This graph shows how the very large excess of remand suicides in the first month of custody is largely explained by the almost equally large excess, at any one time, of remand prisoners who have only been in custody for a month or less. The actual excess of observed deaths over expected deaths, under the null hypothesis that deaths are evenly distributed over time in custody, is only 20 per cent, that is, an observed proportion of 42 per cent compared with an expected proportion of 35 per cent. It is possible to conclude that there is an elevated degree of risk of suicide in the early days of custody but that it represents only a relatively minor variation in a graph that for the most part indicates that risk tends to be constant over time in custody. In short, given the actual level of increased risk in the early period of custody, any overstatement of suicide risk

AVERAGE DAILY POPULATION 1972-1990
(THOUSANDS)

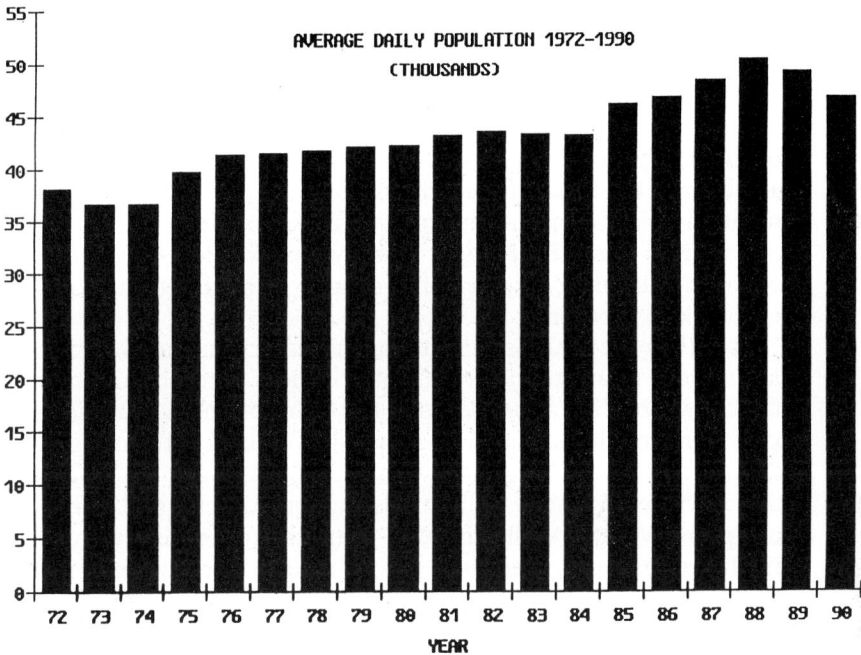

in comparisons between the prison and general populations is likely to be fairly inconsequential.

A separate aspect to be considered was how serious a matter it would be if it had been found that the increased risk in the early days of custody was indeed very great. This issue can best be illuminated in the context of an examination of the second problem with the daily average population rate, that is, the theoretical possibility that the rate can exceed 100 per cent. This is a potentially serious problem which also arises from the fact that in the prison situation the man-year is usually shared by several persons. However, this problem is amenable to solution through a relatively straightforward procedural operation. This entails the fixed allocation of prisoners to specific units, for example beds or prison places, which are then taken to constitute the daily average population total.

In other words, to solve this problem the incidence of suicide must be measured in terms of unit-years, for example, prison-place years, which substitute for shared man-years but are equivalent to unshared man-years in some important respects. Only units and not individual prisoners count towards the suicide rate and each unit can only count once because it is equivalent to an unshared man-year which can only sustain one suicide. Thus, if a prisoner committed suicide when allocated to a unit (prison place) in which another prisoner had earlier in the year committed suicide, the second suicide would not be counted towards the annual rate. This procedure offers a complete solution to the problem. As it happens suicide is such a rare event that it will usually be possible to dispense with this kind of adjustment, despite the fact that it is theoretically required.

It is the conceptualisation of the shared prison man-year as a unit year with fixed allocation of prisoners, that illuminates the question of the seriousness of any overstatement of suicide risk which might be due to greater risk of suicide in the earlier days of custody. We have seen that the prison man-year, even if it is shared by many individuals, can be properly and fairly compared with the unshared man-year spent by one individual in the community, when the risk of suicide is constant over time in custody. However, the present question is how serious it is when risk is far from constant over time in custody. This amounts to asking how important it is to maintain the fiction that the prison shared man-year is equivalent to the general population man-year in every respect. In fact, structurally it is impossible to fully match a normal prison population with the general population on the time dimension. Even in the unlikely event that every prisoner spends exactly one year in prison, they will be arriving and leaving at more or less random points during the year and so often not contributing a full man-year over the period of the observation year. In other words, comparisons between prison population and general populations are always at best comparisons between unit-years or shared man-years and unshared man-years, between prison places observed for a year and people observed for a year. This is an unavoidable state of affairs.

A greater level of risk in the earlier period of custody will invalidate any assumption that the prison man-year can be taken as equivalent to the general population man-year, but this is an almost meaningless fiction in the first place. In reality the comparison between prison and general populations always involves a comparison between unit-years and man-years, and what can be considered an overstatement of suicide risk when the prison man-year is supposed to be strictly equivalent to the general population man-year, becomes the appropriate estimate of risk when the prison man-year is more correctly understood as a unit-year.

We have seen then, that in England and Wales the actual excess of risk in the early period of custody may not be large enough to seriously undermine the assumption of equivalence between prison and general population man-years. However, even if it were large enough, this would not present a serious problem for the daily average population rate so long as the rate is conceptualised as a measure, in terms of unit-years, which allots risk to prison places rather than to prisoners. This limits the significance of comparisons with the general population but in an entirely realistic way, congruent with the structural exigencies of the situation.

The evidence against the daily average population rate then, is not as strong as it may first appear and it is by no means sufficient to justify its abandonment. It is much to be preferred over the receptions rate for comparisons with the general population rate. In addition, Table 1 presents five hypothetical situations that illustrate the superiority of the daily average population rate for comparisons between prisons or prison systems.

Table 1

	No of suicides	Daily average pop'n	Receptions	Daily average pop'n rate	Receptions rate	Mean no sharing man-year
A	10	1,000	5,000	1,000	200	6
B	10	1,000	500	1,000	2,000	1.5
C	10	1,000	1,000	1,000	1,000	2
D	10	1,000	0	1,000	0	1
E	20	2,000	6,000	1,000	333	4

It can be seen that the daily average population rates for the five different prisons are equal because they have been standardised in terms of unit-years. Given the underlying figures for population and number of suicides, this appears to be a reasonable, desirable and readily comprehensible outcome. The reception rates, on the other hand, vary widely, from an absurd zero to an equally unjustifiable 2,000 per 100,000. In the case of examples A and B the reception rates vary by a factor of ten. It clearly makes no sense to suggest, as these rates do, that the suicide problem in prison A is ten times less serious than in prison B or that prison D (a long-term prison) has no suicide problem at all.

We can conclude that the daily average population rate offers the more meaningful, stable and reliable method for assessing the relative seriousness of prison suicide rates. It is properly standardised in terms of people in the only available way, that is, in terms of unit-years. It is stable in comparisons between prison systems and between different years for the same prison system. Nevertheless, whilst endorsing the daily average population rate, it appears to be a reasonable precaution to recommend that the mean number of prisoners sharing each man-year should always be stated alongside the daily average population rate. This is so because it represents a significant difference between prisons or prison systems, which may be related to differences in suicide rates, although not necessarily because it is related to the number of prisoners in the early stages of confinement.

Finally, there remains the question of the different results given by the two rates for comparisons of suicide risk between remand and sentenced prisoners. The receptions rate shows little difference between the two types of prisoner and this is related to the fact that a similar proportion of remand prisoners as sentenced prisoners commit suicide. The daily average population rate indicates a major excess of suicides amongst remand prisoners because it compares the time spent at risk for the two groups. The present argument clearly supports the latter view that remands are at greater risk, firstly, because the empirical evidence suggests that risk of suicide is not sufficiently elevated in the early period of custody as to provide an explanation for the excess of suicides amongst remands, a greater proportion of whom, we know, are doing early time; and secondly, because, even if the evidence had fully supported this time-based explanation, it would not affect the significance of the differential, it would only suggest that the differential is not due to any differences between sentenced and remand prisoners as such but rather to differences between the early and later periods of custody.

To choose the receptions rate interpretation would be to pre-empt any further investigation of the topic, because this interpretation begs the question by dismissing the possibility that there are significant differences between remand and sentenced prisoners with respect to suicide risk. Clearly not only does the daily average population rate present the best estimate of risk but it is also essential to the study of the intricate questions that pervade this topic. This rate specifies time and without time specification it is impossible to illuminate any of the vital issues surrounding time, such as whether or not custody is more likely in the early period of custody.

To summarise our current state of knowledge in this areas we can conclude that:

1. the risk of suicide is considerably greater for remand than for sentenced prisoners;
2. part of the excess risk, but a relatively small part, is explained by the fact that there is a somewhat elevated risk of suicide in the early days of custody and that more remand than sentenced prisoners are doing early time;
3   other differences between the populations of remand and sentenced prisoners must account for the greater part of the excess risk for remands.

Finally, it is clear that the daily average population rate will be essential to the testing out of these differences and their proper elucidation.

Five (i)

Deaths in police custody in prisons in Holland

Gerard de Jonge

INTRODUCTION: TOO MANY CORPSES

Those who consider the Dutch criminal law system as (perhaps a bit too) humane and scrupulous in respecting the rights of suspected persons and prisoners may find it hard to believe that there is a serious lack of accountability of police and prison personnel for people dying in their custody or as a consequence of violent encounters in arrest situations.

Alarmed by a sequence of deaths in police cells, Mrs. Ineke van den Brûle, member of the Hague Bar, conducted a pilot study into the problem of deaths in custody, widening her scope to deaths resulting from violent encounters between suspects and the police (van den Brûle, 1989).

On the basis of her preliminary findings and inspired by the work of the British INQUEST organisation (about which one of its 'founding fathers', Tony Ward, gave a series of lectures in Holland), a research committee recruited from a national group of critical defence lawyers[1] set out to investigate the problem on a larger scale. The committee was asked to do research on the causes of deaths resulting from police encounters and during custody. Furthermore, the committee was to evaluate the formal investigative procedures that are the sequel of such events and (if it proves necessary) develop new methods by which such fatal events can be investigated in a way satisfying not only the needs of the authorities involved, but also of the next of kin and the general public.

Since 1990, this committee has been recording and documenting death cases as they are reported in the Dutch press.[2]

THE FACTS, AS FAR AS TRACEABLE.

It is very difficult to find reliable figures about the deadly incidents that are the committee's object of research. Public statistics are only available concerning deaths in prison. Deaths resulting from violent police operations or in police cells are not centrally recorded.

The killing force of the police

Up until now, the press has been our most dependable source regarding 'police' deaths.

The available data show four different situations in which confrontation with the police may end fatally.

One category consists of people who kill themselves while being chased by the police. A sad example of this occurred on October 6th, 1991, near the city of Roermond, when a 21-year-old illegal Moroccan man jumped into a lake while trying to flee from police who were chasing him and six others to check their papers. Another example was the fatal car crash against an Amsterdam tree on December 21st, 1991, which ended the young lives of two men suspected of speeding who were being chased by a police car.

A second group of people is killed in violent arrest situations. The story is always the same: cornered suspect allegedly draws weapon, police shoot suspect - end of story and suspect's life.

Then there are the people who don't manage to leave the police station alive. They can be divided into two groups: those who hang themselves during their relatively short stay (3-4 days) in police detention and those who die from (hidden) injuries or an (undetected) overdose of drugs and/or alcohol.

During 1990, the committee counted nine deaths connected with police operations as meant above; during 1991, the toll was 14.

A very big problem in trying to assess the scale of fatal police encounters is the lack of (public) registration of these events. Although each shot fired must be accounted for, the police reports made on these occasions remain hidden from the public eye somewhere in the Ministry of Justice and the Home Office. From the scarce research in this field, we may draw the very shaky conclusion that an average of two persons are killed by police-bullets each year (van der Vijver, 1987; van Koot, 1988).

The same problem obscures the proportions of the phenomenon of people dying in police cells. First of all, the exact number of police cells is nowhere to be found in our public statistics. Neither is the daily average population of these cells made public. No official data are available on the number of people dying in police cells each year, but the non-official source of the press can give us an idea. The research by Ineke van den Brûle mentioned above and the registration of cases by our committee result in a (rough) estimate that an average of seven people die in Dutch police cells every year.

In August, 1989, the Home Office promised to launch a thorough investigation into deaths in police custody and acknowledged the need for a central and public registration of these occurrences. The investigation was carried out but considered to be too faulty to be published and nothing ever happened after that. This led to intervention by the Dutch League for Penal Reform 'Coornhert-Liga', which urged the Home Affairs Minister to come forward with a sound registration system for lethal incidents in police cells.[3]

But, alas, the Minister did not speak up, so the Coornhert - Liga decided to lodge a complaint against him with the 'Nationale Ombudsman', who is to give his opinion on this matter in 1992.

Dying in prison cells

We will now look at the deaths in prison, including remand centres.

Here we have official and public figures: the 'Gevangenisstatistiek' or, in English, 'Prison Statistics'.

These statistics (Netherlands, 1992) provide data about detainees (all categories) who die during their imprisonment. They do not, however, specify the causes of those deaths, for which one has to look at other sources.

During 1988, 18 people died in prison, out of a daily average population (d.a.p.) of 5,061; in 1989, three people are reported to have died in prison (d.a.p. 5,734), while in 1990, 11 detainees died during their imprisonment (d.a.p. that year, 6,616).

The department of statistical information of the Ministry of Justice gave (by telephone) the following data on prison suicides: in 1988, 8; in 1989, 6 people. A report of the Medical Inspection department of the Ministry of Justice mentions that 5 people committed suicide during 1990 inside the prison walls out of a total of 13 deaths in the prison population that year (Netherlands, 1991: 13).

The differences in these reported data indicate two things:

1. that a uniform and dependable registration method is called for;

2. that there is no reason to suppose that the number of people dying in prison cells is alarmingly high.

However, one can easily reply to this last statement by objecting that a zero death rate should be the ultimate aim of everyone involved.

A summary evaluation of the facts

On the basis of the data gathered, the committee takes as a working hypothesis that between 10 and 25 persons die in Holland every year by or in 'the arms of the law'.[4]

It will hardly surprise anyone that the research committee stresses the need for a uniform national and public registration of deaths occurring by police violence or during custody. Whether this can ever be made a priority with the Ministries of Justice and Home Affairs is a question yet to be answered. A few spectacular incidents may be needed before awareness breaks through on these bureaucratic levels.

INVESTIGATION PROCEDURES

It seems obvious that all deaths as meant in this article should be investigated by an independent authority, such as the Coroner in countries with a Common Law tradition or the investigating magistrate[5] in the countries belonging to the so-called Romano-Germanic 'family of law' (see David and Brierly, 1985). However, nothing like this has happened in Holland.

There are no special legal provisions concerning the investigation of deaths in which police or prison personnel could be held responsible. There is no independent authority or body of officials designated by law to conduct investigations in such cases.

In practice, whenever law enforcement officials might be involved in such deaths, the case is taken over by the public prosecutor of the district court within whose jurisdiction the death has occurred. The first reports will be made by the local police, but after that the public prosecutor will ask for an investigation by a special police force called the Rijksrecherche. There are five offices of this special investigation service (totalling about 50 police officers), each of them attached to one of the offices of the five Procurators-General, who control the work of the 19 district public prosecution offices. The reports from Rijksrecherche to the public prosecutor are not made public. Whenever the public prosecutor considers it necessary, an autopsy of the body will be performed by pathologists of the Judicial Laboratory. It is up to the discretion of this public prosecutor to decide whether the reported facts will lead to the prosecution of the law enforcement official(s) concerned. It must be stated that this public prosecutor is not considered to be 'a judge or other officer authorised by law to exercise judicial power' within the meaning of article 5 (3) of the European Convention for the Protection of Human Rights.[6]

Although the prosecutor is called 'public', there is no public supervision of the handling of these cases. A countercheck of the post-mortem is virtually impossible, since most of the relevant parts of the body will have been destroyed by the first autopsy and, besides, there are no public funds available to finance such counterchecks requested by the family.

As a consequence, the relatives of the deceased and the general public are often left with lots of questions about the true causes and circumstances of those deaths.

The Need for a Public and Impartial Investigation Procedure.

Although the reports of the Rijksrecherche are not public, anyone can try to obtain copies of or access to them on the basis of the Dutch Act on the Publicity of Government (Wet Openbaarheid van Bestuur), which dates from 1978. The main theme of this law is that every request to a public authority for information should be granted. Of course, the law contains exceptions to this rule,[7] which the Minister of Justice has used to deny access to written information on death cases requested by the lawyers research committee. No copies of the reports of the Rijksrecherche have been disclosed. But the minister did not refuse all information: in the cases about which more information was asked, he provided the committee with a global description of what had happened (in his view), so a bit was gained.[8]

Another possibility for obtaining information is given by the 1981 Law on the National Ombudsman (Wet Nationale Ombudsman).[9]

Everyone has the right to file a complaint with the Ombudsman regarding an act or omission of a governmental body and, in almost all cases, the Ombudsman is obliged to investigate the case. Every public authority is obliged to give all the information the Ombudsman asks for. But whether or not he publicises all he comes to know is up to the Ombudsman's discretion. He can force people to testify and he can ask the opinion of any expert he thinks can shed more light on the cases presented to him. His final report is public and contains a verdict on the act or omission of the public authority that has been complained about. His (moral) judgment has no legal force whatsoever. In most cases, it takes a lot of time before the Ombudsman has dealt with the cases presented to him. He is legally empowered to start investigations by virtue of his own office, but he has not been known to do so in all cases of death where law enforcement officials might be involved.

Though the Dutch research committee is aware of the drawbacks[10] of the British inquest procedure (based on the Coroners Act), it appreciates at least four elements of it: (1) the obligation to investigate all (seemingly) unnatural deaths by (2) an independent judicial authority in (3) a public hearing, resulting in (4) a public verdict.

The introduction of these elements into the Dutch legal system seems essential. The most feasible way to do so would be to make it mandatory for the examining magistrate (the rechter-commissaris, who normally investigates complicated cases until they are ready for trial) to start an investigation every time somebody dies in relation to police (in)activity. The next question is how to introduce proposals of this kind in a political climate in which the 'law and order' pendulum has made a formidable swing to centre-right during the last decade and seems to be stuck there.

Perhaps inspiration for change in this direction can be found on an international level.

The United Nations on Deaths in Custody.

On December 8th, 1988, the forty-third session of the General Assembly of the United Nations adopted the 'Body of Principles for the protection of all persons under any form of detention or imprisonment'

Of great importance to our present subject is Principle 34, which reads as follows:

> *Whenever the death or disappearance of a detained or imprisoned person occurs during his detention or imprisonment, an inquiry into the cause of death or disappearance shall be held by a judicial or other authority, either on its own motion or at the in stance of a member of the family of such a person or any person who has knowledge of the case. When circumstances so warrant, such an inquiry shall be held on the same procedural basis whenever the death or disappearance occurs shortly after the termination of the detention or imprisonment. The findings of such inquiry or a report thereon shall be made available upon request, unless doing so would jeopardise an ongoing criminal investigation.*

Perhaps Dutch legislators should draw their own conclusions from this Principle 34, even if it is not per se legally binding.

Notes

1. In Dutch: *Landelijke Werkgroep Verdediging in Strafzaken*. The author is secretary to this working group.
2. To put the following data in their proper perspective, the Netherlands have about 15 million inhabitants.
3. Letter from the Coornhert-Liga to the Minister of Home Affairs of 11 December 1991.
4. This term is, of course, borrowed from the title of the book by Scraton and Chadwick (1987).
5. Better-known is the French expression *juge d'instruction* which, via the introduction of the *Code Pénal* in 1811, found its place in the Dutch judiciary under the name of *rechter-commissaris*.
6. This question is dealt with in the decision of the European Court of Human Rights of 29 November 1988 (*Brogan and Others v. UK*), Publ. CEDH, A-series, vol. 145-B).

7. For instance: the requested information will not be given if doing so might frustrate ongoing criminal investigations or might jeopardise the right to privacy of persons concerned.
8. Letter of the Minister of Justice to the Landelijke Werkgroep Verdediging in *Strafzaken*, 23 July 1991.
9. A notorious case handled by the National Ombudsman is the so-called 'Hans Kok' case of a squatter who died presumably due to lack of care in an Amsterdam police cell on 25 October 1985: Public Report No 87/R276, 30 March 1987. The Ombudsman did not manage to get more information out of the police officers involved than was already known to the lawyer of the family. The responsible officers still go free.
10. For instance: the relative 'inequality of arms' of the parties involved, due to a lack of access to police reports and the lack of publicly funded legal aid; the limited range of verdicts possible; the use of a jury.
11. United Nations, press release GA/7814, 16 January 1989.

Five (ii)

Deaths in Dutch prisons

H.R. Kleinjan and R.E. de Smidt

INTRODUCTION

There is something very sad and unclean about dying in the custody of justice.

It should not happen while staying in a police cell or in a prison or remand house, so one feels. The custody of justice is not in general, and certainly not in the Netherlands, meant to be such a final and harsh one. We deprive of liberty not of life. So deaths in custody, the theme of this conference, are the subject of continuous attention and debate in the Netherlands too.

I will be talking about deaths in the Dutch prison system. A fellow countryman of mine, Gerard de Jonge of the University of Limburg, has spoken, earlier on, about deaths in police custody in Holland. Comparing the situation and conditions in the Dutch prison system with those existing in Dutch cells the differences are obvious and quite remarkable. It is very strange to note the gap between those two custody systems which, incidentally, fall as far as the quality of the police cell is concerned under the authority and responsibility eventually of the same Minister of Justice.

If I focus upon deaths in Dutch prisons and remand houses, this is not so much because of the size of the problem, but more because of its very existence and nature. Every death inside is an unwanted one; and since it cannot be undone, we would like to prevent it.

I would like to start off this presentation with some recent figures on the occurrence of deaths in Dutch penitentiaries. I will switch then on to suicides as a cause of death. I will reflect upon some explanations for suicidal behaviour inside our institutions.

The emphasis of my paper lies on the prevention of suicidal behaviour, and particular at prevention on a general level.

SOME DUTCH FIGURES

In 1989 15 inmates died while in custody in the Dutch prison system: 6 as a result of a suicide, 9 as a result of other causes (natural deaths). These figures mean very little without more background data and information. So let me give you some.

Data gathering

In respect of gathering data about deaths in custody there are two sources for the central headquarters of the Dutch prison system, working independently from each other.

Firstly there are the yearly reports of the medical inspection of the prison administration. These yearly reports are based on the confidential data delivered by the medical services in the prison and remand houses. Secondly there exists a central registration of every serious incident of any kind in any penitentiary. The institutions have the duty to report these incidents (which include deaths) not only to the central headquarters but also to the public prosecutor.

We think these data gathered from two sources and compared, are reliable. That is they give a reliable picture. Some improvements could be made in the way of registration. Our prison system is too open to hide anything serious for a large period of time. These data serve as a base for developing and evaluating our policy in this field. In this regard I would like to add that in 1986 for the first time to my knowledge, an exploratory research was done by the university of Leiden on the phenomenon of the self-destructive behaviour (including suicides) of inmates in our penitentiary establishments. As a follow-up to this study, in 1989 a working party published a report on the prevention of so called (para) suicidal behaviour. Its recommendations are introduced in our prison system. Back to the figures, reliable as we think they are. I'm using figures from the medical inspection of the prison administration.

For the five year period of 1985 to 1989, the yearly average number of suicides was 6.8. In comparison, the yearly average number of suicides for the period of 1980 to 1984 was 6.0, so the last decade has seen a slight increase of suicide (from 6.0 to 6.8).

For the period 1985 to 1989, the yearly average number of deaths by other causes than suicide was 6.6. In this period *one* incident has been registered concerning the killing of an inmate by another inmate. The rest of this category concerns natural deaths and accidents. So in general if prisoners do die in a violent way, they do so in our system by their own hand. The most frequently used method of suicide by inmates is hanging.

Much higher in the same period was the yearly average number of serious incidents not resulting in deaths, like suicide attempts, self-mutilation, food refusal and swallowing of strange objects; this occurred on average 241.4 times a year.

The numbers I have given to you are absolute figures. There are two ways to relate them to the number of inmates. First: a score based on the yearly flow of inmates through our prison system. In this approach the yearly average number of suicides per ten thousand (10,000) inmates was 2.7. Secondly: a score based on the number of places available in our system. In this other approach the yearly average number of suicides per ten thousand (10,000) occupied places was 13.3. I am giving you these two approaches and corresponding figures so that you can compare them with figures from other systems.

Comparing these relative figures with figures of suicides in free society and in psychiatric hospitals in Holland we note the following:

1. Based on 10,000 beds the number of suicides in 1984 in psychiatric hospitals was 40.8. This means three times higher than in our prison system in the years 85-89.
2. In 1985 the number of suicides for men in general in free society was 2.0 per ten thousand. This means 6 to 7 times lower than in our prison system, and 20 times lower than psychiatric institutions.

RISK FACTORS FOR SUICIDE IN THE DUTCH PRISON SYSTEM

Are there special factors which could increase the risk of suicide within the Dutch prison system?

1. As with all prison systems Dutch prisons are also total institutions. Consequently commonly known suicide risk factors like social deprivation, feelings of impotence and lack of possibilities to influence and determine one's situation are - to a degree - inherent to the situation of detention. Escalation of these feelings cannot always be totally prevented.

2. Most suicides take place in our system in remand houses shortly after detention and incarceration, so our figures show. This seems to be caused by the acute disturbance of the persons state of mind. This disturbance is not completely avoidable, given the personality structure of the persons involved and the fact that the transition from free society to a penitentiary always represents a severe shock.

3. The Dutch prison system is based on the single cell - one person to one cell principle. However attractive this principle is from various points of view, an inmate is alone during many hours without being watched or spoken to which enhance the mere opportunity of committing suicide.

4. Half of the total prison population in Holland belongs to an apparently high risk group of *foreigners* and *ethnic minorities,* in terms of suicidal behaviour, as established by research. The negative features of detention in general are intensified by being a foreigner, not speaking the language, not being understood, not having contact with family or friends, the fear of being evicted, etc.

5. Research has shown that susceptibility for drug addiction increases the risk of suicide. The total number of inmates in Dutch prisons with an addiction vary from 30 to 60 per cent.

6. About 3 per cent of our prison population suffers from severe psychiatric disturbances; this means they should be transferred to a psychiatric hospital or at least to a special section where they can be given the attention and care they obviously need. Due to a still existing lack of capacity in psychiatric hospitals and in special hospitals for this category, the transferral cannot always be realised within a short period of time, or realised at all. The risk involved is clear. On the other hand, once transferred, they lower the risk in the prison system.

So it seems there are some general and common and some special risk factors involved in the Dutch situation, regarding suicidal behaviour. What are factors in our system we consider as having a benign influence on the incidence of suicidal behaviour? In other words what are our ways of prevention?

WAYS OF PREVENTION

My contention is that the prevention of suicidal behaviour is at least partly related to the general principles governing our prison system, which flow of course from the objectives you want to reach with the deprivation of liberty.

Let me point out some of the leading principles of the Dutch prison system.

The main objectives of the Dutch prison system are, apart from securing an unhindered deprivation of liberty; humanisation of detention; prevention or at least minimalisation of the harmful effects of detention, preparation of the reintegration of inmates into society. To define this humanisation and the minimalisation of harmful effects more clearly I shall mention some of the general characteristics of the Dutch prison system which probably stem from these two objectives.

1. Due to a large expansion and refurbishing programme since the early eighties and going on into the nineties a tremendous investment is made not only in the enlargement of the capacity but also in the bettering of the housing conditions of inmates and staff. The prison system in Holland has grown from a mere 4,000 places in the early 80s to 7,600 in 1991 and will grow to about 8,400 in 1994. Whatever one may think of this growth the positive effect is without a doubt a sharp rise in the quality of the detention conditions. Sanitation facilities in the cells for example. More important: the decision to build housing units for inmates not bigger than 48, sometimes divided in units of 24 or 12 places. A standard prison nowadays ideally comprises: 3 x 48, 2 x 24, 1 x 12 units. This makes up to 204 places. That is also the standard size of a prison in the years to come. We have, however, also housing units and prison far bigger, remnants from the (recent) past. These housing units of 48 and smaller enable dividing and

selecting inmates according to their needs. As mentioned earlier, all cells are single cells. This has several advantages in terms of privacy, protection, security and individualisation. Moreover the space available for inmates in our modern prisons has increased to 42 sq. metres for each individual inmate, which includes 10 sq. metres for the cell.

2. The single cell principle is counterbalanced, so to speak, by the extent of communal activities and free association for inmates. A very large part of the day the Dutch inmate in a so called 'closed' institution is out of his cell, up to 14 hours in some instances. This point characterises, I suppose, very strongly the Dutch situation. It also prevents in principle the isolation of inmates. And it does increase the risk of escapes from prisons, one should add.

3. Another important feature of the detention in Holland is the strong legal position of the inmate regarding his rights. Decisions of the governor can be overruled (on complaint by the inmate) by an independent body attached to each institution, with a right of appeal for both parties - inmate and governor, to a central independent body. The rights of prisoners relate to virtually every aspect of prison life. As an example I mention the right to telephone the outside world. I could also mention the right to appeal to placement in a certain type of category of prison.

4. A wide variety of activities is offered to inmates during the daily programme, which consists in general of half a day labour, half a day other activities. Specialised staff for various kinds of activities are attached to the prisons and remand houses. More important however is that they work integrated with the prison officers. In principle there are teams of officers and specialised staff attached to the different units.

Executive staff, in a number of 2 to 24 inmates, is - in our opinion: of course - unarmed; they are supposed to work and live among and with the inmates, not only guarding them, but also playing a meaningful role in helping prisoners to learn some skills and offering help or serving as go-between with other staff and with the outside world. This means there is a growing professionalism among the officers which does not only relate to assuring security and control, but also to rendering care and help.

MORE SPECIFIC WAYS OF DEALING WITH DIFFICULT INMATES

Apart from the more general characteristics of the Dutch prison system, a more specific characteristic is the very strong emphasis on ways to categorise the prison population according to their expressed needs (education, training, labour, etc.) and in terms of their personality and aptitude for living in bigger of smaller groups. This last approach offers a way to detect, in an early stage, problem cases.

In most closed penitentiaries, so-called psychosocial teams are rapidly developing or already fully functioning. A psychosocial team consists in general of the psychologist, the psychiatrist and the social worker, who are, as a rule, attached to a prison. Their task is to co-ordinate the special psychosocial care for inmates with psychosocial problems, who are referred to this team by the warden, the medical doctor or others.

The importance of classification of inmates, not only according to their needs (like training or education) but also in terms of their personality and aptitude to function in smaller or bigger groups, is reflected in the existence of several specialised institutions or sections for these categories within the prison system.

1. First there is the possibility of a referral of an inmate to a special hospital within the prison service for these who are suffering from mental disorders (the so called FOBA-institute, capacity 54 places). A placement in the Foba is made while awaiting placement in a psychiatric hospital within the general mental health system or in a special hospital within the criminal justice system for persons who are detained to be treated.

2. Secondly there is a limited number of small sections of prisons (mostly about 12 places) where special and individual care can be given to prisoners who can't function well in a normal prison situation.

3. A special institute furthermore within the prison system exists to deal with crisis intervention, psychological examination of inmates and therapy.

4. Also in a growing number of remand houses small extra attention wards are functioning or set up (capacity about 12 places). Here inmates with psychological problems or behavioural disturbances, who need an extra structured or protective environment, are placed. Staff supervision in

these wards is more intensive than usual. Recently a working party has been formed to supervise the development of special attention wards in the remand houses.

My conclusion is that in recent years within the prison system the importance of the psychosocial climate of our establishments has been fully acknowledged. We seek to better this psychosocial climate by different ways. I mention the housing conditions, the scale of housing units, the double tasks of the staff of guarding and helping the inmates, the special units and special attention wards. The role of management is of course preponderant. Currently, research within our department has been undertaken to develop a scale or inventory for assessing the psychosocial climate in a penitentiary. Of course the opinions of the inmates are an integrated part of such a 'prison environment scale or inventory', as some call it.

Prevention on an Individual Level

As was shown in the study on parasuicidal behaviour and the report of a working party, a timely signalisation of (para) suicidal behaviour is very important. Hereto, upon detainment of a person in a remand centre, if possible, information should be gathered about possible predetentional suicidal behaviour. This information often is not available. Moreover not every suicide can be foreseen. Every inmate undergoes a medical examination after entering a remand centre on the day of his admission or in the following workday. In the first period of stay in a remand centre, the inmate is placed in an 'entry-ward'. There he is observed to determine whether there are particular characteristics which require special attention or problems which need solving, and to determine what ward (in terms of regime and co-inmates) would be most suited to him. Once convicted he can be placed in a special section to be given extra attention and care, as I mentioned earlier on.

When an inmate has shown suicidal behaviour, experiences teach us that executive staff often does not know quite how to react and cope in the future. Often they tend to misinterpret the incident; they fall back on routine procedures and not seldom react to the behaviour of the inmate by putting him in isolation. So there is often impotence with the staff in this regard. This can lead to a repetition of the behaviour from the inmate. Training of staff in the respect of how to handle parasuicidal behaviour is nowadays stressed upon.

So, ideally suicidal inclinations will timely be signalised, and interpreted for what they are, so that appropriate help can be offered.

IN CASE OF DEATH INSIDE

If death has occurred (as a consequence of suicide) there are useful procedures to be followed. A key element is the provision of extensive information to relatives about the course of detention of the deceased. This has to be offered personally, as soon as possible, and, if necessary, several times. Herewith, the mourning process can be helped, and the arising of a strong antipathy to everything and everyone that has to do with the criminal justice system countered.

Attention must be paid to staff members and co-inmates as well. They may also need help in dealing with the incident. As far as staff are concerned, feelings of guilt can easily arise and have to be dealt with. And for the inmates, successful suicides are known to evoke other suicides. Alertness on the part of staff and medical professionals is called for.

FINAL REMARKS

My story is perhaps an optimistic one. The figures for unnatural deaths in the Dutch prison system - suicides mainly - do not seem alarming, if that is the right phrase to use in the case of unnatural deaths. In part this could be related to a very strong emphasis on humane conditions of detention and attention for those who need extra care, in small units. This means extra staff. So this emphasis on humane conditions is made possible by the support of Dutch Parliament, which expresses the willingness, one must assume, of Dutch society.

A willingness to invest and spend a lot of money for those who, sooner or later, will be again among us in daily life.

PART TWO

PRISON SUICIDES IN CONTEXT

The next five chapters share a common theme: they all seek to understand suicidal behaviour by prisoners as a reaction to the situation in which they are placed, rather than in terms of individual pathology. With the exception of Louise Pirouet's chapter, they all discuss suicides within the context of the sociology of prisons.

Both Simon Page and Jean-Claude Bernheim follow Erving Goffman in conceiving the prison as one among many kinds of 'total institution'; although Bernheim, like the French sociologist Castel (1988, Ch.2), prefers the term 'totalitarian institution', with its explicit connotation of political power. Page, on the other hand, comments on the absence of an analysis of power in Goffman's work, while also warning us not to equate the 'total institution with 'total power'. The exercise of power within prison, he suggests, is often the confused outcome of conflicts among inmates and occupational groups - a theme that is also taken up by Deborah Coles and Tony Ward.

While Page draws on his personal experience as a probation officer working in prison, Bernheim bases his arguments on a substantial body of literature which will be unfamiliar to most English readers. Much of it is the work of doctors practising in the French, Belgian, Swiss and Canadian prison systems. As Bernheim pointed out in another paper for the Canterbury conference, 'Reactions to Suicides in Prisons', some prison doctors in these countries have for many years taken a markedly critical attitude to the institutions in which they work. Bernheim's reviews of this literature show that medical discourse is capable of understanding suicide not simply in terms of individual pathology, but as a reaction to a 'pathogenic environment'.

Alison Liebling's study of suicide and self-injury among young prisoners eschews medical and psychiatric explanations in favour of those drawn from sociology and social psychology. Her chapter summarises the results of this research (reported in more detail in Liebling, 1992) and suggests in the light of her subsequent work with Helen Krarup that the model she proposes holds good for young male prisoners up to the age of about 26.

Some of the themes of Liebling's research are taken up in the chapter by Coles and Ward, writing in their capacities as a current and a former Co-Director of INQUEST. Their presentation to the Canterbury conference, on which they collaborated with the parents of two recently deceased prisoners, was not a formal paper but an attempt to bring home - perhaps too forcefully for some delegates' taste - the anger and distress which families often feel both at the treatment of their imprisoned relative and at their own treatment in the aftermath of his or death. Their chapter here is largely a reflection on events which have happened since the conference, but it reiterates some of the main points of their original talk.

The chapter by Louise Pirouet has a rather different emphasis since it focuses on a group of detainees - asylum seekers - whose vulnerability to suicide or self injury seems to have less to do with prison conditions than with the anxiety or hopelessness generated by immigration procedures. Her detailed discussion of these cases is an important reminder of the need for specificity in explaining prison suicide and self-injury. How far the same explanations hold good for different genders (Liebling, 1994), age-groups, categories of prisoners and types of self-destructive behaviour is, as yet, far from clear.

Pirouet's chapter is sadly topical in the light of the case of Omasase Lumumba, a Zairean asylum seeker who died in Pentonville prison in October 1991 and whose controversial inquest ended in a verdict of 'unlawful killing' just before this book went to press (see McFadyean, 1993). Lumumba did not commit suicide; he died (in a way which remains medically obscure) while being held down on the floor of a segregation cell by officers using 'Control and Restraint' techniques while attempting to strip off his clothes. One of the many disturbing aspects of the case is that while the officers who stripped

Lumumba said it was 'standard procedure', the Governor in charge of the segregation block justified it on the ground that he thought as Lumumba was at risk of suicide. Lumumba was not considered by prison doctors to be depressed or suicidal, and the use of control and restraint techniques appears to have been a response to his passive refusal to obey orders. His inquest should alert us to the danger that the risk of suicide may be used to justify inappropriately repressive measures.

Six

Suicide and the total institution

Simon N. Page

INTRODUCTION

I elected to work at Armley prison from July 1988, arriving days after the second death in a month among youngsters in 'B' Wing. During my ten months' work there on B Wing there were three further suicides. I no longer have access to figures of the number of attempts (as they were then still called) but there were dozens. I spent hours sat on the concrete floors or vinyl-covered mattresses of strip cells, talking with young men in great distress.

This paper is based on that experience of individuals, on my work in that prison and the mental and emotional struggle that came with it. The title of this paper sounds perhaps as if I claim academic respectability: I do not. What follows is in fact what my experiences and personal theorising have told me. All that I have done is to check that against the experience to be found in prison studies over the years. It is based on Armley at that time but my reading has demonstrated that my experience was nothing new. What I found is highly unlikely to have disappeared never to re-surface.

SYNOPSIS

I intend to remind us that the prison is a variety of Total Institution, with a particular and powerful history. I shall invite us to consider that this requires us to view the situation as an entity and not merely a set of related component parts. However, I hope I shall not fall into the trap of speaking of the institution as a system without actors. Then I shall consider suicides in terms of a crisis for, and threat to, the institution. I will pay particular attention to the strategies adopted by the institution, and consider the way that institutional sub-culture and values play a powerful role. The impact of this on the handling of those suicides and attempts will be looked at. Finally I shall look at the implications for the work of outsiders inside a total institution, most particularly Probation Departments.

HISTORY AND CONFUSION OF PURPOSE

It is worth paying at least passing attention to the history of our prison system. If, as will become clearer below, I am to argue that role confusion and irresolvable conflict are major factors in the handling of suicides, this history is very important as one of the sources of systemic role confusion. I do not accept that there has been a process of rational enlightenment which more or less alone brought the prison system about from a chaotic squalid disorder based on uncivilised retribution. Nor do I accept the view that the system is the sinister success of a far-seeing conspiratorial and competent ruling class acting in unison. In my view there are three distinct forces:

1. the late eighteenth century discourse on discipline and punishment in the Enlightenment led by the likes of John Howard;
2. the early nineteenth century requirement for a more regulated labour force (along with the Poor Law and Bentham's 'grinding the rogues honest and the idle men industrious');
3. the response to civil disorder from the 1830s onwards.

What has proceeded from these is an erratic line of policy traced out by the outcome of conflict and compromise. The prison system has survived limping along, and regularly staggering from crisis to crisis, because of lack of alternatives or perhaps more because in the political discourse on law and order conflict over the role of imprisonment and its alternatives has been too great to be mediated into effective compromise (Ignatieff, 1981).

TOTAL INSTITUTIONS

I was guilty at one stage in my thinking of equating the notion of the Total Institution with the notion of Total Power. It was but a short step then to see prisons as absolute power absolutely corrupting. I found it helpful to be reminded of Goffman's definition of a Total Institution (Goffman, 1961):

1. all aspects of life are conducted in the same place and under the same single authority;
2. each phase of daily activity is carried on in the immediate company of a large batch of others all of whom are treated alike and required to do the same things together;
3. all phases of the day's activities are tightly scheduled with one activity leading into another, the whole sequence being imposed from above by a system of explicit formal rulings and a body of officials;
4. the various enforced activities are brought together into a single plan purportedly designed to fulfil the official aims of the institution.

Goffman's definition does not rest on Total Power. In fact an analysis of power is conspicuously and problematically absent. Sykes (1958) was right to conclude that:

> ... *the lack of a sense of duty among those who are held captive, the obvious fallacies of coercion, the pathetic collection of rewards and punishments to induce compliance, the strong pressures towards corruption of the guard* ... **all are structural defects in the prison's system of power rather than individual inadequacies** *(my emphasis).*

But Sykes' notion of corruption is still very sinister sounding when you read his detailed argument, and does not equate with my experiences.

Let me bring this problem down to earth, by posing a couple of practical questions that I struggled to answer:

1. Why does a man I talk with every day, who seems an ordinary working chap and decent family man and whom I always find approachable and reasonable; why does he refuse day after day to respond to the orange light outside the cells of young men who do not want to defecate in a bucket in the corner of a small room in the company of two strangers? Why does this reasonable man behave so

unreasonably when he has nothing else to do much of the time?

2. Why does another reasonable man, this time a governor, stonewall the enquiries of a family who have heard rumours that their son has injured himself, yet privately be able to confide that he was not ordered to do so and knew he was doing wrong? Why does this reasonable man behave so unreasonably?

These men might appear to have total power: without being zealously Freudian one might reasonably argue that control over another person's bowels is pretty close to total power (at least to infantilise). Yet total power neither the officer nor the institution in fact possesses. More likely the behaviour is really a futile gesture of power and control in a situation where control is required in the face of conflict frustration and heavily compromised power.

Goffman describes well how in total institutions the formal or official account is very different from the informal and probably more real account. What the formal account suggests is that a prison is uniformly and bureaucratically regulated to achieve a rational purpose and that power is exercised rationally to that end. (Ironically, a conspiracy theory would also have to rest partly on rationality of purpose.) I would suggest that the daily exercise of power in a prison is confused, at times quixotic and deployed to maintain the institution in its normal equilibrium, to maintain individual institutional participants, and reflects the changing compromise outcomes of the conflicts of internal groupings. It is not rational and goal-oriented.

Morris and Morris in their study of Pentonville between 1958 and 1961 found that despairing cynicism characterised prison officer attitudes, not cruelty and victimisation. In their published version they say that 'reformist, punitive and apathetic attitudes are quite fantastically confused' (1963). They described how the positive influence of the Wakefield Prison Officer training was degraded by institutional processes. I can recall very clearly observing the very same at an Open Prison only a very few years ago. I want to lay emphasis on what I see as structurally and inevitably confused roles and exercise of power perhaps particularly in those similar to Armley. There are so many confusions that I shall just give some examples:

1. officers are supposed to be in full charge but in fact rule by consent in large part (Sykes, 1958);
2. officers resent inmates having it too easy but soft treatment is less harsh for staff too (Morris and Morris, 1963);
3. officers share large parts of male urban proletarian culture and are torn by what they have in common and their polarity in role (Morris and Morris, 1963; Klare, 1973); in passing I would observe that the violence I witnessed between officers and inmates resembled pub brawls in origin and responses rather than systematic brutality;
4. officers too are locked into the prison in more ways than one;
5. officers often voice authoritarian views and yet are at the bottom of an authoritarian command structure in which orders are many and explanations rare (Fitzgerald and Sim 1979);
6. there is confusion of management and command structures and of attendant expectations and attitudes, unresolved as yet by Fresh Start.

STAFF VALUES AND SUB-CULTURE

In the face of these confusions and many others (Hawkins, 1976) as well fear and daily hostility from inmates, a culture maintains staff. They desperately need a way of interpreting their institutional world and daily experiences. Their socialisation does not take them over body and soul and does not destroy individuality completely; but in a mad world a sub-culture which offers explanation and security is powerful.

What kinds of values and theories inform this sub-culture? For example:

1. the prison is a powder keg ready to explode at any time;
2. prisoners are always conspiring (Goffman, 1961);
3. all prisoners are deceitful and delinquent by nature and their entry into the prison is proof of guilt in this regard;
4. concessions cannot be made because once one gets it, they'll all want it;
5. prisoners are volunteers here: they brought it on themselves;
6. recidivism is a form of ingratitude (Morris and Morris, 1963);

7. officers are successes and prisoners failures: they have little in common;
8. the difference between prisoners and officers is one of moral/personal superiority (Klare, 1973);
9. staff are grossly overworked;
10. civilians know nothing (Fitzgerald and Sim, 1979);
11. outsiders know nothing (ibid).

In sum the prevailing staff sub-culture denies the existence of a social order in the institution in which all participate. There are only buildings, staff, procedures and criminals. There is little recognition that prison is an actor and itself induces unreasonable behaviour. It is scarcely conceded that prison is 'a threat to the life goals of the individual, to his defensive system, to his self-esteem, or to his feelings of security'. (Maslow, cited in Sykes, 1958). Yet we know that prison brings many losses: of citizenship, of autonomy, of consent in relationships, of goods and services, of usual sexual habits, of all normal social boundaries etc.

As an example let me briefly consider bullying. The Staff sub-culture see it as a part of the criminal nature - not as one of a whole series of adaptations by individuals to the social order of the prison which turn up in well documented argot roles of manipulative, reactive coping behaviour.

The staff sub-culture is communicated in elaborate layers of code, ritual, totems and superstitions. It seems to me that the principle carriers of the sub-culture (which will vary to some extent over time and from one institution to another) are the staff who are:

1. most identifying with the institution (Waddington, 1977);
2. who occupy the most impermeable positions in the institution i.e. those at the centre roughly of the staff hierarchy (Goffman, 1961).

These will be the staff just below the break between the old Governor and Chief officer grades, where the uniformed/civilian dress divide has shifted recently and where management and command systems meet.

In the restriction of coping mechanisms normally available to any individual in their social environment in the community, the institution not only causes major problems to inmates but compounds this by cutting off available options to deal with those problems. (Loyd, 1990, p.31) Individuals are forced to 'maladapt' and seek new responses (or perhaps find that their limited emotional and behavioural repertoire is exhausted). Yet the institutional sub-culture interprets much coping behaviour (e.g. argot roles) as inappropriate and culpable manipulation. To this degree the institution cuts off further avenues of escape (Goffman, 1961). Perhaps we should ask not why there are so many suicides, but why there are so few. Perhaps it is a tribute to the frightening adaptability of the human animal.

Flight and fight are classic descriptions of two coping mechanisms. In fact it is illuminating to consider 'flight' and 'escape' as almost interchangeable in the prison setting. 'Escape' could in fact be the best way of describing the motives for many of the youngsters I interviewed. Many prison officers would agree from a different perspective, and leads many to see it as essentially a discipline problem. 'Escape' from an intolerable situation (by death or manipulation) must be the main reason. Charles Lloyd (1990, p.27) as good as observes this but only in passing. The research strives endlessly to look for improved aetiologies; and the direction of research still seems likely to concentrate on mapping individual pathology and not the pathology of the social order in various institutions. What statements there are in this regard concentrate on the intolerability of the slop bucket and so on.

CRISIS AND THE ORGANISATION

It is appealing to hold one of two views of a prison as an organisation:

1. as a crisis held within limits, which seems to underly many Prison Officer Association public statements;
2. as a social system, a self-regulating mechanism in which disturbances bring about changes which restore equilibrium.

Sykes (1958) sees them as remaining in corrupt equilibrium but for crisis. I would suggest that this is closer to the truth. He would suggest that the institution's responses almost inevitably worsen the situation, normal compromises break down, finally social and formal authority may break down and the scene may be set for major disturbance. Even if one is cautious of

Sykes' tendency to the lurid, this is borne out by Morris and Morris' description of the Pentonville riot of 1959.

Riots and escapes constitute the most common crises for a prison, but suicides are too. Judge Tumim (Home Office, 1990c) captured some of the flavour of it:

> *B-Wing staff were understandably on edge, anxiously waiting for the next incident. Tension showed in their faces and in the faces of the young men they were looking after ... and, say the other inmates it was hardly surprising if they cut or tried to hang themselves ...*

In crisis the prison's efforts actually undermine some of the cohesive factors at work (e.g. by increasing the level of scrutiny of letters, creating a feeling of deprival of rights). There is a tangible feeling of excitement and disturbance in the air. Staff and inmate sub-cultures produce increasingly hostile stereotypes. Role confusion increases, particularly for the more liberal-minded staff. Secrecy, suspicion and hostility to outsiders increase, most particularly perhaps for more liberally-minded staff. Secrecy, suspicion and hostility to outsiders increase (Fitzgerald and Sim, 1979), perhaps most particularly at the level of greatest identification with the institution i.e. the impermeable middle order referred to above (although the history of the crises of the past quarter century demonstrates that the tradition of para-military secrecy is encouraged at the highest levels.)

Moral considerations apart, suicides pose a number of threats. Suicide can be seen as representing defiant choice in the face of a supposedly regulated social order with control in the hands of staff. It threatens to bring invasion of territory by Managers, civilians, outsiders. Outsiders demand to have information and influence. Careers and reputations can be threatened. Not least suicide causes real pain for staff, and the sub-culture is about as unsupportive as could be (Klare, 1973). It was pointed out to be by an Officer in fact that suicides bring about collective allegations of moral and functional bankruptcy.

In crisis the myth of the monolith can be seen for what it is - but not necessarily from the outside. In fact the divergence between the official and unofficial accounts of life in the institution is probably at its greatest. With norms of understanding negotiation and behaviour perceived to be breaking down, the role of the staff sub-culture becomes clearer.

The sub-culture, the institutional theories of human nature, come into play as major actors in attempts to regain control. They also function to alleviate individual staff in their personal pain, moral dilemmas and role discomfort. These processes are yet again confused and contradictory (to outsiders) but can still lead to similar outcomes. Below are some examples that I observed:

1. Denying the institution. This involves portraying the institution only as a set of individuals struggling in awful conditions. This leads to the interpretation of any criticism of the institution as criticism of particular individuals each of whom can be portrayed as doing their individual best in impossible circumstances.

2. Denying that suicide could be rational. This involves interpreting the institution as ordered and rational, and the individual inmate as pathological. This can in fact appear to be a benign response. Staff see suicides as caused by 'depression', 'depression' as being 'medical', and 'medical' problems requiring the Hospital. Thus the inmate is removed from the Wing, along with his attendant dilemmas.

3. Claiming that suicide is rational. This involves labelling the behaviour and the inmate as 'manipulative' and culpably so. With this come second order theories of 'doing it just to cause trouble' or 'just to get bail'. It requires denial that the inmate's situation really is all that intolerable or unreasonable. The behaviour is seen as rational but unreasonable and the perceived underlying demand is seen as unreasonable and/or irrational. The inmate may be seen as too risky to keep on the Wing: he is likely to be sent to the Hospital, whose role it is to identify and deal with malingerers (Sim, 1990).

4. Treating suicidal behaviour as a form of extortion or hostage-taking. This is an extreme form of 3.

5. Distancing and scapegoating. This involves concentrating on locating the blame rather than dealing with the problem. The list of the blameworthy include: the Home Office, the Government, the lack of sanitation, the families of prisoners, the Courts, the Press. The important thing is that the institution should not appear on the list at all.

6. Complaining that no-one understands or sympathises.

This relates to (1). At the same time staff will maintain that prisons can only be comprehended from inside.

7. Increasing the need for secrecy: in order to maintain stability and avoid putting the idea of suicide into other inmates' heads.

The role of the Hospital is a special one and repays study in itself. The important thing to remember is that the Hospital is an institution within an institution, an analogue of the main prison. It is an intimate part of the control and authority structure of the prison and is itself one of the more impermeable and even secret parts of the institution (Sim, 1990). The Hospital responds to the suicidal in two contradictory ways. Its 'medical' response is to try to diagnose the problem. Once in crisis the Hospital staff become very frustrated because they know that the majority by far are not conceivably 'medical' but that they cannot really stop the Wing shipping the problem out. At this point the other Hospital role and response come to the fore. It has deep-seated roots as the part of the institution with a duty to identify and punish malingerers. In fact the response of the Hospital can be much more punitive than the Wing: the Wing can at least avoid the problem by shipping the suicidal inmate out. Some responses are plain punitive e.g. by declaring a self-injury as manipulative, and interpreting the injury as a refusal to work, wages can be stopped. Some are punitive and covert e.g. rough handling and verbal abuse. Some responses are punitive but parade as therapeutic e.g. 'we'll leave him in strip cells for a couple of days to consider the consequences of his actions.'

Verbal abuse takes two forms. There is straightforward cursing, which is the informal punishment most usually meted out by Hospital Orderlies, who are in fact discipline staff. Those staff interpret self-injury as a breach of discipline for which there is no formal punishment, only informal. For these staff the breach of discipline consists of an act of defiance and also an Escape from normal location. The other form of verbal abuse is the professional sort of which 'labelling' is a part. This consists of calling the inmate 'immature', 'inadequate', 'manipulative', 'attention-seeking' and so on.

In any event the most significant response at Armley was the use of strip cells. This was to deal with the requirement to discipline malingerers. But also the Hospital was dumped with a problem that the institution failed to manage at all. The ethical requirement for doctors to engage with individuals in their care remained; but I would suggest that it was overwhelmed by the institution's need to eliminate the means and opportunity for further self-injury regardless of the cost to those inmates; and regardless of the fact that strip cells repeated and worsened conditions of the worst of life in the main prison; and regardless of the fact that strip cells intensify the features of imprisonment most associated with suicidal reactions (HMSO, 1990a, p.39).

OUTSIDERS INSIDE: PROBATION STAFF

I would identify the main outsiders inside as the Probation and Education Departments despite the wish of some of their staff to become increasingly identified with the institution. I exclude the Prison Medical Service and Chaplaincy as they have such deep-rooted roles within our prison system; I exclude them despite the outward-looking attitude of many of their individual staff. Outsiders inside have strong professional and power bases outside the prison but spend almost all their working week within the prison. They straddle the boundary of the prison, and are accountable to two systems; they have partial inside knowledge whilst bringing outsider forms, values and behaviour. Boards of Visitors and visiting professionals (e.g. Consultant Psychiatrists) have limited access to the inside of the prison and what they see can often be manipulated. That said, some members of Boards of Visitors can be unusually tenacious - which they have to be to be effective.

In normal times Governor grades will express a welcome for outsiders inside, as a check against abuse and a reminder of non-institutional perspectives on the prison. But in crisis this official line is weakened, although not officially dropped. As the varying layers and groupings within the prison staff try to wrest the institution back to normal, other needs become more important. Stability of the institution becomes paramount. At the bottom of the Officer grades there is much apathy toward outsiders inside. A typical response might be along the lines of: 'I just do my job and wish it weren't made harder by interference'.

In the thick of the institution are those with the greatest identification with and investment in the institution, and who are the most crucial actors in the maintenance and development of staff sub-culture. These staff manage much of the information at the interface between command and management structures and methods. I would suggest that it is here that one finds greatest hostility to outsiders, particularly in crisis. Outsiders inside are expected to declare themselves either for the institution or against. There is little room for divided loyalties, mixed feelings or uncertainty. Outsiders are pushed or inveigled into finding a role within the institution's framework: 'don't rock the boat', 'things are difficult so join us in putting them right', 'we'll help you with the things you want.' The response that is being sought is :'We are part of a team within a highly structured situation whose ultimate responsibility and control do not rest with us. *To be successful we have to integrate* and work within the structure.' (Hutchinson, cit. in Walker and Beaumont, 1981, my emphasis.)

Alternatively the outsider may engage in direct confrontation. This is equally satisfactory because the institution is close to guaranteed success and the crusader can be despatched before too long if he/she does not succumb to the personal pressures anyway.

There is little point on trying to prescribe strategies for Probation staff in an institution in crisis. If the Department is in that situation then it is too late and probably irretrievably so until the crisis has passed. The problem for us is in trying to find a purpose when the normal state of affairs is that the local Probation Service has no cogent view of what we should be doing; and the institution has no demand other than to do Welfare, do parole write-ups and not rock the boat.

Probation inside has two major roles in common with Probation outside:

1. to negotiate between the State and individuals in conflict with the State;
2. to 'individualise' offenders in the face of institutions which tend to 'standardise'.

Probation staff must develop their own counter-culture and not simply act like chameleons. Professional distance must be maintained by checking valued constantly against outsider counterparts. Staff must not evaluate 'success' by institutional measures. Staff must maintain behavioural and attitudinal distance, call prisoners 'Mr.', avoid prison slang, give equal credence to prisoners and so on. Departments must strive to have a collective voice and, equally, deal with the institution structurally and not merely by personalities.

It is only on the basis of such a position that a Probation Department has any effective way of responding to a suicide crisis and responding to the inmates concerned; without independent culture values and behaviour the Department will be pulled into being one of the mechanisms that respond to institutional need to restore normality, at the expense of individuals in crisis.

CONCLUSION

I would argue that Total Institutions are as good as incapable of generating change internally. Until the institutions are more effectively opened up to outside influence and control, crises will be a major route to change.

The vary nature of institutions such as those where suicides most commonly occur must be broken up in a planned way. By a different route. Judge Tumim (HMSO, 1990b) comes to some of the same conclusions. His arguments about creating large prisons out of flexible smaller 'communities', for example, is one way of attacking some of the elements of a Total Institution. There must also be abolition of the Official Secrets Act, abolition of Crown Community for prisons and abolition of the Prison Medical Service. The use of category B institutions for local prisons and YOI allocation must stop. Much more access to communication is needed via telephones, visits and outside agencies working inside the prison without direct accountability to the prison (e.g. Samaritans, CAB etc.) Command-based structures and functions need to be shifted further toward management orientation, along with communication lines.

Secretly perhaps the notion of community prisons could contain the germ of something more than marginal change; and the possibility (although not yet the reality) of managers from outside the Prison Service could help. For all this, however, if the unofficial reality of staff values, sub-culture, behaviour and power are likely to remain at best only secret targets for change, then the full implications of a Total Institution analysis will not have been grasped.

Seven

Suicides and prison conditions

Jean-Claude Bernheim

PRISON: A TOTALITARIAN ENVIRONMENT

It has been demonstrated that suicides and attempted suicides are comparatively more frequent in isolation cells and high-security prisons. We consider it important to study these findings more closely, in particular as Doctors Cosyns and Wilmote (1973, p.38), responsible for the Suicide Prevention Centre in Brussels, see prisons as a 'totalitarian structure'.

As early as 1957 Dr Bruno Cormier, at that time psychiatrist at St Vincent de Paul penitentiary in Canada, stated that according to his personal experience:

> *A fascist society has some qualities in common with penal institutions. Both are dictatorial, and both rely for their existence on the restriction of liberty. There are, however, some essential differences. For instance, no dictatorial society has yet been sufficiently absolute to prevent men from overthrowing by killing or extensive revolution the abusive power. . In prisons, on the contrary, no riot has yet succeeded in restoring liberty.*
>
> *Within our present democratic society, then those groups of people who are confined to penal institutions are leading an existence governed by an absolutely different principle from the one which governs the rest of our society. The penal institution, as we know it today, deprives its members of social and individual freedom which form the foundation of our society.*
>
> *Prisons differ from concentration camps in that prisons are permanent institutions in our society, while concentration camps*

are temporary institutions existing only during wartime. (In dictatorial societies, however, concentration camps are permanent during the life span of the dictatorship.) (p.140).

In *The Society of Captives*, Sykes (1958, p.xiv) states in his introduction 'the detailed regulations extending into every area of individual's life, the constant surveillance, the concentration of power into the hands of a ruling few, the wide gulf between the rulers and the ruled all are elements of what we would usually call a totalitarian regime'. In addition Goffman (1968) carried out an in depth study of the characteristics and functioning of different types of totalitarian institutions that can be found in our western societies.

He defines a 'total institution' as follows:

... a place of residence and work where a large number of like-situated individuals, cut off from the wider society for an appreciable period of time, together lead an enclosed, formally administered round of life. Prisons serve as a clear example, providing we appreciate that what is prison-like about prisons is found in institutions whose members have broken no laws (p.xiii).

Totalitarian institutions can be classified in five groups:

1. Institutions established to care for persons felt to be both incapable and harmless; these are the homes for the blind, the aged, the orphaned, and the indigent.
2. Places established to care for persons felt to be both incapable of looking after themselves and a threat to the community, albeit an unintended one: TB sanitaria, mental hospitals, and leprosaria.
3. A third type of total institution is organised to protect the community against what are felt to be intentional dangers to it, with the welfare of the persons thus sequestered not the immediate issue: jails, penitentiaries, POW camps, and concentration camps.
4. Institutions purportedly established the better to pursue some worklike task and justifying themselves only on these instrumental grounds: army barracks, ships, boarding schools, work camps, colonial compounds, and large mansions from the point of view of those who live in servants' quarters.
5. Finally, there are those establishments designed as retreats from the world even while often serving also as

training stations for the religious; examples are abbeys, monasteries, convents, and other cloisters (p.16).

Several doctors have commented on the totalitarian aspects of prisons. For Dr. Schaub and Landau (1972, p.45) prisons are a highly 'pathogenic environment'. Doctors Colin, Gonin and Ducottet (1975, p.3) consider that prisons 'can be defined as a perversely structured psychotic universe'. As for the effects of these institutions on the inmates, Dr Cormier and his colleague Jean-Paul Williams (1966, p.472) note that 'the loss of freedom is accompanied by an emotional regression which varies according to each individual, but which is a constant phenomenon nonetheless'.

More recently, Dr. Eichenberg (1972) concluded that the 'pathogenic effect of imprisonment' is a result of general prison conditions and loss of freedom. It is generally accepted today that present prison conditions create 'abnormal living conditions' (Dorlhac de Borne, 1984, p.30).

Consequently, the following question should be asked: Is the high number of suicides and suicide attempts not the result of bad prison conditions and its totalitarian structure?

In a paper on psycho-pathological reactions to captivity, Carrot et al. (1949, p.376) state that 'it is difficult to confuse captivity [in war] and detention in a prison' even if 'the tendency is to establish a link between the mental state of captivity of the group and prison psychoses'.

However, prison conditions to which prisoners of war studied by Carrot and his colleagues were submitted are curiously similar to those experienced by the political or common law prisoners we have studied:

The prison environment is grey, horizons are blocked off. In addition to the monotony, the separation from families and the anxiety this causes, the close crowding of prison life and the inevitable conflicts this engenders, there is the long duration of the war, where months run into more months and where hopes of liberation go through various alternatives: desires to escape, unsuccessful escape attempts, deceptions and jealousies which arise as a result of unfair and inequitable discipline, restricted and censored mail, depressing propaganda and, above all, the permanent feeling of constraint, the guards who are omnipresent, sometimes good-natured, sometimes brutal, but always unpredictable (p.377).

This description could well apply to custody and prison conditions and there is no reason to believe that these abnormal conditions do not exert a pathological influence, both on prisoners of war and on prison inmates.

Carrot et al. state in their study (1949) that:

> ... *lack of privacy (in addition to anxiety caused by separation from families) has also been revealed to be very pathogenic: individuals who feel they are suspected of stealing, who think everybody mistrusts them, that everything is an allusion on their lives, their behaviour or their families. In this type of situation, incidents have provoked suicide attempts (p.383).*

Even if after World War II psychiatrists believed that the effects of captivity were not the same for war prisoners as for common law prisoners, this can no longer be the case today.

For Dr. Cormier (1957, p.146), a psychiatrist, 'normal offenders are quite comparable to political prisoners in their reaction to deprivation of liberty'. He defines a 'normal offender' as 'first offender with no history of criminal tendencies'.

However, Dr. Cormier (1966, p.480) considers that even if 'the wider psychology of political prisoners, concentration camp detainees and criminals is different...the symptoms of psychopathological states we have encountered in these men are similar'.

Dr Thorburn (1984, p.40), who at the time was doctor at the San Quentin prison hospital, USA, wrote that the study of self-mutilations in prison was 'an opportunity to evaluate the disease characteristics' of prison conditions.

Lastly, the vast majority of doctors having worked or are working inside prisons and who have written on the subject of suicide attempts in prison consider this institution as a pathogenic environment which generates 'human behaviour modifications that only the individuals with strong and well structured personalities can tolerate without too much difficulty' (Eichenberg, 1978, p.116).

SUICIDES AND THE DEGREE OF SECURITY IN PRISONS

We shall now take a closer look at the kind of prison where suicides reported in Canadian, French, Belgian and Swiss prisons have occurred.

Generally speaking, western correctional systems cover a

wide range of institutions of various degrees of security, according to their 'vocation'. For example, minimum security prisons, medium security prisons, which are more restrictive, but still allow a certain degree of freedom of movement; maximum security prisons which totally or almost totally restrict all movement of inmates. It is in the latter type of institution that are to be found detainees or prisoners considered to be dangerous or who present a high escape risk.

It goes without saying that prison conditions worsen as security becomes more restrictive and the number of hours spent in isolation or locked up increase.

Canada

Table 1 shows that from 1960 to 1983, 71 per cent of suicides in Canadian penitentiary occurred in maximum security institutions and that the average percentage of suicides in these prisons is 1.5 times higher than the percentage of people detained there. As we know, the suicide rate almost doubles if one refers to the number of admissions. It can therefore be concluded without risk of error that most suicides occur in maximum security prisons or at least a certain number of them.

In addition, 139 of the 206 suicides which took place between 1960 and 1983 (67%) occurred in 6 maximum security prisons which are well-known for their severity: Dorchester, St-Vincent de Paul, Archambault, Kingston, Prince Albert, and British Columbia.

Burtch and Ericson (1979) calculated the suicide rates in the 4 most ancient maximum security prisons in Canada. Their results are shown in Table 2.

Let us now take a look at six institutions involved.

1. Penitentiary of British Columbia

On the subject of suicide attempts and self-mutilations, Dr. Scott, a psychiatrist employed by the Canadian Correctional Service, and who testified in the case of *McCann v. The Queen* in 1975, revealed that in 1974 at BC penitentiary, 11 per cent of the inmates in the Special Correction Unit (SCU) had cut their wrist or other parts of the body compared with 1 per cent of the rest of the prison population; whereas 6.4 per cent of SCU inmates tried to commit suicide 'only' 0.9 per cent of the general prison population did so (Jackson, 1983, p.79).

Table 1
Relation between the % of suicides within maximum security
penitentiaries and the % of the carceral population detained
within maximum security penitentiaries in Canada from 1960
to 1983

year	% of suicides in maximum security pen. (a)	% of the carceral population detained in max. sec. pens. (b)	a/b
1960[1]	100	8	1.20
1961[1]	100	77	1.30
1962[1]	100	74	1.35
1963[1]	100	71	1.41
1964[1]	100	71	1.41
1965[1]	100	71	1.41
1966[3]	90	62	1.45
1967[3]	100	56	1.79
1968[2]	94	52	1.81
1969[1]	83	55	1.51
1970[2]	89	44	2.02
1971[2]	71	36	1.97
1972[2]	86	36	2.39
1973[2]	55	41	1.34
1974[2]	57	39	1.46
1975[2]	50	41	1.22
1976[2]	100	40	2.50
1977[1]	50	41	1.22
1978[1]	33	36	0.92
1979[1]	22	39	0.56
1980[2]	70	33	2.12
1981[2]	50	35	1.43
1982[2]	55	36	1.53
1983[2]	63	35	1.80

Sources:
1. Statistics Canada, Catalogue 85-207 *annual, 1960 to 1965, 1968-69, 1977 to 1979.*
2. Annual Report, Solicitor General Canada, *1969 to 1976 and 1980 to 1983.*
3. Statistics Handbook, Canadian Criminal Justice, *Solicitor General Canada, 1977, p. 63.*

Table 2
Suicide rate for four Canadian penitentiaries from 1960 to 1975

Penitentiary	No. of suicides	%	Rate per 100,000 DAP
St-Vincent de Paul (1960-73)	48	52	528.4
Prince Albert (1960-75)	18	19	209.7
British Columbia (1960-75)	14	15	186.5
Kingston (1960-72)	13	14	163.5
Total	93	100	$\mu = 272.0$

Source: Burtch and Ericson(1979), p. 8.

Compared with the average annual suicide tare in Canadian prisons it can be observed that the rate at BC Penitentiary (Table 2) is 1.8 times higher (186.5/104.6) for the years 1960-1975.

Referring to prison conditions, Judge Heald of the Federal Court of Canada, declared in a famous judgment in 1975, that 'confinement ... in the Solitary Confinement Unit at BC Penitentiary constitutes amounted to the imposition of cruel and unusual treatment or punishment contrary to section 2(b) of the Canadian Bill of Rights' (*McCann v. The Queen*, 1976, p.614).

BC Penitentiary was closed down by the Canadian Correctional Service in 1980.

2. Kingston Penitentiary

Kingston Penitentiary was studied very closely after the uprising there in April 1971. We shall be referring to this study, given that 14 of the 17 suicides which occurred there between 1960 and 1983 took place up to and including 1971. In their report Swackhammer et al. (1972, p.60) stated that:

> *Inmates at Kingston penitentiary were forced to spend at least 16 hours daily, practically isolated, in their cells. In this limited and confined environment, they were only permitted to sleep, read, write 'authorised' letters and to have one pastime, on condition that they received permission and had the financial means ... Even within the confines of the cell and concerning external appearance, the list of regulations was so long that the inmates had in fact become a series of pawns, programmed to adopt identical personal habits and lifestyles.*

Their report also mentioned 'the substantial reduction of privileges' of inmates following the 'spontaneous' demonstration in 1967 (p.40). It is to be noted that 2 and 3 suicides in 1967 and 1968 occurred during the period when prison conditions were becoming more severe.

At Kingston penitentiary the average annual suicide rate for the years 1960-1972 (Table 2) is 1.6 times higher than the average rate in other prisons during the same period (163.5/104.5).

3. Archambault Penitentiary

At Archambault penitentiary, where conditions have deteriorated since the work strike by inmates which lasted four months in 1976, and where the inmates' committee was forbidden from giving support to inmates who had suicidal tendencies, the number of suicides has increased in the past years. The events of 1982, during which three prison guards were killed, did nothing to improve the situation. On the contrary, as Amnesty International (1983, p.32) reported:

> *The A.I. delegation found that there exists at least 'reasonable grounds to believe' that there was within the meaning of United Nations Declaration on Torture, torture or other cruel, inhuman or degrading treatment or punishment in the Archambault institution during the period beginning 26 July 1982.*

Following the mission by AI, the then Solicitor General, Mr. Bob Kaplan, appointed a correctional Inquirer, whose office is part of the Ministry of the Solicitor General, to inquire into 'the allegation of bad treatment of inmates at Archambault penitentiary following the incidents of 25 July, 1982.

In this report Mr Stewart (1984) states that there are reliable elements of proof that inmates placed in isolation were subjected to bad treatment in July and August 1982. However it is impossible to determine the extent and gravity of maltreatment (pp.48-49).

He states in his recommendations: 'it is essential that there be meaningful attitudinal changes and improvements that come from the administration and filter down to all levels' (pp.185-86).

It is fair to state that prison conditions became considerably worse at Archambault after 25 July 1982.

Between 1980 and 1985 there were 11 suicides, an

Table 3
Total number of suicide for Archambault penitentiary since its
founding in 1968 to 1985

Year	No. of suicides	Rate per 100.000 DAP
1969	0	
1970	0	
1971	0	
1972	1	
1973	1	
1974	1	
1975	1	
1976	0	
1977	0	
1978	0	
1979	0	
1980	0	
1981	2	
1982	3	
1983	3	
1984	3	
1985	0	
Average (1969-85)	0.9	207.6
Average (1969-80)	0.3	78.4
Average (1980-85)	1.8	431.4
Total	15	

Sources:
Canada(1976). Recueil statistique - aspect choisis de la question
pénale. *Ottawa, Solliciteur général du Canada, Division des
statistiques, 1976, 8 mars, p. 69*
*Phone call with Michel Lauzon, Correctional Service Canada, Quebec
Region, September 1986.*

approximate average annual rate of 431 suicides per 100,000
persons in custody, for an average daily population of 425
sentenced individuals (Table 3).

For the period 1980-85 therefore the average annual rate of
suicide is double the average annual rate recorded since the
penitentiary was opened in 1960 (431/207.6) and 2.6 times
higher than the average annual rate in Canadian penitentiaries
during the same period (431.4/168.5).

It is to be noted that from the opening of the penitentiary until 1980 the suicide rate there was lower than the average annual rate in Canadian prisons: respectively 78 per 100,000 persons sentenced (1969-1980) and 114.6 (1970-1979).

4. Prince Albert Penitentiary

'This institution has had disturbances throughout its history' (MacGuigan et al., 1977, p.20). These were the terms used in the Parliamentary Subcommittee's Report which summarised the history of this prison, opened in 1911.

The report notes: 'in 1976 there was a tragic, but non violent occurrence when three native Indians died in one week, one after choking on food and the other two by committing suicide' (p.20).

An enquiry carried out by the John Howard Society of Saskatchewan (1975) shows that all six suicides which occurred between 18 November 1972 and 16 June 1973 took place in the isolation units. The enquiry also highlights the deplorable prison conditions at the prison during that period.

For the period 1960-1975 the average annual suicide rate (Table 2) was twice the average annual rate of Canadian penitentiaries (209.7/104.6).

5. St-Vincent de Paul Penitentiary

Between 1960 and 1983 40.7 per cent (60/147) of the suicides in maximum security penitentiaries took place in a single institution: St-Vincent de Paul penitentiary. Between 1975 and 1983 a quarter (24.5%) of all suicides in maximum security prisons occurred at this prison, i.e. 12/49.

Compared with suicides in the general Canadian penitentiary population for the years 1960-1983, 29 per cent of the total number of suicides (60/206) occurred at St-Vincent de Paul, which is a staggering figure. Between 1975 and 1983 the percentage went down to 13 per cent, which is 'respectable'.

In Canadian penitentiaries the average suicide rate for the years 1960 to 1973 is 104.5, i.e. five times lower the rate at St-Vincent de Paul for the same period. On 3rd October 1983 the prison director at St-Vincent de Paul, Mr. Marc-André Lafleur, wrote to an inmate in the segregation wing, i.e. in isolation for administration reasons, 'I agree with you that it is inhuman to live in pavilion no.1'

Since the publication of the Archambault report in 1938 no

Table 4
Number of suicides in British Columbia prisons from 1970 to 1980

Prison	No. of suicides		%
Oakalla	24		68.6
west wing		14	
south wing		5	
east wing		3	
segregation unit		2	5.7
Lakeside	2		5.7
Alouette	2		5.7
Wilkinson Rd	3		8.5
Prince George	2		5.7
Kamloops (1976)	1		2.9
Haney (closed in 1976)	1		2.9
Total	35		100.0

Source: Scott-Denon (1983), p.109.

one would contest the poor living conditions at St-Vincent de Paul. For fifty years there has been talk of improving or closing it down, and this kind of discourse has justified the construction of several other penitentiaries.

6. British Columbia

In his report for the Correctional Service of British Columbia, Scott Denon (1983) indicates the number of suicides in the various prisons of the province. These figures are shown in Table 4.

Once again one observes that the majority (69%) of the suicides in the provincial prisons of British Columbia occurred in a maximum security institution, the Lower Marinland Regional Correctional Centre; generally known as Oakalla.

In 1975 Dr. Guy Richmond, who was a doctor at Oakalla for several years, wrote that in the 1950s major improvements and renovations were called for at the prison. The isolation area was in such a bad state that it was impossible to ensure the health of inmates. As the piping for the heating system ran through this area the temperature was higher than the safety limit permitted and rats were the sole companions for inmates. It was not until 1954 that a new isolation unit was built, which only had a bucket as a toilet (Richmond, 1975, pp.48-49).

Despite this, Dr. Richmond continued to believe that 'this type of punishment (isolation) is not only useless but produces more aggression and depression, especially in the case of the younger offender' (p.49).

Because of the bad living conditions at this prison the provincial government of British Columbia announced that it would be closed down.

France

For France the figures are not so complete. They do however allow us to continue our demonstration.

Tournier and Chemithe (1979) reported on the number of suicides in France per region. Table 5 summarises their figures for three institutions.

Fleury-Mérogis prison was built over a period of several years and was finally completed at the end of July 1973. For advocates of clean incarceration, Fleury-Mérogis was the prototype of the ideal prison, combining modern standards of detention with modern construction techniques and sophisticated surveillance means.

In spite of the hopes inspired by this state of the art prison, troubles soon began. As the ex-Secretary of State for prisons from 1974 to 1976, Madame Dorlhac de Borne, admitted in 1984, 'at this prison which no one now calls `a model prison' there are more suicides than elsewhere' but slightly fewer than at the Santé, it must be pointed out (p.36).

When talking about Fleury-Mérogis in 1981, Favard admitted that 'modern achievements do not prevent suicides occurring as in any other prison' (p.172).

He reported 48 suicides between 1968 and 1979, more than 12 per cent of the total number of suicides (396) which took place in French prisons during the same period.

Taking into account the figures between the final completion of the prison in 1973 up until 1979, there were 40 suicides, which is equivalent to a suicide rate of 186/100,000 detained persons (Table 6). This rate is 7.7 times higher than the suicide rate among men in the general population (24), whereas for the whole of French prisons during the 1970s the suicide rate was 4.9 times higher. Fleury-Mérogis prison is clearly more dangerous than all of the other prisons put together.

In 1976 there were 12 suicides in this modern prison: '30% of

Table 5
Number and rate of suicide in three prisons in France, 1975-978

Prison	No of suicides	Rate 100.000 DAP
Fleury-Mérogis	27	219.4
La Santé	16	238.9
Fresnes	12	131.2
Total	173	145.9

Source: Tournier et Chemithe (1979), Vol. II, p. 11.
Table 6
Number and rate of suicide at Fleury-Mérogis (France) from 1973 to 1979

Year	No. of suicides	Daily population	Rate 100.000 DAP
1973	5	3076*	162.5
1974	3	3076	97.5
1975	9	3076	292.6
1976	12	3076	390.1
1977**	4	3076	130.0
1978	2	3076	65.0
1979	5	3076	162.5
Mean	5.7	3076	185.8

* *Estimation from Tournier and Chemithe (1979).*
** *Opening of the reception centre.*
Source: Favard (1981), p. 173 and Tournier et Chemithe (1979), Vol II, p. 13.

the total number of suicides in French prisons'. In lights of this dramatic situation the administration finally reacted by setting up a reception centre for new admissions and 'trying to diversify living conditions and relaxing the regulations' (Favard, 1981, p.173).

As a result the suicide rate went down, from 236 per 100,000 incarcerated for the years 1973 to 1976; and to 119 for the years the 1977, 1978 and 1979. This shows that when prison conditions improve the suicide rate goes down.

Given the short periods of time studied and the restricted figures available, this observation could appear circumstantial and it is important to carry out further studies to verify whether they apply generally to other institutions.

In France as in Canada, whether it is in old insalubrious

prisons dating back to the 19th century such as La Santé or St-Vincent de Paul, or 20th century dehumanising 'model prisons' such as Fleury-Mérogis or Archambault, prison conditions are so bad that certain inmates see no solution other than suicide or attempted suicide to put on end to an 'intolerable situation' that they are unable to control. Guignet (1981, p.5) wrote: 'in many cases suicide is truly considered to be the only way out, the final rational act in world where there is no other real alternative.'

Belgium

On December 17, 1979, in Belgium, 'the Minister of Justice officially inaugurated a new prison in Lantin, near Liège ... [He] considers that the prison service has made great efforts to create an institution which responds in the best possible way to humanitarian needs. We have tried to adopt prison life to social progress' (Bulhù and Janssen, 1984, p.66).

However, the figures provide the true picture. According to the statistics of the Belgian Ministry of Justice (Belgium, 1985) there were 2 suicides in 1979 at Lantin prison and at a total of 5 for the first 61 months of operation. Given an average daily rate of 300 persons incarcerated, this provides an annual suicide rate of 327/100,000 incarcerated persons, which is double the average annual rate for all prisons in Belgium (327/163).

Switzerland

For the situation prevailing in Switzerland we referred to the information on the 'model prison' at Champ-Dollon which was officially opened on 8 June 1977. Between the opening in 1970 and February 1980 there were 7 suicides, corresponding to an annual rate of the order of 1,866 suicides per 100,000 inmates of the average daily population. Compared with the other prisons in Switzerland, Champ-Dollon prison is the cause of four times more deaths (1866/465).

ANALYSIS

The results presented so far show that the suicide rates are higher in maximum security institutions, where regulations are more severe, resemble a totalitarian-type regime.

In his analysis of suicidal behaviour at the Santé prison in

France Dr. Hivert (1970, p.372) wrote:

> *In every instance, suicidal behaviour is an expression of the difficulty in establishing communications within a structure where relationships are established on an authoritarian basis and where messages are only transmitted one way.*

Swackhammer and his colleagues (1972, p.38) noted that at Kingston penitentiary in Canada, 'dialogue is impossible between inmates and guards, guards and professional staff and this has led to the inevitable destruction of the programme and the deterioration of prison conditions'.

Dr. Eichenberger (1978, p.115) stated:

> *We must admit that unfortunately inside prisons there are other means of expression than talking: self-mutilation, hangings or other suicide attempts, hunger strikes, violent action (fights, weapons, hostages), escape attempts etc. In all of these means of expression the common denominator is a state of tension where the only means of expression is this symbolic language. Expression by violent means is unusual for a normal person because when free he can resort to a whole range of possibilities before finally resorting to violence. For a person with personality or character problems however (incomplete mental development) where pathology consists of expression through acts rather than words, the symbolic language of violence is usual, as it is for a normal person in a situation of duress.*

This breakdown of dialogue, which has been emphasised by others, is placed in the prison context by Dr. Eichenberger and appears to be more specifically related to high security institutions. When studying the Special Correction Unit of Quebec (Canada), Dr Cormier (1971: 6) noted in a preliminary report that the objective of narrowing the gap between 'guards and inmates' had not been achieved.

Another factor linked to imprisonment is isolation, punitive or administrative, or judicial as in some European countries. Many authors consider this to be a determining cause in the number of suicides in prison. We know that at least 20 per cent of suicides occur in isolation cells. However, to have a better idea of the impact of isolation we must compare the percentage of people held in isolation cells with the number of suicides in isolation. This comparison is possible for Canada and shows that there are proportionally 3 times more suicides or attempted suicides in isolation than elsewhere.

When the question of isolation is mentioned prison authorities refer to it as a particular situation resulting from a special measure applied to a specific person and which involves specific conditions of imprisonment for a specific place. These special measures result in the isolation of inmates from other inmates. But can it be said that people who are locked in their cells 16 hours a day, which is part of the normal functioning in places such as Kingston penitentiary, are not also in isolation? We do not believe so but in order accurately to assess the effect of isolation on the number of suicides we must first establish a definition of actual prison conditions which is not based merely on administrative definitions. Such an analysis goes beyond the present study. We can, however, present the opinion of certain specialists.

The effects of isolation on men and women who are submitted to treatment have been the object of studies for decades and are worth noting.

For Cormier and Williams (1966, p.472) imprisonment or 'the loss of freedom' for whatever reason is a traumatic experience 'which leaves nobody indifferent'. But what should we think of an isolation experience in a totalitarian environment such as a prison?

Existing literature on the effect of isolation is not unanimous on the negative effects, especially regarding isolation in prisons (Crelinsten, 1981). However, it must be pointed out that the most ardent defenders of isolation in prisons are the staff of Correctional Services, such as the Canadians Chuny Roy and Peter Suefield, and that opponents of isolation are people who are independent of the prison authorities at the time of taking a position, such as W.E. Lucas and Richard R. Korn, ex-assistant director of a prison.

Some opponents of the use of isolation inside prison have adopted a very radical position, describing it as cruel, inhuman and degrading, or comparing it directly to torture. In an article in 1976 Lucas stated: 'Solitary confinement is a form of torture ...' (p.153), provoking a strong reaction by Suefield (1978).

In the McCann case (1976) Dr. Peter Suefield testified that the effectiveness of such measures was so doubtful as to merit their abandonment. He stated 'I would be happy for one to see it removed from the repertoire of punitive techniques' (p.599).

In the same case, referring to prison conditions at the Special Correction Unit (SCU) at British Columbia penitentiary in Canada, Dr. Korn wrote that for inmates there 'this experience is a most exquisite form of torture' (p.3).

Professor Fox noted that the use of 'continuous illumination (as practice at the SCU) ... it is something that is employed in international torture' (in *McCann v. The Queen*, 1976, p.595).

Judge Heald wrote in his judgment:

Even if it served some penal purpose, I still think the treatment herein described would be cruel and unusual because it is not in accord with public standards of decency and propriety, since it is unnecessary because of the existence of adequate alternatives (p. 606).

The government of Canada did not appeal against this judgment.

The European Commission of Human Rights stated in its report on the *Ireland v. United Kingdom* case, brought before the Committee of Ministers of the Council of Europe on 9 February 976, that: 'Total sensory deprivation combined with total social isolation can without any doubt destroy personality and constitutes a form of inhuman treatment, which cannot be justified by security reasons' (Amnesty International, 1980, p.13).

Therefore, there is support for the opinion that the use of isolation cells, as practices in certain prisons, is a form of torture, especially as Amnesty International (1973, 1974) considers isolation as a torture technique.

As for the effect of isolation as practised at the SCU in British Columbia (Canada), Dr. Korn states that '...the evidence simply is if that you keep people long enough, they will engage in self-torture, simply to focus the pain' (in *McCann v. The Queen*, 1976, p.592).

Maltaverne (1982) confirmed this statement in his report on a specific case:

He briefly explained all these suicide attempts (phlebotomy, swallowing of foreign bodies) as an overwhelming need to suffer, the pain easing an internal tension which had become unbearable (p.184).

Dr. Fox wrote that inmates subjected to such conditions

'most of them prefer to die, they hang themselves rather than sustain it' (McCann, 1976, p.596).

The connection between the use of isolation and suicides in prisons is not recent as already in 1922 Hobhouse and Brockway wrote 'a close connection between isolation and suicidal tendency is evidenced in many of the reports' (p.558).

Since then, several authors including Wilson and Pescor (1939), Schaub et al. (1971), New York(1972), Cooper (1974), Johnson (1978), Gayda and Vacola (1984), Harding (1984) have confirmed the close link between inhuman prison conditions, material as well as psychological, and suicides in prisons.

Following the events of 25 July 1982 at Archambault penitentiary in Canada, renovations were carried out aimed at isolating still further the inmates from prison staff; and the severity of the new regulations which were adopted has also contributed to reducing contact between inmates and outside visitors. Every effort has been made to increase the physical and social isolation of prisoners. The number of suicides has also considerably increased. Given the knowledge and information we now have, it is difficult not to believe that there exists a link between cause and effect. Just as for Fleury-Mérogis in France it would be useful to be able to confirm this observation.

CONCLUSION

From the statistics and information gathered it is now no longer possible to question the fact that the high suicide rate in certain prisons or categories of prisons is directly and without any doubt related to inhuman prison conditions.

There is only one way to put an end to these deaths, which are too numerous: radically change the inhumane prison conditions in those institutions most affected; first and foremost, abolish all forms of isolation.

Eight

Suicide and suicide attempts amongst young prisoners: The UK experience

There is no doubt that the first few days in a remand centre or young offenders institution have a devastating effect. The new prisoner is bewildered, disorientated and lost; it shows on their faces. They lose their appetite and they often cry. They are no longer the hard man putting on a brave face in court (Little and Bullock, 1990, pp.11-12).

Young prisoner suicide has been a neglected area of research and interest in the UK until the recent explosion of coverage given to the topic by media and campaigning organisations in the late 1980s and early 1990s. Few studies look explicitly at 'the young' as an identifiable and vulnerable group in their own right.[1] A recent study carried out in England over a three year period has as its focus the particular vulnerability of young prisoners to suicide and self-injury. It is this research which has informed the argument of this chapter: that young prisoners present a specific vulnerability to suicidal thoughts and feelings, and that many of these feelings are related to identifiable aspects of the prison situation (Liebling, 1992). A second neglected area has been the management of suicide risk by staff; their responses to and perceptions of the problems posed by those apparently at risk of self-harm.

Recent interest in young prisoner suicide in the UK began in the early 1980s, when the Glenochil Young Offenders

Institution suffered from a series of self-inflicted deaths (see Scottish Home and Health Department, 1985). A Working Group Report noted that there was:

> ... *no remarkable change in the national trend in 1981 that would help to explain the deaths at Glenochil over the past few years. In any case, it is clear that the rates within the complex are much higher than in the general population (SHHD, 1985, 15).*

Soon after this series of deaths, a similar series occurred in England and Wales. In Hull, Leeds, Hindley, Swansea, and elsewhere: that is in busy local and remand centres and not primarily in establishments accommodating young sentenced prisoners, tragic self-inflicted deaths and an escalating number of suicide attempts occurred (see Grindrod and Black, 1989; Home Office, 1988b; Davies, 1990; Liebling, 1992). Increasingly, young prisoners were committing suicide in apparently disproportionate numbers to those occurring either in the community or in prison.

Table 1
Summary of Numbers of Suicides and Self-Inflicted
Deaths in Prison 1985-1989*

Year	1985	1986	1987	1988	1989
Local/Remand	25(21)	16(13)	35(33)	24(22)	34(23)
Dispersal	-	2 (1)	3 (2)	3 (1)	2 (2)
Cat B	2 (2)	2 (2)	4 (3)	4 (4)	2 (1)
Cat C	-	1 (1)	1 (1)	4 (3)	5 (4)
Open	-	-	-	-	-
Female	1 (-)	-	-	-	-
YOI**	1 (-)	-	3 (3)	2 (1)	5 (3)
Total	29(23)	21(17)	46(42)	37(31)	48(33)

*   *Source: Adapted from Home Office, 1990d, pp.50-51.*
** *The self-inflicted deaths in YOIs includes only a small proportion of all young prisoner deaths (see below); many occur in local and remand centres. The figures in brackets are deaths confirmed as suicide by Coroners Inquests.*

Table 2
Self-Inflicted Deaths of Young Prisoners 1987-1990*

1987	7
1988	9
1989	11
1990	10

* *Up-dated from Home Office, 1990d, p.22; Prison Reform Trust, 1990, p.5.*

Several possible explanations were put forward for these deaths and for the increasing number of suicide attempts and self-inflicted injuries occurring amongst young prisoners. Official discourse maintained that there was 'no common link' between the suicides, whether or not they took place within particular establishments and wings, or over short periods of time within a small number of prisons (see McHugh, 1989; also Liebling, 1992). Bullying and harassment of young prisoners by each other was clearly evident from the Working Party Report, as was on occasion, incitement of prisoners by cell-mates to hang themselves. Such behaviour was a feature of the 'inmate sub-culture' (see especially SHHD, 1985; but also Liebling, 1992; Shine et al., 1990; Johnson, 1973; McGurk and McDougal, 1986; Bowker, 1980; and more recently, Liebling and Krarup, 1993). The Scottish Working Group described how after one or two self-inflicted deaths in an establishment:

> ... both staff and inmates become very sensitive to the possibility of suicidal behaviour; staff anxiety rises and leads to increased surveillance and security, which may be counter-productive; among inmates, the initial shock gives way to an acceptance of self-injury and suicide, so that at times of stress it becomes a more likely reaction (SHHD, 1985, p.16)

In Glenochil, increased staff sensitivity towards all acts of self-injury arising as a result of the first few deaths, and a conscientious adherence to stringent guidelines in the recent Circular, gave rise to an unprecedented number of inmates who declared themselves to be suicidal, or who injured themselves superficially in order to remove themselves from difficulties they were experiencing in the mainstream of the young offenders institution. Such activities inevitably resulted in a certain level of 'compassion fatigue' in many establishments amongst some of the staff. In other words, staff found it increasingly difficult to respond to self-inflicted injuries without the additional complications of feeling manipulated, exasperated and vulnerable. A culture was set up of officers referring potentially suicidal inmates to the prison hospital. A doctor or psychiatrist would interview the inmate and conclude that he was not psychiatrically ill or clinically depressed. The inmate would be sent back to the wing. There, amidst frustrated staff, his suicide risk would continue.

It became increasingly apparent to the Scottish Working Party that the 'suicide problem' was not a psychiatric one. It was a management problem. This recognition signalled the beginning of a crucial transformation in the understanding of young prisoner suicide, reflected in the sorts of conclusions drawn by His Honour Judge Tumim in his review of suicide prevention procedures published in 1990. This move away from an exclusively 'medical' or psychiatric understanding of the problem of prison suicide has had far-reaching effects on policy and practice (see in particular, Liebling, 1992; Liebling and Krarup, 1993; also Home Office, 1990c; Prison Service, 1992).

Importantly, four studies were carried out in the UK which added weight to a growing argument that prison suicide was distinct from suicide in the community, particularly in this respect (Backett, 1987; Dooley, 1990a; Liebling, 1992; Liebling and Krarup, 1993). In almost 90 per cent of suicides in the community, a history of psychiatric treatment or illness was evident (Barraclough and Hughes, 1987). In prison, only a third of self-inflicted deaths were found to have a history of psychiatric illness, despite the elevated levels of psychiatric treatment found in the histories of the prison population (Backett, 1987, 1988; Dooley, 1990a; Gunn et al., 1978; Prison Reform Trust, 1991). Amongst young prisoners, this figure was found to be 13 per cent (Liebling, 1992). Clearly, some other set of explanations was required for these deaths.

In May of 1990 the Samaritans published a report showing that suicide amongst young males in the general population had increased by over 50 per cent over the last 10 years, from 10 per 100,000 to 15 per 100,000 (Samaritans, 1990). Mortality Statistics for England and Wales showed that the suicide rate for all males aged between 16 and 44 had increased from 26 per 100,000 in 1986 to 28 per 100,000 in 1988 (OPCS, 1990). At least 600 young men between 15 and 24 killed themselves in 1989. In 1992, the reported suicide figures for young males were even higher (Samaritans, 1992). Amongst the under 25 age group, suicide amongst males increased by 75 per cent between 1980 and 1990. A research team from Edinburgh had illustrated that much of the increase could be accounted for by young men in social classes four and five: those at the socially and economically disadvantaged end of the demographic spectrum (Kreitman et al., 1991). This illustrated a significant point: those young men most at risk of suicide in the community were also those people most at risk of imprisonment.

YOUNG PRISONER SUICIDES: A SPECIAL CASE?

Studies differ as to whether the under 21 group are at particular risk of suicide in prison. Circular Instructions tend 'not to distinguish between arrangements for adult and young prisoners' (Prison Reform Trust, 1987, p.3). Lloyd argued in his literature review of suicide and self-injury in prison that young prisoners appear to be less at risk of completed suicide than other groups (Lloyd, 1990). Recent research and events, however, have highlighted the special risks posed by young offenders, who are increasingly likely to use hanging as a method of self-destructive behaviour, both in prison (Wool and Dooley, 1987) and outside (McClure, 1984). The evidence suggests that the early adult years (up to the age of 26) are a particularly at risk time for prisoners (Hatty and Walker, 1986; Hayes, 1983; Liebling, 1992).

The remand population are disproportionately at risk of suicide. Young prisoners make up a third of the remand population in England and Wales on any one day (see Table 3). At present in the UK, 22 per cent of the sentenced prison population are under 21. The proportion of under-21 annual receptions is disproportionately high, as the average sentence served by young offenders is shorter than those served by adults. Young prisoners provide a large 'pool' of potential suicide risks.

Table 3
Sentenced and Unsentenced Young Offenders as a Proportion
of the Total Prison Population 1988

	Male no.	Female no.	Total no.	Young offenders no.	%
Remand	9,982	430	10,489	3,439	(33)
Sentenced	37,006	1,276	38,282	8,346	(22)
Total	46,988	1,706	48,771	11,785	(24)

Source: Prison Statistics England and Wales, 1988.

Table 4
Young Offender Prison Statistics and Suicides 1972-1987

	1972-75	1976-79	1980-83	1984-87	% Increase '72-75 to '84-87 [A][1]	[B][2]
Total receptions (annual averages)						
Remand	22,728	25,496	27,595	29,690	(31)	
Sentenced	20,123	25,191	27,837	26,101	(30)	
Total	42,851	50,687	55,432	55,791	(30)	(23)
Average daily population						
Remand	1,935	2,032	2,241	3,029	(56)	
Sentenced	8,971	10,161	10,397	9,786	(9)	
Total	10,906	12,193	12,638	12,815	(18)	(22)
Suicides	5	6	8	12	(140)	(121)
Suicides / 100,000 *Receptions*	2.9	2.9	3.6	5.4	(86)	(80)
Suicides / 100,000 ADP	11.5	12.3	15.8	23.4	(103)	(81)

1. Young prisoners
2. All adults and YOIs
Source: Prison Statistics England and Wales 1972-1988.

YOUNG PRISONER SUICIDE IN ENGLAND AND WALES 1972-1987
The most recent study of prison suicides in England and Wales
included 295/300 consecutive prison deaths receiving suicide

Table 5
Suicides in Custody: Backgrounds

Prison	Young offender suicides		All suicides		Sentenced population
	No.	%	No.	%	%
Stage of custody					
Remand	16	(52)	139	(47)	(11)
Convicted	5	(16)	16	(5)	(4)
Sentenced	10	(32)	140	(48)	(83)
Sex					
Male	30	(97)	290	(98)	(97)
Female	1	(3)	5	(2)	(3)
Marital status					
Single	29	(94)	158	(54)	nk
Married	2	(6)	63	(21)	nk
Separated	-	-	58	(20)[a]	nk
Not known	-	-	3	(1)	nk
Ethnic origin					
UK White	27	(87)	247	(84)	(83)
Afro-Carrib.	2	(6)	18	(6)	(9)
Asian	1	(7)	30	(10)	(8)
Not known	1	(7)	-	-	-

a. A further 13 (4.4%) of all prison suicides had killed their spouse.

verdicts (Dooley, 1990a). Thirty one (10.5%) of the 295 prison deaths receiving suicide verdicts occurring between 1972 and 1987 and studied by Dooley (1990a) were under 21. All of the 31 young prisoner deaths by suicide died by hanging. Some of the deaths were clustered in particular establishments. It has been possible, using Dooley's figures, and Prison Statistics for England and Wales, to show how young offender suicide rates compare with all suicides in prison between 1972 and 1987. The rate of young prisoner suicide has increased since 1972, and this increase has been slightly larger than that shown for all prison suicides.

Some of the increase can be attributed to the increasing proportion of remand prisoners in the young prisoner population: the sentenced young offender population has decreased since 1972; the remand population has doubled (see

Table 6
Under-21 Suicides in Custody: Details

	Young offender suicides[a]		All suicides[a]	All sent'd suicides[a]	Sent'd prison pop'n[a]
	No.	%	%	%	%
Offence (/Charge)					
Burglary/Theft	14	(45)	(34)	(39)	(61)
Murder	3	(10)	(19)	(16)	(4)
Rape	2	(6)	(5)	(4)	(2)
Other sexual	1	(3)	(5)	(1)	(3)
Arson	1	(3)	(4)	(6)	(1)
Wounding/GBH[c]	1	(3)			
ABH[c]	1	(3)	(17)	(24)	(15)
Robbery	2	(6)			
Criminal damage	1	(3)	(4)	(3)	(2)
Other (indictable)	5	(16)	(12)	(9)	(13)
Sentence length[b]:					
Less than 18 mths.	2	(20)	na	(16)	(54)
>18mths- <4 years	5	(50)	"	(27)	(28)
>4 - <10 years	1	(10)	"	(25)	(12)
>10 years	-	-	"	(7)	(1)
Life	-	-	"	(26)	(5)
Borstal	2	(20)	"	-	-
Psychiatric history	4	(13)	na	(33)	(20-30)
Previous self-injury					
Non-custodial	6	(19)	na	nk	nk
During previous custody	5	(16)	"	"	"
During present custody	6	(19)	"	(22)	"
Total	17	(55)	"	(43)	"
Type of accommodation:					
Single cell	12	(39)	na	nk	nk
Multiple cell	9	(29)	"	"	"
Single-hospital	6	(19)	"	"	"
Segregation	4	(13)	"	"	"

a. 1972-87 average
b. 18mths.-3yrs for young offenders
c. GBH = Grievous bodily harm; ABH = Actual bodily harm

Table 4). The percentage increase for all suicides in prison between 1972 and 1987 are given in the last column.

From the details given in the Table above, it is clear that the major increase in the young offender prison population has been amongst remand prisoners. The average daily population of sentenced young prisoners has actually fallen since 1976-1979. Since 1972-1975 the number of remand receptions has increased by almost one third; the average daily population of young remand prisoners has increased by over a half. Young offenders are being remanded into custody in greater numbers in 1984-1987 than in 1972-1975, but they are also spending longer there and in more crowded conditions, often in local prisons intended for adults.

Half of the 31 young prisoner suicides in Dooley's study were on remand at the time of death (the figure for all suicides was 47 per cent); five (16%) were convicted and awaiting sentence, and 10 (32%) were sentenced (see Table 3). The corresponding figures for all suicides were five per cent and 48 per cent respectively. In other words, 11 per cent of all those suicides by sentenced inmates receiving verdicts of suicide were accomplished by young offenders. 11 per cent of remand suicides were accomplished by young offenders. 31 per cent of suicides amongst convicted prisoners awaiting sentence occurred amongst young suicides. All of the ethnic minority deaths received suicide verdicts.

As seen in Table 6, almost half of the suicides were accomplished by young offenders charged or convicted with burglary and theft (45% compared with 34% of all suicides). Few of the young offender suicides were charged with or convicted of offences of violence, compared with the sentenced prison population, or with all prison suicides.

Half (of those sentenced prisoners receiving suicide verdicts) were serving sentences of between 18 months and three years. Only four prisoners (13%) had a recorded history of psychiatric treatment. This is substantially less than that found in the records of all prison suicides. Over half had a history of self-injury (55%); 19 per cent had injured themselves during the current sentence. Over a third (39%) of the suicides occurred in a single cell, but nine of these deaths occurred in multiple cells (29%).

Table 7
Under-21 Suicides in Custody: Timing

Timing of suicide		Young offender suicides		All suicides	
		No.	%	No.	%
Year	1972-1975	5	(16)	nk	
	1976-1979	6	(19)	"	
	1980-1983	8	(26)	"	
	1984-1987	12	(39)	"	
Time of day	00.00-08.00	17	(55)	140	(47)
	08.00-16.00	6	(19)	74	(25)
	16.00-24.00	8	(26)	76	(26)
	not known	-	-	5	(2)
Stage of custody	< 1 week	2	(6)	51	(17)
At time of death	> 1 week < 1 month	6	(19)	33	(11)
	> 1 month < 3 mths	12	(39)	67	(23)
	> 3 mths. < 1 year	10	(32)	76	(26)
	> 1 year	1	(3)	68	(23)

TIMING

No particular pattern was apparent regarding the day of death (four deaths occurred on a Monday, nine on a Tuesday, six on a Wednesday, seven on a Thursday, five on a Friday, five on a Saturday and nine on a Sunday). Most of the deaths occurred between midnight and 8 a.m. (see Table 7).

Most (65 per cent) of the young prisoner deaths occurred within three months of reception into custody, but many (10) occurred after that. More young offenders committed suicide earlier in the sentence than adults (with the exception of the first few days). Few young prisoners committed suicide after one year of their sentence.

Young prisoners differed slightly in terms of apparent motivation for the suicide from all prison suicides. Almost half of the young prisoner suicides were attributed to prison pressure, slightly more than all prison suicides (see Table 8). Guilt for the offence was less likely to be a major motivation, and mental illness was slightly less likely to be a main motivating factor.

Table 8
Under-21 Suicides in Custody: Motivation

	Young offender suicides		All suicides	
	No.	%	No.	%
Imprisonment intolerable	14	(45)	118	(40)
Outside pressures	5	(16)	45	(15)
Guilt for offence	2	(6)	37	(12)
Mental illness	6	(19)	66	(22)
Not known	4	(13)	29	(10)

DISTINGUISHING CHARACTERISTICS OF YOUNG OFFENDER SUICIDES

To summarise, young prisoner suicides differed from a total group of prison suicides in the following respects: they have increased slightly more than all prison suicides. They are more likely to cluster in particular establishments. They are more likely to be located in particular establishments, or wings within particular locals and remand centres, however. They are more likely to occur amongst convicted unsentenced prisoners; they are more likely to be charged with or convicted of acquisitive offences. They are likely to be serving slightly shorter sentences and to end their lives within one month or at most one year of reception into custody. Young prisoner suicides are much less likely to be found to have received psychiatric treatment (13% as opposed to almost a third of all prison suicides).

Gunn found that violent, sexual and drug-related offences were more often associated with psychiatric disturbance than were property offences (Gunn et al., 1978, p.318). The offences of these young suicides and the infrequent presence of a psychiatric history, together suggest that psychiatric illness plays a minor role in their deaths (SHHD, 1985; Dooley, 1990a; Fawcett and Mars, 1973; Diekstra, 1987). Slightly more of the young offenders have a past history of self-injury, but they are no more likely than all suicides to have injured themselves during the current sentence. They are slightly more likely to die between midnight and 8am (55% as opposed to 47% of all suicides). Almost half of the suicides are attributed to prison pressures (40% of all suicides were so ascribed).

Several other studies support the argument that the under 21 age group differ in significant respects from adults, and may have a different susceptibility to suicide in prison. Their offences are found to be less serious: usually property offences (Hayes, 1983), their attempts more frequent (Phillips, 1986), and they are more likely to occur in clusters (Grindrod and Black, 1989; SHHD, 1985; Home Office, 1988b). Australian research shows that when prison suicides are divided into types, one 'atypical' but high risk group emerges which departs from the profiles otherwise associated with prison suicides. This atypical group (found by Hatty and Walker, 1986; Australian Office of Corrections, 1985) is the young offender with a history of convictions for property offences. He is single, with no job or family support; he has a history of self-injury.

There is evidence that young prisoner suicides are more likely to occur in isolation or segregation areas (Hayes, 1983). Young prisoner suicides may differ from adult suicides in other respects, such as impulsivity (Fawcett and Mars, 1973), and the influence of 'contagion' (Diekstra, 1987). They are likely to have fewer ties (children, spouse, etc.) than the adult population. Importantly, the suicides of young offenders may be more 'situation-specific' (Dooley, 1990a; Diekstra, 1987).

In most prison suicide and attempted suicide studies, suicide attempt groups are found to be younger than prison suicide groups, and are more likely to use cutting as a method (Phillips, 1986; Correctional Service Canada, 1981). However, young offenders in Wool and Dooley's study were more likely than adults to use hanging as a method of deliberate self-harm. In a UK study by Thornton (1990) one in 20 inmates in 21 closed male YOI's from three prison regions were found to have injured themselves during the current sentence. He found that one in eight of the young offenders had a history of self-injury. One in 12 reported having injured themselves during their current sentence (including remand; see Table 9). About half of these inmates reported that they intended to kill themselves. His study does not distinguish between types, degrees or frequency of self-injury.

Wool and Dooley (1987) argued that suicide attempts are motivated by 'some form of emotional stress relating to poor communication with family and friends' (p.297). 43 per cent of all attempts were apparently motivated by domestic worries - including close relationships being threatened, visits or letters not arriving, or other bad news. A quarter of the suicide attempts in their study were due to prison pressures, such as

Table 9

Percentages of Attempted Suicide and Self-Injury Amongst
Male Sentenced Young Offenders

		Attempted suicide	Self injury
		%	%
Current sentence:	remand	2.7	4.7
	local prison	0.9	1.1
	YOI	1.6	3.1
	Total	5.2	8.9
Previous institutions		1.8	4.3
Outside		8.3	13.0

Source: adapted from Thornton (1990, p.8)

boredom, or finding the prison situation intolerable. Five per cent were due to an apparent psychotic illness; 16 per cent were attributed to some other emotional disturbance, such as fear, guilt or temper. In nine per cent of cases the reason was unknown, or not given. Isolation and difficulties in communication may contribute to the distress felt by those undergoing domestic worries.

Power and Spencer found in their study of young prisoners in Scotland that half of their sample of self-injurers attributed their 'parasuicidal behaviour' to 'anticipated friction with fellow inmates' (Power and Spencer, 1987, p.231). Strict Suicide Observation (placement in a hospital location with protective clothing and frequent observation) provided an escape from such threats. 18 per cent of these prisoners said they had experienced some form of emotional upset (for example, a consecutive sentence, the death of a relative, etc.) before the incident. Other motives included 'manipulation', according to the authors of this study:

28% of parasuicidal inmates reported a degree of manipulation associated with their behaviour; for example, deciding to opt out of the regime by being placed on SSO; expecting to avoid loss of remission following placement on misconduct report; or expecting transfer to more convivial surroundings such as the prison hospital (Power and Spencer, 1987, p.231)

The authors concluded that the motivations for prison parasuicidal activity included 'avoidance of subjective situational threats'.

Johnson found that his sample of 143 young 'crisis-prone' (self-destructive) prisoners differed significantly from their 168 adult counterparts in three ways: they were disproportionately prone to what he called 'Isolation Panic'; they were more prone to crises indicating 'last-ditch efforts to reinstate flagging social supports'; and they were disproportionately prone to 'crises which marked a declaration of psychological bankruptcy in the face of social pressures and threats' (Johnson, 1978:463). Johnson's study was based on semi-structured interviews with self-destructive young inmates. He found that:

> ... *youths displayed distinctive patterns of psychological breakdown related to concrete coping tests posed in the prison environment and self-esteem problems posed when imprisonment strained interpersonal links or undermined feelings of social competence (Johnson, 1978, p.463)*

He argued that segregation proves more unmanageable for young inmates than for adults because of their especially strong needs for social contact and support:

> *The conditions of solitary confinement can directly undermine preferred coping strategies. Some adolescents rely heavily on activity as a mode of adaptation. Their goal is to immerse themselves in prison life and to ignore disquieting outside concerns (ibid., p.466)*

Johnson concluded that prison creates special problems for young offenders, a particularly vulnerable group (see also Johnson, 1976):

> *Many youths need social support, shared activity, acceptance ... Prison ... is an arid human environment, presenting obstacles to adaptation and threats to self-esteem. It symbolizes community rejection, closes off opportunity and stunts interpersonal growth (ibid., p.481)*

Rates of bullying and victimisation in young offender establishments and in prisons which accommodate young offenders are high and may be increasing (Johnson, 1978; McGurk and McDougal, 1986; Shine et al., 1990; see also

Bowker, 1980). Bullying and 'baroning' are particularly likely during reception and during the first few days after arrival on a new wing (Shine et al., 1990). Baroning is a mode of economic gain whereby tobacco or canteen goods are loaned and borrowed, with high rates of 'interest' expected in return. Inmates may be threatened with violence if they default on payments. 'Taxing' involves the forcible removal of inmates' goods. (Shine et al., 1990, pp.119-20). Young inmates may be particularly susceptible to threats or attacks from others, having few of the resources and skills necessary to avert such behaviour (Johnson, 1978; Bowker, 1980).

Previous research has been dominated by the search for psychiatric explanations for suicides in prison. It has omitted to investigate, for example, whether the experience of imprisonment may be different for the potentially suicidal. Research carried out at the Cambridge Institute of Criminology compared the results of extended interviews with young prisoners who had attempted suicide or injured themselves sufficiently gravely to require hospital treatment with the results of similar interviews with inmates from the general young prisoner population. Both groups were asked in detail about all aspects of their backgrounds, their current situation within the prison and their perceptions of the sentence. Did they have friends, contacts with family, work in prison, how did they spend most of their time? Did they have problems sleeping, few hopes for their release?

The results showed that a group of young prisoners who show a marked vulnerability to suicide can be differentiated from the general young prisoner population by the extent of the background deprivation they report (rather than the presence or absence of these measures), but more importantly, by almost every measure of their inability to cope with or make any constructive use of their sentence (see Liebling, 1992). These findings are consistent with previous studies of young males, both in the community and in prison. They are found to have poor coping skills, to find the constructive use of time difficult, and to be especially prone to pressure from their peers (Willis, 1988; Zamble and Porporino, 1988).

The vulnerable group in the study reported here had less contact with family, friends or the probation service whilst in custody. They found prison life more difficult, and were in every sense worse off than the comparison group, spending

Table 10
Activity in Prison

		Suicide attempt group		Comparison group	
		No.	%	No.	%
Do you do	Yes-Like	26	(52)	46	(92)
physical	None	9	(18)	2	(4)
education?	Yes-Dislike	15	(30)	2	(4)
Totals		50	(100)	50	(100)
				p<.0001	
How much time	Minimum	3	(6)	16	(32)
do you spend	Some	21	(42)	20	(40)
in your cell?	Most day	26	(52)	14	(28)
Totals		50	(100)	50	(100)
				p<.005	
Are you ever	Often	41	(82)	25	(50)
bored?	Sometimes	9	(18)	16	(32)
	Never	-	9	(18)	
Totals		50	(100)	50	(100)
				p<.001	
Are you 'active'	Active	23	(46)	45	(90)
whilst in your cell?	Inactive	27	(54)	5	(10)
Totals		50	(100)	50	(100)
				p<.0001	
What can you do	Nothing	28	(56)	25	(53)
when bored?	Positive	11	(22)	19	(40)
Negative	11	(22)	3	(6)	
Totals		50	(100)	47	(100)
				p<.05	

more time locked up in their cells and feeling more hopeless both about their opportunities in prison, and their prospects outside.

The above Table shows some of the differences to emerge: the suicide attempt group were much less likely to either do or to enjoy physical education - a sign of the problems and fears they experienced there. They felt bored and became more so as the sentence went on. They could think of no way of relieving these feelings. They occasionally resorted to 'cutting-up' or banging their fists or heads against the wall out of sheer desperation at the prospect of continuing confinement. On a variable ('Active') constructed after the interviews, based on their responses to many different questions about ways of passing the time, the suicidal group scored markedly more negatively than the comparison group.

The most vulnerable inmates were found to be in the worst situations. Many had no job or activity in prison, and many received very little contact from their families. They made few friends, experienced more difficulties with other inmates, and described the prison experience as particularly distressing. Most significantly, they were unable to generate any constructive defence against the boredom of confinement. Where others could read, write, exercise, study and create, some simply despaired.

It was the combined effects of hopelessness, their histories, their current situation, and the fact that they could not generate any solution to their problems that propelled these young prisoners towards suicide, and suicidal thoughts. In this context, situational triggers may be decisive in a suicide attempt. Prisoners have different thresholds, depending on their vulnerability and the sort of problems they encounter. For the vulnerable, a sudden change of location, threats from other inmates, or even a delayed visit, can be crucial. The significance of each of the three constituents of a 'pathway to suicide' (see Liebling, 1992): vulnerability, prison pressures and situational triggers, may vary in each case, so that for the particularly vulnerable, only an apparently 'trivial' situational trigger may be sufficient to drive someone to despair. If their first expressions of distress are ignored, prisoners may be propelled along this pathway at an even faster rate.

Young prisoner suicide is rarely a psychiatric problem: it is also a problem of coping. The experience of prison is not uniform: inmates' own resources and opportunities vary. A lack of the necessary skills with which to endure a sentence of imprisonment may fall within the boundaries of 'normal mental health'. Asking how prisoners spend their time in their cells, how they get along with other prisoners, what sort of plans they have for their release and how much contact they have with their families outside, may provide important clues as to how the prisoner is coping with the experience of imprisonment. The pains they feel may be indicated in several different ways. A self-inflicted injury may be a 'cry for help': an attempt to escape from an intolerable situation. If the cry is not heard, it becomes a 'cry of pain': a despairing indication that one cannot go through the next hour (Diekstra and Hawton, 1987).

Notes

1. For the purposes of this paper, 'the young' will refer to the under 21 age-group, as defined by Home Office Rules. The arguments outlined in this paper may be of equal significance to other 'young' groups of prisoners, up to the age of about 26. See Liebling and Krarup (1993), for further elaboration.

2. The analysis of these figures is my own, but would not have been possible without the kind assistance of Dr. Enda Dooley in extracting this data from his study of all prison suicides, 1972-1987. The comparison is limited by the fact that significant differences between the adult and young offender suicides could not be explored without separating them from the original total figures given in Dooley's paper.

Nine

Failure stories: Prison suicides and how not to prevent them

Deborah Coles and Tony Ward

It is in the nature of suicide prevention that its failures are easier to identify than its successes. This is especially true for us, since our main sources of information are the families who turn to INQUEST for help after the deaths of prisoners, and the evidence at the inquests on those deaths.[1] It is not the purpose of this chapter to disparage the good work of those prison service staff, prisoners, and voluntary organisations who are trying hard to tackle the problem of suicide and to help distressed inmates. We intend, however, to focus on some recent cases in which good practice has been conspicuously lacking. We believe that these cases highlight not merely the failings of individuals, but inherent features of the prison system which pose formidable obstacles to well-meaning efforts at reform.

In order to relate our case studies to this wider context, let us briefly outline what we take to be some fundamental and well-established features of the modern prison. One feature of particular relevance to suicide is the prison's tendency to individualise the problematic behaviour which it seeks to contain. Historically, the development of prisons has gone hand in hand with the development of a body of knowledge about prisoners as individuals, through a battery of techniques of surveillance, examination and documentation (Foucault, 1977). Deviant behaviour, whether in the form of rebellion (see Scraton et al., 1991; King and McDermott, 1990) or suicide, tends to be ascribed to disturbed individuals rather than disturbing situations, and remedies are sought in the better identification of those individuals, and in their isolation and surveillance under special regimes. Nowhere is this emphasis on isolation and surveillance more apparent than in the techniques of suicide prevention developed in the Victorian penitentiary, and all too readily recognisable today. In 1878 the Chief Surgeon of Pentonville described how the prisoner showing suicidal tendencies was:

> ... *sent to a cell called a medical observation cell, the trap door of which is kept constantly open, and certain directions are given to the officers that the prisoner is to be specially watched ... The furniture of his cell is always removed ... (Royal Commission on Penal Servitude, 1878, qq.1924-5)*

At least the Victorian prisoner kept his clothes. The inquest on the death of Frankie Terenzio, a remand prisoner found hanging in his cell in June 1992 despite a 15-minute watch (instructions to officers to observe him at 15-minute intervals), was told that he had, without proper authorisation, been placed for three days in an unfurnished 'strip' cell, clad only in a canvas suit. Prison officers at the recent inquest on Omasase Lmumba (see Introduction to Part 2, supra), testified that it was 'normal procedure' in Pentonville to remove the clothing of prisoners who were put into strip cells, irrespective of whether they were suicide risks or not; this is contrary to prison rules.

The individualisation of prisoners as objects of surveillance is not, however, matched by their individualisation as objects of treatment (Garland, 1985). The conventional prison is not geared to treating prisoners as individuals, but to treating large categories of individuals in more or less uniform ways (Hudson, 1987, pp.33-35). The knowledge that is gained of individuals is routinely reduced to a decision to assign them to one of a small number of categories and regimes (high risk/ some risk/no risk/hospital/special supervision/normal location). Once made, these categorisations may be changed only reluctantly; behaviour that could lead to a change of categorisation and hence of regime may be viewed with suspicion, as a deliberate attempt to manipulate the system (Sim, 1990; Power and Spencer, 1987, cited by Liebling, this volume).

Moreover - and as our case studies illustrate - the apparatus of surveillance and categorisation within prisons is not a single, smoothly functioning machine. Power and knowledge are dispersed among penal agents whose activities are often poorly co-ordinated. Though the conflicting priorities and interests of medical, disciplinary, medical and welfare staff and management should not obscure the extent to which all these groups work together towards a common end of discipline and control (Sim, 1990) they do introduce a significant degree of friction and inefficiency into the system.

A further elementary feature of the prison which must not be forgotten in discussing suicide is its violence. The maintenance of order and discipline rest ultimately on techniques such as the 'control and restraint' methods which led to the death of Germain Alexander in Brixton in 1989 and the unlawful killing of Omasase Lumumba in Pentonville in 1991. The 'legitimate' use of force to maintain order is backed up on occasions by techniques which are plainly illegitimate (Sim, 1991; King and McDermott, 1990). Probably more significant in relation to suicide among young males is the bullying and 'baroning' described by Liebling (this volume).

Imprisonment subjects prisoners to multiple deprivations which gravely threaten their personal relationships and sense of self (Goffman, 1968; Sykes, 1958; Johnson and Toch, 1982; Genders and Player, 1988). Coping with these deprivations, as Liebling (this volume) points out, takes skill; and some prisoners are more skilful than others. One of the more remarkable (and encouraging) findings of prison research is how resourceful many prisoners are in the art of 'psychological survival' (Cohen and Taylor, 1972; Sapsford, 1978). We can perhaps take some comfort from the fact that despite the material and emotional poverty from which many young prisoners come (Liebling, 1992, p.130), despite the bleak regimes under which they live, and despite the apparent rationality of suicide as a means of escape from intolerable pain (Scraton et al., 1991, p.63), only a small minority of prisoners resort to it.

PRISON DEPARTMENT CIRCULAR CI 20/1989

The deaths discussed below all took place during the period when the Prison Department Circular Instruction on Suicide Prevention, CI 20/1989, was in force. A revised version of procedures introduced in 1987, it is still in effect at the time of writing, although a new Instruction should be operative in all prisons by April 1994. As the Prison Service Suicide Awareness Support Unit points out, the introduction of new procedures in 1987 coincided with a sharp rise in the number of self-inflicted deaths in prisons: from 1980-86 there were between 21 and 29 self-inflicted deaths each year; from 1987-92 the figure fluctuated between 37 and 50 (Prison Service 1992a, para. 1 and Annex B). The central feature of the Circular is its emphasis on the medical role. All prisoners should be screened for suicide risk on reception, first by a hospital officer and then by the Medical Officer. Thereafter,

> *It is the responsibility of all staff who come into contact with an inmate who shows some signs of being at risk to refer him or her to the Medical Officer.... Staff are not required to assess the significance of the inmates' behaviour; that is a matter for the Medical Officer. It is a matter of acting quickly and effectively on any sign of suicidal feelings, for example if an inmate becomes upset or withdrawn after receiving a 'Dear John' letter, or talks of or threatens suicide (para. 21).*

Inmates thought to be suicidal may be located in hospital under 'special supervision', or in a cell under 'intermittent supervision', being observed at approximately 15 minute intervals. Inmates at 'marginal risk' may be located in normal accommodation with a 'compatible cell mate' (para. 31). Where the inmate's behaviour or lack of staff make these measures impracticable, an 'actively suicidal' inmate may be placed in a protective or stripped room, but this is recommended 'only for short periods, since the sense of isolation is unlikely to promote long-term recovery from suicidal feelings' (para. 33).

Other preventive measures are also placed under the Medical Officer's auspices, though (like the prisoner's response to a 'Dear John' letter) they have no obvious medical significance:

> *Governors should ... consider allowing suicidal inmates special letters or visits where the Medical Officer considers that this would be helpful (para. 37).*

> *[A]rrangements may be made, subject to the Medical Officer's approval, where local groups of Samaritans have indicated their willingness to help inmates. It should of course be*

understood that the prison visitor's or Samaritan's role is to befriend the inmate, but not to offer the kind of professional counselling which is the responsibility of the Medical Officer (para. 38)

So far as we are aware, few if any Medical Officers have training or qualifications in counselling.

The Prison Service (1992a, para. 7) now accepts that 'the new procedures may have been somewhat counter-productive'. They are gravely flawed in at least two respects. Firstly, although it is no doubt sensible to make some interim assessment of risk on reception, too much weight is placed on what is often, in practice, a very superficial interview (INQUEST, 1990). This seems to reflect an assumption that 'being a suicide risk' is a characteristic prisoners carry with them, rather than a product of their interaction with the prison. Secondly, by giving Medical Officers responsibility for what in many cases are non-medical problems, the Circular encourages buck-passing between medical and discipline staff. Liebling (1992), in her interviews with prison staff, found that poor communication was seen as a major problem. Discipline staff complained of 'the generally low level of communication and information-sharing' (p.217) while hospital staff felt 'that uniformed staff expected the hospital to provide a 'refuge' for discipline and control problems, and inmates not surviving on the wings' (pp.217-18). Lack of communication, and confusion over what was a medical and what a discipline problem, are recurring themes in the following case histories.

It will quickly become apparent that a number of these case histories do have a significant medical or psychiatric dimension. Such deaths are likely to over-represented among instances of conspicuous bad practice, for the simple reason that they are more likely than others to be prefigured by obvious 'warning signs' which staff may either act on or ignore, and which are subsequently revealed by the inquest. The subtler indications of despair given by prisoners who are not grossly disturbed may go unnoticed both at the time and in hindsight.

SEVEN CASE HISTORIES

1. Patrick Murphy

Our first example is a relatively undramatic case which typifies the type of death which we believe could have been averted if the lessons of other young prisoner suicides and self injuries had been learned. Patrick Murphy, aged 16, was found hanged in his cell at Deerbolt Young Offenders Institution on 3 May 1992. He had been involved in petty crime since the age of 11, and his parents had long sensed a certain 'oddness' about him; they wondered if he might be autistic. His six-month sentence for a spate of petty thefts and burglaries of schools, passed despite pleas from his juvenile justice worker, was his first experience of custody, and he was serving it an institution 130 miles from home. After sentence was passed Patrick was found in the police cells below the court with an anorak cord around his foot and neck. The police treated this as a serious suicide attempt and warned the prison of it by a POL 1 form, but did not tell his parents. Patrick was interviewed on reception by a Hospital Officer who had no training in suicide prevention and had not seen CI 20/1989. The Officer described the incident on the screening form as a 'poor attempt in police custody at self strangulation ... apparently using his foot to strangle himself!!!' implying that it need not be taken seriously. He did not indicate that Patrick was a heavy drinker and smoker, that it was his first time in custody or that he expected his family to have difficulty in visiting him all of which could be interpreted as 'risk indicators' under CI 20/1989. He did, however, tick the box for 'some risk'.

The part-time Medical Officer who spent 10-15 minutes with Patrick the following day merely noted that he was 'not suicidal'. Despite the fact that he was the first doctor to see Patrick since he had attempted suicide, and despite the Circular Instruction's guidelines on the importance of family contact in suicide prevention, he did not consider contacting the police for more information or informing Patrick's parents of the attempt. The result of his decision was that Patrick was sent to a wing where staff had no information about the suicide attempt.

Patrick reacted badly to imprisonment. He was particularly upset at being deprived of cigarettes and went on hunger strike because of this. He became dishevelled and slept in his clothes. He naively - meaning it as a joke - told other inmates that he was a 'beastie' (sex offender): an example of poor 'coping skills' if ever there was one. A prison officer told Patrick's parents after his death that on the last afternoon of his life he had been bullied and involved in a scuffle with other inmates; abrasions to his face found by the post-mortem are consistent with this. Prison reform groups had brought the problem of bullying at Deerbolt to the attention of the Home Office.

2. Iain McKinlay

Iain McKinlay was one of two young men who died by hanging in adjacent cells in Hindley Remand Centre on 25 June 1990. An 18 year old remand prisoner facing a rape charge, he had been transferred to Hindley from Strangeways after taking part in the riot there in April 1990. He had made a suicide attempt while serving a sentence at Chelmsford and on arrival at Strangeways he had been assessed as a suicide risk. When he arrived at Hindley he was placed in solitary confinement, where he remained for the last seven weeks of his life. The Governor, Alfred Jennings, justified his decision at the inquest by saying he feared McKinlay would cause 'another Strangeways' at the prison (though there was no suggestion that McKinlay had been any kind of 'ringleader' in the Strangeways protest). He added that 'solitary confinement can do a lot of good', that he would do the same again and had no regrets. It emerged at the inquest, however, that the last four weeks of Iain's time in solitary had not been authorised by a member of the Board of Visitors and the Governor was therefore in breach of Prison Rule 43.

A fellow prisoner testified that Iain was taunted, abused and threatened by both prisoners and staff, after officers told prisoners he was a sex offender. Iain had gone on hunger strike after - according to the fellow-prisoner - he found a razor-blade in his food. Letters from Iain to his friends referred to this abuse (making what appears to have been a coded reference to sexual abuse) and expressed a wish to kill himself. Iain's probation officer and a Salvation Army officer warned the Governor that Iain might harm himself. Two of his friends in the prison spoke to members of staff, including the chaplain, about their fears that Iain was suicidal but none of this information was passed on to medical staff. A prison officer wrote 'please observe' on a roll board after a warning from Iain's girlfriend that he might kill himself. At no time, however, either on arrival at Hindley or subsequently, was Iain assessed for suicide risk. The Senior Medical Officer admitted at the inquest that there had been wholesale breaches of CI 20/1989, which neither he nor the other doctor who saw Iain during medical visits to the punishment block had ever read. Iain left a note before he died stating that he was going to kill himself because 'The screws are letting open the cell and letting the other cons up my arse'.

3. Phillip Knight

Phillip Knight, aged 15, was found hanging in his cell in Swansea prison on 13 July 1990. He had been imprisoned under an 'unruliness certificate' after absconding from care and being charged with theft of a handbag. He had been placed in care as his adoptive parents found great difficulty in controlling or communicating with him; he was regarded by his parents and social workers as a very disturbed boy.

Two of Phillip's social workers spoke to the police and to the prison officer in charge of the young offenders unit at Swansea, warning them that Phillip might kill himself. The police filled in a POL 1 form warning the prison that Philip had 'suicidal tendencies'. By the time the social workers spoke to the prison officer, however, Phillip had already passed through the reception process and been assessed as presenting 'no suicide risk at this time.' In response to the social workers' warning, the officer gave an oral instruction that staff should keep an eye on Phillip and ensure that he was placed in a cell with another prisoner.

Two days later Phillip had a fight with his cellmate and erected a barricade. He was placed in a single cell in the punishment block. A personal officer was assigned to him, but this officer knew nothing of the warnings that Phillip might be suicidal, and spent only ten minutes a day talking to him. At the inquest this officer gave evidence to the effect that the personal officer scheme could not work properly at Swansea owing to lack of staff time.

On 6th July, after seven days in solitary, Phillip cut his left wrist so badly that he could have bled to death had he not rung his cell bell to summon help. On his way to the prison hospital he told a prison officer that he wanted to die. This was recorded on a form (F210) filled out by the officer who found him. The prison doctor did not, however, consider Phillip a suicide risk and interpreted his wrist slashing as an 'expression of anger and resentment' (inquest testimony). The doctor had not seen the POL 1 form and could not recall at the inquest whether he had read the F210. Phillip was placed in a strip cell with nothing except a mattress and a canvas jacket. The inquest testimony of the doctor, chaplain and prison staff indicated that Phillip was seen as a discipline and control problem and his self-injury as attention seeking and manipulative.

On the day of his death Phillip appeared in court, expecting to be sent to a secure unit for juveniles. He was sent back to Swansea as no place could be found for him.

It should be mentioned here that since the inquest Swansea prison has made notable efforts to improve suicide prevention, which will be discussed later.

4. Paddy O'Grady

Paddy O'Grady, a 24-year-old former council caretaker, hanged himself with a strip of sheet tied to the anti-suicide grille in front of the window of his single cell on 27 May 1991. He was the 14th prisoner to take his own life in Brixton prison since January 1989.

Paddy, a fit, healthy young man and a keen footballer, was arrested in January 1991 on a charge of attempted burglary and remanded to Wormwood Scrubs. According to his visitors he coped well with the regime there. On 6 March he was transferred to Brixton. One result of the transfer was that his daily visits were reduced in length from 75 to 15 minutes. This increased his anxiety about his relationship with his pregnant girlfriend Caroline.

Caroline gave birth to a daughter on 7 April and brought her to the prison to visit Paddy. Paddy, however, became increasingly depressed. He was concerned that Caroline might leave him and that he was an inadequate father. On 7 May Paddy was convicted and remanded to await sentence. As a convicted prisoner his visits were reduced to just one a month.

On their last visit, two weeks before his death, Caroline and Paddy's brother Jim were shocked by his condition. They were taken to F wing (Brixton's hospital wing, which has since closed), where Paddy was being held in a single cell. He had a swollen face, dried blood on his chin, unbandaged slashes on his wrists and cigarette burns on his legs. He was wearing the canvas shift garment issued to inmates in strip cells. It emerged at the inquest that Paddy had tried to cut his wrists on the perspex panes on the doors of two strip cells.

Jim O'Grady told the inquest, 'I couldn't believe how anyone could let someone deteriorate like that. You wouldn't treat a dog that way. He was very, very depressed. He just kept crying and saying `I need to be in hospital. I need help''.

Paddy had demanded a lot of attention from the prison medical staff. He complained of physical ailments including severe headaches and repeatedly asked to be transferred to a hospital. During 82 days in prison Paddy had 25 consultations with eight different prison doctors. Yet at no stage did those doctors hold a case conference to discuss an inmate who was falling into deep depression and had proved capable of injuring himself. One doctor who gave Paddy paracetamol for his headaches told the inquest that he did not consult the inmate medical record and had no idea where such records were kept.

The visiting consultant psychiatrist in charge of the case admitted a series of errors, including placing Paddy in a single cell and not arranging for him to have extra family visits as he could have done under CI 20/1989. He also said he had been wrong not to consider Paddy a serious suicide risk.

A solicitor's clerk told the inquest that his firm had written to the prison on behalf of Paddy's mother who was worried about her son's health. No reply had been received. A probation officer who visited Paddy four days before his death was so alarmed by his physical appearance and anxious behaviour, and by what seemed to be 'some kind of rope burn or mark of ligature' around his neck, that she told officers: 'In all my experience I cannot remember seeing anyone so much at risk of killing themselves'. Her fears were communicated to staff on F wing, but neither the probation officer who worked on the wing nor three members of staff who found Paddy hanging were aware of it.

None of the staff on duty on the night of Paddy's death had been trained in the use of the defibrillator installed at the prison after previous suicides. The one member of staff who emerged with some credit at the inquest was a discipline officer who had been sufficiently concerned about Paddy to visit him on F wing, although he worked in another part of the prison.

5. Caroline Wood

Caroline Wood, aged 19, was found hanging in Styal prison on 22 June 1992.[2] She was heroin dependent. Prison Service guidelines issued in 1991 recommend that such inmates be given methadone during a detoxification programme lasting seven days. Styal's Medical Officer disagreed with the guidelines. No methadone was given to women withdrawing from drugs, nor was there any counselling or support for women suffering drug withdrawal, and the detoxification process was considered to be over in two days. Some days before her death a prison officer had noted that Caroline appeared depressed, but no action was taken as a result.

HM Chief Inspector of Prisons has commented on staff shortages at Styal and the lack of a personal officer scheme (Home Office, 1992). At the time of her death there was only one officer in duty in the unit where Caroline was housed, and that officer was busy with administrative duties. Caroline was not seen for two hours before she died.

6. Kwaku Ohene

Kwaku Ohene was a 31 Year Old Ghanaian prisoner in Swaleside. He was convicted of attempted murder in 1991 although it was accepted at his trial that he was mentally ill at the time of the offence. A leading forensic psychiatrist, Dr Coid, prepared a report for the court stating that Kwaku was suffering from an 'intermittent but serious psychotic illness' and that if it recurred the prison medical service should contact him. This report apparently never reached any of the 13 prisons in which Kwaku was held at different times. While at The Mount prison Kwaku suffered a serious psychotic illness. He told medical staff that he had been treated by Dr Coid at Hackney Hospital, but they wrote to the wrong hospital.

Kwaku made frequent complaints about racist treatment at the hands of the prison service.

In Swaleside, prison officers became very worried about Kwaku's mental state. He was hearing voices, mumbling incoherently and saying he could not cope on the wing. When he was found to have cut his wrists staff took him to hospital, expecting that he would be seen by a psychiatrist. Instead he was seen by a doctor who considered his wrist cutting as common behaviour in prison, said the cuts were superficial even though they needed stitches, made no psychiatric assessment at all and, to the surprise of prison officers who thought he was a clear suicide risk, returned him to the wing with no special instructions.

Later the same day staff again became concerned when they

saw him in his cell 'crouching with fists clenched, pacing about the cell, incoherent, wringing his hands, almost crying' (inquest testimony). Again he was taken to the hospital but there was no room for him there so he was sent to the segregation unit where there were no medically trained staff on duty and where prisoners were kept in virtual isolation.

The following day he was again taken to hospital. This time a nurse put him on a 15 minute watch (i.e. gave instructions that he be checked at approximately 15 minute intervals). She said at the inquest that this was for purposes of 'general observation' and not because she considered him a suicide risk. He was not seen by a doctor and the nurse made no attempt to contact one. That night he was found hanging by a night patrol officer who was alone on duty in the hospital and had no suicide prevention training and no keys.

7. Delroy McKnight

Delroy McKnight died in Wandsworth Prison on 19 January 1991 at the age of 29, five months from the end of a three year sentence for burglary. Doctors at Highpoint prison had diagnosed him as an acute paranoid schizophrenic with suicidal thoughts and delusions and put him on regular doses of largactil. He was transferred to Wandsworth (on the authority of a prison officer) on the ground that Highpoint did not have adequate medical facilities to treat him; but the reason for his transfer was not communicated in writing to Wandsworth, nor was the Medical Officer at Wandsworth alerted to Delroy's active medical problem. Staff at Wandsworth were under the impression that he had been transferred for disciplinary reasons.

On arrival at Wandsworth Delroy was assessed by a Dr Rashid, who prescribed continued doses of largactil. He did not consider that Delroy needed to be in hospital. Instead he was placed on normal location, locked in a shared cell for 23 hours a day.

Three months before Delroy's arrival at Wandsworth another prisoner there had killed himself and a review of suicide prevention measures had been carried out as a result. In spite of this, Dr Rashid admitted at the inquest that he had not followed, nor even read, the procedures laid out in CI 20/1989.

A toxicologist's report after Delroy's death revealed that he had not taken any largactil for some days, but when he stopped taking it could not be ascertained as the relevant record card had been lost. The Medical Officer did not know that Delroy had stopped taking medication. He did not carry out any review of the case.

His cellmate told the inquest that Delroy had become more and more withdrawn until he would not leave the cell even to slop out but lay in his bunk, amid his excreta, endlessly reading the bible.

There was confusion in the prison system as to Delroy's whereabouts. His family were not told he had moved to Wandsworth and sent his Christmas cards and presents to Highpoint. They were returned unopened. Two days before his death a probation officer who had been concerned about Delroy's health at Highpoint arrived at Wandsworth to visit him, but was wrongly told he was no longer there.

A month after his transfer, Delroy cut his throat with a broken piece of glass from his cell window.

CONCLUSION

We hope it will be apparent why we consider that in each of these cases staff failed to take action which could have averted a death. There were failures of communication, failures to follow Prison Service guidelines on suicide prevention (or the care of drug users in Caroline Wood's case), failures to take self-injury and other warnings seriously, failures to involve family and friends who could have helped care for prisoners, failures to perceive the human needs of inmates who were seen as discipline problems. All these contributed to what the inquest juries in the Ohene, O'Grady and McKnight cases branded as 'lack of care'. So, more broadly, did the criminal justice system's failure to find more humane ways of dealing with people several, if not all, of whom were inappropriately imprisoned in the first place. But deaths like these can be, and often are, presented as failures of another sort: those of individual prisoners to 'cope' with the prison regime.

In taking issue with the individualisation and medicalisation of suicide, we are not seeking to argue that individual differences are irrelevant. On the contrary, the characters and circumstances of each of the seven people we have discussed, and in some cases their psychiatric histories, are crucial to understanding why they died. Alison Liebling rightly points to differences between inmates in their 'coping skills' as an important factor in explaining self-injury and suicide among young prisoners, though one of which the importance (if any) varies greatly from one case to another. But given the bias towards individualist explanations that is inherent in penal discourse, and in the legal and medical discourses of the coroner's court, there is always a danger that what should be merely one facet of an understanding of suicide will be over-emphasised and distorted:

> *Many of the inquests on deaths in prison, particularly suicides, which we have researched focus on the 'individual' in terms of personality, background and ability to 'cope'. It is assumed that people take their own lives not out of any rational response to brutal regimes, harsh conditions or round-the-clock isolation but through a personal defect in character or background which renders them as individuals inadequate in meeting the reasonable demands of essentially fair regimes (Scraton and Chadwick, 1986, pp.106-7).*

To counter this view, what needs to be stressed is the essential *un*fairness of a system which, in the name of 'just deserts', imposes the same deprivations on individuals some of whom will 'do their bird' with relative ease, or 'successfully' adjust themselves to the most brutal and exploitative aspects of institutional life, while others will endure physical and psychological torment and despair. Of course the coroner's court is not the most suitable forum to raise issues of this kind. A court where (as in one recent inquest on a death in Winson Green prison), counsel are not permitted even to refer to the report of an inspection carried out at the time of the death (Home Office, 1992c) can hardly serve as inquiry into the fundamental iniquities of the penal system, and can all too easily degenerate into a nasty exercise in scapegoating. This is not the place for a detailed critique of the inquest system (see Scraton and Chadwick, 1987; Tweedie and Ward, 1989): suffice it to say that the level of conflict at many prison inquests would in our view be reduced if the Prison Service displayed greater openness beforehand.

There is, no doubt, a danger that too great an emphasis on the deep-rooted features of the prison system which contribute to suicide will lead to defeatism, a view that nothing can be done short of fundamental reform or abolition. However, while the reasons for the rise in prisoner suicides throughout the

1970s and 1980s (Liebling, this volume), and their sharp increase from 1987 onwards, are not fully understood, these phenomena do indicate that the present rate of suicide is not an inevitable consequence of imprisonment. Judge Tumim's report of 1990 marked an important break with the previous medical understanding of suicide and set out a realistic programme of short-term reforms, many of which were reiterated in the Woolf Report.

Both Liebling (1992) and a recent report by the Howard League (1993) emphasise the role of prison officers in picking up clues that prisoners are distressed and possibly suicidal. Liebling's study was carried out in Young Offender Institutions where, she suggests, 'a core of the prison staff ... share some enthusiasm - if recently jaded - for notions of welfare and reform' (p. 197). We doubt whether the staff culture in some other institutions would be equally conducive to this aspect of Liebling's approach. We also doubt whether the problems posed by the staff culture will be overcome in the way suggested by the Howard League (1993, p.66), by creating an elite of specially qualified Personal Officers whose roles would be 'more of a Probation Officer than a Prison Officer'. What is not in doubt is that good quality staff who have the time and the motivation to get to know their charges as individuals could make an important contribution to suicide prevention. This is a point to be borne in mind when assessing the new private prisons (Ryan and Ward, 1989).

Another approach which has found some favour lately is to involve prisoners in suicide prevention, as in the 'listener scheme' at Swansea prison and the 'care support scheme' at Ranby (Prison Service, 1992a, pp.19, 26; Home Office, 1993b, p.92). In both schemes, selected inmates are trained, with the help of the Samaritans, to support other inmates who are under stress. We are in no position to evaluate what seems a promising initiative, but our one reservation about it is that it may place a share of the responsibility for suicide with prisoners without giving them any say in the measures that might prevent it; although a few establishments (including Swansea) do now have a prisoner representative on their Suicide Prevention Management Groups.

Another group who have an important part to play in suicide prevention are prisoners' families and friends. As the stories of Patrick Murphy, Paddy O'Grady and Delroy

McKnight all illustrate, there are cases where much more could and should be done to keep families and friends informed and to respond to their concerns about an inmate. The discretion to allow extra visits under CI 20/1989 could be more widely used. Of course, not all potentially suicidal inmates have supportive relatives and friends.

Our disagreement with the Prison Service is less over what should be done about suicides in the short term, than over whether anything significant actually is being done in many of the worst establishments. It is difficult to convey, without multiplying case histories *ad nauseam*, the exasperation we feel as inquest after inquest, year after year, reveals the same administrative and medical blunders, the same failures of communication, the same almost wilful blindness to prisoners' distress. Of course this is not true of every case: there are many deaths where everyone concerned seems to have acted quite reasonably within the constraints of the system, and where any suspicions the family may have could probably be defused by greater openness in advance of the inquest. But it is true in too many cases, and the lessons of these cases do not seem to be learned. Further evidence of this can be seen in the depressing series of four suicides at Feltham chronicled by INQUEST for the Howard League (1993).

If little seems to have changed this is, we suggest, attributable not merely to individual incompetence but to a combination of factors - bureaucratic inflexibility, the priority of discipline over care, a view of prisoners as potential manipulators and malingerers, mistrust and poor communication between different groups of staff, bullying and extortion among prisoners - which are endemic to prison society. It is difficult to be optimistic about eradicating these factors until we have far fewer prisoners and a more constructive approach to those that remain. The recent chilling of the ideological climate with regard to 'law and order' in general and young offenders in particular makes that seem a sadly distant prospect.

Notes
1. We would like to acknowledge the help of the prisoners' families in compiling the case histories in this chapter.
2. We are grateful to Prison Watch for information about this case.

Ten

Suicide and attempted suicide by asylum seekers detained by the UK authorities

Louise Pirouet

A refugee is defined in international law as anyone who has a 'well-founded fear of persecution for reasons of race, religion, nationality, membership of a particular social group or political opinion, is outside the country of his nationality and is unable or, owing to such fear, is unwilling to avail himself of the protection of that country' (UN Convention Relating to the Status of Refugees, 1951, Art. 1).

However, the presence of refugees may cause problems in relations with the countries from which they have fled, with the result that the only refugees who are welcome are defectors from those countries which are identified as the enemy, and whose defection offers the host country some political advantage. The United Nations Convention Relating to the Status of Refugees, 1951, and the 1967 Protocol, set out an internationally accepted framework for the recognition, treatment and protection of refugees, though not all member states of the UN have signed and ratified the Convention and its Protocol.

The vast majority of the fifteen or so million refugees in the world today are found in the poorer countries of the world, especially in Africa and Asia, but the number of people seeking asylum in Western Europe has risen steadily from c. 13,000 in

1972 to c. 500,000 by 1991, with a steep rise from 1989 onwards. A major part of this influx consisted of ethnic Germans who had a right to enter (West) Germany; an increase from the third world is almost certainly connected with new expectations raised by the fall of the Berlin Wall, though the precise relationship may be difficult to determine. It is also partly due to the far greater availability of cheap air travel which has grown up to meet the demands of the Western tourist industry. So long as the majority of refugees were from the Eastern Bloc and were relatively few in number, Western European countries accommodated them quite easily. A steady rise in the numbers of people seeking asylum from the third world and from what were perceived as alien cultures, and from countries with which the West had trading links, together with a substantial rise in the overall numbers, has resulted in growing hostility towards refugees by Western governments and a growth in the administrative obstacles put in the way of those seeking asylum. In three countries of Western Europe, Finland, Denmark and the UK, there has been a growing use of detention, and in the UK in particular, this may be for long periods, sometimes exceeding a year (Jolly and Nettleton, 1990, p.15). Currently some 150 asylum seekers are probably detained at any one time, and the government plans to increase the number of detention places by 300.

It will be argued here that asylum seekers who are held in detention centres and prisons and who become clinically depressed, inflict self-injury, attempt suicide, or succeed in committing suicide do so for different reasons from people held on remand or serving prison sentences after conviction. For this reason, little in Judge Stephen Tumim's Report on *Suicide and Self-Harm in Prison Service Establishments* (Home Office, 1990e) is of relevance to our subject. The Report specifically excludes consideration of Harmondsworth Detention Centre and of motives for suicide. Because their motives are different from those of other prisoners, the remedy will also need to be different. What detained asylum seekers share with, for instance, young remand prisoners, is extreme vulnerability. There have not, to our knowledge, been any suicides among immigration detainees other than asylum seekers during the last few years. We find this significant.

In the period 1987 to mid 1992 three asylum seekers held in detention in the UK have killed themselves, and many others have become clinically de- pressed, have attempted suicide or injured themselves. Although no statistics are available, one psychiatrist working for the Medical Foundation for the Care of Victims of Torture saw some seven detained asylum seekers during February 1991 whom he diagnosed as severely depressed. The number of deaths is tiny by comparison with the number of suicides among convicted and remand prisoners, but as a proportion of the total number of asylum seekers detained, it is possibly higher than the incidence of suicide in the prison population as a whole. In any case, even one death, particularly of someone who came to this country to seek asylum, is too many. The distress represented by cases of clinical depression and attempted suicide cannot be quantified.

We must first ask why some asylum seekers, who are in no sense of the word criminals, should be detained without charge or trial by the Immigration Service, becoming, in the words of Judge Tumim (Home Office, 1990e), 'unconvicted and unsentenced prisoners ... held on the direction of immigration officers and not of magistrates or judges'. One reason given by the Home Office for detaining asylum seekers is that the Immigration Service believes someone will not fulfil the conditions laid upon him by the terms of temporary admission (TA), or because no suitable sponsor can be found.[1] Such detention is lawful under the 1971 Immigration Act. A second reason for detention is that a decision to deport has been taken. An asylum seeker granted TA may therefore be lawfully detained at some future date: the TA notice he is given is entitled 'Immigration Act 1971 Notification of Temporary Admission to a Person who is Liable to be Detained', and the recipient is further informed:

> *Although you have been temporarily admitted, you remain liable to be detained. You have NOT been given leave to enter the United Kingdom within the meaning of the Immigration Act 1971.*

Asylum seekers may also be held because of irregularities in their travel documentation (however, as Sir John Donaldson, Master of the Rolls, pointed out in a Court of Appeal ruling given on 26 October 1987, the possession of false documents is not in itself a reason for detention since there may be no other way in which asylum seekers can leave their country of origin). A rapid rise in the number of asylum seekers detained at any one time is often a Home Office response to an influx from a particular area (Sri Lanka in 1987, Turkey in 1989, Zaire in 1991).

Detention is also lawful under the European Convention on Human Rights. Article 5(1)(f) allows 'the lawful arrest or detention of a person to prevent his effecting an unauthorised entry into the country or of a person against whom action is being taken with a view to deportation or extradition' (for the text of the Convention see Brownlie, 1987, pp.184-85).

However, if the purpose of detention is to deter other asylum seekers or if it is intended to intimidate people, then detention will be unlawful (Coker, 1987; Cohen and Goulbourne, 1987, pp.15-22). Fears have been expressed that it is sometimes used as a deterrent. There have been reports that immigration officers at Harmondsworth Detention Centre and elsewhere have tried to persuade asylum seekers to withdraw their applications, and warned them that if they do not, they will remain in detention for months. Although proving that a detention was unlawful is very difficult, immigration detainees have been released from detention on a court order (JCWI, 1990-91, p.11).

Although detention may be lawful, the way in which it is used may not be ethical and sometimes seems to be in contravention of the Guidelines issued by the Office of the UN High Commissioner for Refugees (UNHCR). The 37th Session of the Executive Committee of the UNHCR held in 1986

(a) Noted with deep concern that large numbers of refugees and asylum seekers in different areas of the world are currently the subject of detention or similar restrictive measures by reason of their illegal entry or presence in search of asylum, pending resolution of their situation. [2]

Their concern arose out of Article 31 of the 1951 UN Convention on Refugees which states:

The contracting states shall not impose penalties, on account of illegal entry or presence, on refugees who, coming directly from a territory where their life or freedom was threatened in the sense of Article 1, enter or are present in their territory without authorisation, provided they present themselves without delay to the authorities and show good cause for their illegal entry or presence (Brownlie, 1981, p.61).

The Executive Committee then went on to express the opinion that 'in view of the hardship which it involves, detention should normally be avoided'. Whilst they recognised that it might be temporarily necessary in cases where asylum seekers lacked proper documentation, they stressed

(d) ... the importance for national legislation and/or administrative practice to make the necessary distinction between the situation of refugees and asylum seekers, and that of other aliens;

(e) Recommended that detention measures taken in respect of refugees and asylum seekers should be subjected to judicial or administrative review;

(f) Stressed that conditions of refugees and asylum seekers must be humane. In particular, refugees and asylum seekers shall, wherever possible, not be accommodated with persons detained as common criminals, and shall not be located in areas where their physical safety is endangered.

Moreover the Home Office's own instructions are to keep detention under continual review so as not to prolong it.

But these guidelines are not always followed. One factor leading to stress and attempted suicide is the length of time often taken to process the asylum applications of those held in detention, (and, indeed, of asylum seekers in general). Judge Tumim (Home Office, 1990b, p.18), reporting on Haslar, where asylum seekers and other immigration detainees are held, noted:

Detainees were not entitled to Legal Aid and relied upon various immigration welfare agencies to provide legal help and advice. Immigration Service procedures were perceived as slow at best but often inadequate. As a result detainees showed signs of anxiety and stress, became depressed or 'demonstrated' by refusing to take food. We accept that this is a matter for the Immigration Service to resolve. However, they have a firm commitment continually to monitor cases and ensure that the need for continuing detention is regularly reviewed. We saw little evidence of this at Haslar and have some sympathy with the view expressed to us by staff and detainees that having been sent to Haslar they were out of sight and out of mind.[3]

Extreme anxiety about the future is well-known as a factor which may precipitate suicide.

It must be further noted that asylum seekers are not always separated from 'common criminals' as the UNHCR Guidelines suggest they should be. They have been held in Exeter, Gloucester, Winchester, Lewes, Pentonville and Risley Remand Centre, all ordinary prisons. The Home Office claims that by placing them on the remand wing, it is keeping to the Guidelines. In late 1990 a group of men who came in through Dover were held for up to three months in Canterbury Prison which was persuaded to accept them because Immigration Officers said the men would be there for only a week. There have been reports of hostility towards asylum seekers by other inmates both at Canterbury and elsewhere. Some asylum seekers have reported their revulsion at the violent attitudes of the criminals among whom they have found themselves, and have commented on this additional cause of stress on top of finding themselves incarcerated in a common prison. Asylum seekers are regularly held in Haslar Prison which is used solely as an immigration detention centre, and where no distinction appears to be made between them and other immigration detainees, a distinction also recommended in the UNHCR Guidelines. The Home Secretary rejected Judge Tumim's suggestion that, because asylum seekers and other immigration detainees were greatly distressed to find themselves held in prison, Haslar should be redesignated a detention centre ('Response by the Home Secretary' in Home Office, 1990b).

In spite of Home Office insistence to the contrary, there is good reason to believe that much detention is arbitrary. In October 1987, 78 asylum detainees, many of them Sri Lankans, were detained on the disused carferry, the Earl William, at Harwich. During the hurricane which occurred that month the ship broke her moorings, was damaged, and was rendered unsafe. The detainees could not remain aboard. Instead of being moved to other places of detention, they were all released and allowed to go to the friends and relatives who had offered them accommodation all along. Nothing about their cases had changed, but it had become inconvenient to continue to detain them.[4] If they could be released after the hurricane, why did they have to be detained before it? The arbitrary nature of detention was again illustrated in 1989. On 8 October one of two Turkish Kurds detained at Harmondsworth detention centre died of burns received when he and another asylum seeker, threatened with being returned to Turkey, barricaded themselves into a room and set it and themselves alight. That evening, between 7.00 and 8.00 pm, all the Kurdish asylum seekers held in Gloucester Prison were released on the orders of the Home Secretary. The remaining Kurds held in Haslar, Harmondsworth and elsewhere were released either then or within the next couple of days.[5] Once again it must be asked why they needed to be detained in the first place. In 1991 a group of thirty-three asylum seekers were rapidly released from Pentonville Prison the day before a planned vigil by church groups outside the jail which ITV had promised to film (JCWI, 1990-91, p.7). The frustration and despair of detained asylum seekers is not difficult to understand. Judge Tumim mentions hunger-strikes in his report on Haslar, but there have also been cases of attempted or threatened suicide there, and of self-injury.

There is further evidence that the UNHCR Guidelines are not being followed. The Medical Foundation for the Care of Victims of Torture has had to visit a number of prisons as well as the regular immigration detention centres to examine people who claim to have experienced torture. Even after a medical report has been submitted, and a psychiatrist has pointed out that continuing detention is adding seriously to almost unbearable trauma, weeks or even months may pass before a decision on the case is reached. The longest period of detention that Charter '87 knows of for an asylum seeker is 17 to 18 months; the person concerned had suffered torture before fleeing to the UK, and a report on this had been submitted to the Home Office months before his release.[6] In January 1991 a solicitor representing a detained asylum seeker who had suffered torture won a decision in principle that bail should be granted, but the sum required as a bail surety was set impossibly high. The Medical Foundation is having to give long-term psychotherapeutic treatment to a number of people for the trauma of anxiety suffered whilst in detention in the UK on top of that resulting from the torture from which they had fled (Bracken and Gorst-Unsworth, 1991; see also Medical Foundation for the Care of Victims of Torture, 1992, Case 4). The willingness of asylum detainees to stick it out in detention rather than be returned to their country of nationality is eloquent witness to their fear of renewed persecution if forcibly repatriated (though the Home Office refuses to accept this).

The physical conditions of detention and the unsatisfactory state of British prisons do not appear to be among the factors which lead to suicidal thoughts and suicide itself. But the fact of being detained in the country where they had hoped to find freedom may directly contribute to suicidal thoughts. Conditions may be bad (though Haslar has a good regime), but they are usually much better than prison conditions in the countries from which asylum seekers have fled, and whose prisons they have often experienced at first hand. What they fear is forcible repatriation, and anxiety mounts as days and weeks and sometimes months go by without their applications being processed. But worse still is the receipt of a letter which tells them that the Secretary of State is 'minded to refuse' them asylum (and poor initial decision-making means that these letters are given to a great many people who are later permitted to stay). Trapped in detention, this may be the point at which a suicide attempt occurs. A final removal notice kills all hope.

The 'minded to refuse' letter needs some explanation. In the words of an immigration officer explaining why such notices are given, 'The Immigration Service and the Refugee Unit at the Home Office modified their practices to accord with dicta expressed by the courts in the case of Thirukumar and Others as to what constitutes a fair and just manner for dealing with asylum applications'.[7] In other words, before a ruling by the Court of Appeal forced the Home Office to do otherwise, asylum seekers were being refused asylum without even being told why. The 'minded to refuse' letter was introduced to meet the court's objections. This letter is a threatening document which is sometimes very difficult to follow. Most of those of which Charter '87 has copies are pro forma letters with a space in the middle into which someone has written, often by hand, and sometimes in very poor handwriting, a summary of what the Home Office understands to be the asylum seeker's story, and then a statement of why that does not, in the view of the Home Office, constitute a valid claim to asylum. These comments sometimes reveal ignorance of the circumstances obtaining in the country from which the asylum seeker has fled, or a statement which, in effect, says, 'We do not believe your story', with no reasons given. Until recently the all important Political Asylum Questionnaire (PAQ), on which the asylum applicant was required to set out the grounds of his application, was filled in, not by the asylum applicants themselves, but by immigration officers during an interview soon after arrival which may have been conducted through interpretation. The result was that asylum seekers were not always able to present their cases properly, and, when given a 'minded to refuse' letter, had great difficulty in getting correct versions of their stories believed. In Autumn 1991, after complaints from many quarters over a long period of time, this procedure was changed. Now, in the majority of cases, asylum seekers are given PAQs and told to return within eight weeks. During this time they may get help from specialist solicitors or one of the refugee agencies to complete the PAQs. The exceptions are those asylum seekers who are held in detention, and in these cases the PAQ is still filled in by the immigration officer, with all the possibilities for misunderstanding which that involves.

The quality of decision-making illustrated by the examples of 'minded to refuse' letters which Charter '87 has seen is not encouraging. In one case, for example, a point of major importance had been misread by the immigration officer, and the asylum seeker's story was poorly presented. No wonder that a 'minded to refuse' letter may be the cause of a suicide attempt by an asylum seeker held in detention.

We should now turn to a consideration of the three cases in which asylum seekers have killed themselves since 1987. The first was a Ugandan, Mr Ahmed Katongole. He arrived in the UK during September 1986 and was given TA. He claimed membership of a group which had opposed President Obote of Uganda, and which had attempted to join with President Museveni after Obote was toppled in January 1986. He fled to the UK claiming that his life was in danger. Experts on Uganda found his story credible. In March he was summoned to see the immigration officer at Gatwick for what he was told would be a routine interview. On arrival he was informed that he would be removed on the next flight back to Uganda. In desperation he took an overdose of the paracetamol tablets which he had with him and had to be taken to Crawley Hospital for emergency treatment. From there he was sent to the Beehive Detention Centre, thence to Latchmere House, and finally to Pentonville Prison's hospital wing. A psychiatrist saw him and said he needed to be with his friends in the community. Mr Musoke of the Uganda Refugees' Welfare Association tried to find out where he was being held, but was repeatedly refused this information. Mr Katongole was not told that an MP, Mr Ron Leighton, had taken up his case (a piece of the safety-net for asylum seekers which the Home Secretary removed soon after this). On the morning of 22 March Katongole was found hanged in his cell. The inquest jury brought in a verdict of suicide 'aggravated by official indifference and lack of care' (*Independent*, 26 March 1987, 2 July 1987). Charter '87 has been unable to obtain any comment from the Home Office other than disclaimers of responsibility and a statement that it would be 'inappropriate' (inconvenient?) for the minister to comment further.[8]

Some consideration of this case is called for. The first attempt at suicide occurred before Ahmed Katongole was detained. He took an overdose of paracetamol for no other reason than that he was in mortal fear of being returned to Uganda. In view of Uganda's appalling record of human rights abuse, his fear would seem to have been well-founded. The government in Uganda had changed, but after fourteen years of the intensity of violence Uganda had experienced, it would be foolish to imagine that respect for human rights could be restored overnight. Detention made matters worse for Katongole. A psychiatric report noted the trauma of isolation, which is far more acute in the case of foreigners than in the case of Britons. 'Lack of care' must include the failure to tell Katongole that an MP had intervened on his behalf, as well as to the failure of the prison staff to carry out the routine surveillance which is required when a prisoner is known to be suicidal.

In October 1989 a further death in custody took place. When an influx of Turkish Kurds began to arrive in the summer of 1989, the then Home Secretary announced in Parliament that many of them were simply economic migrants looking for a better life, although it is unclear how he could have known this, since practically none of the asylum claims had been processed at the time he made this statement. A number were persuaded to return to Turkey, but the vast majority of those who reached the UK had experienced persecution and were fleeing for that reason (see McDowell, 1989). The hostile attitude of the UK government added greatly to their fears and anxieties. Among those detained in Harmondsworth was Mr Siho Iyiguven and a friend, both of whom were threatened with removal back to Turkey. In despair they barricaded themselves into a room and set it and themselves alight. Both were severely burnt. The friend, who received 30% burns, recovered; Siho Iyiguven received 60% burns, including inhalation burns, and died two days later on 8 October in Mount Vernon Hospital. It was over a year before the inquest was held and the verdict was one of misadventure. Whatever the verdict, as far as the Kurds are concerned Iyiguven is a martyr who committed suicide, as he had said he would, rather than be returned to Turkey. Harmondsworth is run down and depressing, but it is no worse than most prisons in the UK. It was not the circumstances of his detention that drove Siho Iyiguven to take the action which led to his death, but the prospect of being returned to Turkey. His wife and children are now refugees in this country as a result of fresh persecution following the return of his body to Turkey, which strongly suggests that the decision to refuse him asylum was wrong.

The third death was of a Zairean, Mr Nsimba Kimpua, who arrived at Heathrow on 10 June 1990. An immigration officer became persuaded that because he had come via Lagos and because his French was bad and his Zairean identity card was forged, he was not a Zairean at all (although she did not know enough about Zaire to know that Lingala, the language which he claimed to speak, is its most widely spoken language). On 11 June the immigration officer noted, 'We have no Lingala interpreter on our books and I am reluctant to go to the trouble (and expense for HMG) of finding one especially only to discover that [he] does not after all speak this language'. The notes continue, 'I told the passenger that we are unable to proceed with his asylum application until he tells us where he really comes from, who he is and what nationality he is, because of the problem of finding an interpreter'. The notes do not record what language was used or whether Nsimba understood what was said. The immigration officer's notes show that he felt unwell and was traumatised, though she does not appear to have recognised his state. A request for an interpreter was eventually made by the Immigration Service a day or two later to Zairag (a Zairean community association), the Refugee Arrivals Project, and the School of Oriental and African Studies, but none of them was able to produce one. On the morning of 16 June Nsimba Kimpua was found hanged in a toilet in Harmondsworth Detention Centre, 22 hours after he was first noticed to be missing. The post-mortem showed that he had eaten little for some days. Had he been referred to one of the refugee agencies, they would have been able to provide an interpreter and this death might have been avoided. The refugee agencies have asked repeatedly that all arrivals shall be referred, but the Home Office refuses to undertake that this shall be done. Charter '87 wrote to the Parliamentary Under-Secretary of State with responsibility for refugees on 27 June 1990 about Mr Kimpua's death, asking to be told the date of the inquest. No reply has ever been received in spite of several reminders and a promise by the head of the Refugee Unit that a reply would be sent.

The inquest on Nsimba Kimpua, held on 4-5 March 1991, showed that no one had any overall responsibility for Nsimba (or, presumably, for anyone else at Harmondsworth); although his absence was noted at Friday evening's meal and his name was called over the tannoy, he was not found until 22 hours later, and then by chance. Group 4 Security officers who run Harmondsworth have only five days training, and no training in suicide prevention (this is the group now chosen to run the UK's first privately administered prison). There is no on-the-spot medical care. The inquest jury found, on the basis of photographic evidence provided by members of Nsimba's family that he was indeed the Zairean who he claimed to be, and brought in a suicide verdict. They were not able to enquire into the state of mind which drove him to take his own life, though they brought in a rider to the verdict, saying, 'A search had been made when he was missing. This was inadequate, and he was not found until the next day. The level of communication with the person who died was a matter of concern in the days from 11-15 June 1990'. One wonders if it was any better between his arrival and 11 June. If there was no 'lack of care' in the technical sense, the system plainly permitted neglect.[9]

The final topic to which we must turn is the treatment of asylum detainees who attempt to commit suicide. Charter '87 first learned of the way in which those who attempted suicide were treated in the prison system before the use of strip cells became common knowledge, and they were unable to credit what they were hearing from solicitors and others. In one case it was reported that an asylum seeker was left wrapped up in a plastic foam blanket in a strip cell for three days, and that when his brother eventually managed to see him, he stank, apparently because he was covered in excrement. By the time a worker from one of the refugee agencies saw him he was too traumatised to speak. When we discussed these reports with psychiatrists and a psychotherapist, some were at first disinclined to believe that such practices were still possible. Now, of course, the whole scandal has emerged and the UK has been questioned by the United Nations Committee on Torture about the use of strip cells.[10] The British Medical Association (1990, p.28) has welcomed the promised phasing out by the prison system of the use of strip cells, but as yet there seems to have been little change in practice.

We will look in detail at one case where an asylum seeker, diagnosed as a suicide risk because of his fear of removal, was treated in this manner. Mr O arrived in the UK on 31 May 1989 and applied for asylum. His claim was that if he were returned to his country of nationality, he would again suffer imprisonment and torture as the police would again try to make him divulge the whereabouts of his brother who belonged to a proscribed organisation. He feared that he would break down under torture and divulge his brother's whereabouts. His case was an almost exact parallel to two other cases in which asylum was granted, but Mr O was refused asylum and ordered to be removed. However, the Office of the UNHCR considered him to be a mandate refugee who should have full refugee status, and a high-level intervention was made from Geneva. His removal was stopped shortly before take-off was due, and the Home Office agreed to a five day stay of removal. Mr O had already been held for some time under strict supervision lest he attempt suicide (the death of Siho Iyiguven had occurred only two days before Mr O's removal was due). He was now taken from Heathrow Airport to Pentonville Prison, having no idea of what was happening to him, and was reported to be nearly out of his mind with fear and anxiety. When his lawyer saw him that evening he had been stripped of his own clothes and was dressed only in 'some sort of a blanket'. A letter about him had been sent by Dr Tom Landau of the Medical Foundation to the Home Office describing him as harbouring suicidal notions, deeply depressed, and therefore by definition potentially suicidal, but this was not, of course, the sort of treatment the Medical Foundation would have recommended. By the next morning he was reported to be wearing his own clothes and sharing a cell with another man who was also believed to be a suicide risk. Eventually arrangements were made for him to apply for asylum in another member state of the European Community (that is no longer possible under the Dublin Convention: asylum seekers refused in one member state are now refused in all).

Little comment on this case is required. It is difficult for anyone to imagine the state of mind of this man both before and after the attempt to remove him on 12 October. Stripping him of his own clothes and placing him in isolation will have added to his distress. A psychotherapist consulted by Charter '87 said such treatment was 'destructive of the personality'. There have been other less dramatic incidents in which asylum detainees have attempted suicide or been diagnosed as suicide risks and been similarly treated. We have urged researchers currently engaged on a Home Office-funded project on the resettlement of refugees to include in their sample people who have suffered detention and been treated in this way when they were diagnosed as potentially suicidal. We believe that this sort of treatment may have long-term results.

It will now be clear that the remedy for suicide and attempted suicide by asylum seekers detained in the UK is two-fold. First, they should not be held in detention except in the most exceptional circumstances, and if there are circumstances which require asylum seekers to be detained, they should be informed in writing of the reason for their detention and the detention should be reviewed by an independent judicial authority. Amnesty International has published a detailed statement of what should be the rights of asylum seekers with regard to detention.[11] In a statement made to the Annual General Meeting of INQUEST on 25 November 1989, Dr Tom Landau stated on behalf of the Medical Foundation for the Care of Victims of Torture:

Many of our patients, who have come here in the belief that the United Kingdom represents freedom, respect for human rights and their final desperate hope for survival, find themselves again detained, in prison or a detention centre, sometimes for many months and for no very apparent reason. The psychological effect of this is not hard to imagine, nor is it difficult to understand that a survivor of torture who, having escaped to 'Freedom' and being incarcerated with apparent removal of his final hopes, will seriously consider suicide as the only possible alternative to deportation and further torture with violent death as a further possibility. 'It is better to die here than in my country' is a statement which we hear distressingly often.

Nothing has improved since then. In 1991 an article was published in the *Psychiatric Bulletin* entitled 'The mental state of detained asylum seekers' (Bracken and Gorst-Unsworth, 1991), but the only development has been planning by the Home Office to provide 300 extra detention spaces for immigration and asylum detainees.

Secondly, there needs to be a change of policy regarding the granting of asylum. Though detention puts a greatly added strain on asylum seekers, there have also been many cases of asylum seekers who are not detained becoming clinically depressed and suicidal when months grow into years and their applications for asylum remain undecided, or are refused. That is why those concerned with the welfare of asylum seekers welcomed a long-overdue increase of staff in the Home Office Refugee Unit. On one occasion parents brought their two young children to one of the refugee agencies on receiving a refusal notice; the father slashed his wrists, and the distraught mother asked how she could kill herself and her children because she could not face the torture which she was sure they would suffer if returned. Strenuous representations eventually resulted in the family being permitted to stay, but the psychological damage to the children who witnessed their parents' despair and inability to protect them has been done, and psychiatrists believe that such damage may well be life-long. Suicide attempts like this are not 'a natural expression of disappointment at not being allowed to settle in the UK' as a Home Office official once claimed. Until the Home Office takes such fears seriously, we believe that suicide and attempted suicide will continue. That Home Office decisions are not always safe is evidenced by recent cases where decisions have been altered on appeal. But for those who apply for asylum at a port of entry there is no right of appeal until after they have been removed back to the country from which they fled. The Asylum Bill presented to Parliament in 1991, and which fell because of the General Election of Spring, 1992, offered only a right to apply for leave to appeal, although a full right of appeal had been promised to Parliament earlier that year.[12] The Refugee Unit of the Home Office needs to be as concerned with protection as with keeping down the immigration statistics; as concerned not to send people back to persecution and torture as with excluding 'bogus' refugees (sometimes simply people who have not been persecuted quite sufficiently to meet the

Home Office's rigorous standards); it needs to be more concerned with human rights and less concerned with disparaging those who seek to protect them.

In these circumstances perhaps the best that we can ask for is that good psychiatric practice be followed for those detained asylum seekers who are at risk of suicide. It is easy to see that present practice is flawed. It is harder to see what might constitute good and relevant practice. It is virtually impossible for prisons and detention centres to make a full appraisal of the extent to which an asylum seeker may be a suicide risk because such an assessment would involve an understanding of the person's cultural background and of his or her personal history. Ideally a friend is needed to help make such an assessment. But it may be taken as axiomatic that asylum seekers are particularly vulnerable. Friends and refugee welfare personnel need good access. A person at risk should not be placed alone or in a strip cell. Strenuous efforts should be made to find sympathetic interpreters when the detainee knows no English. But when all is said and done, how can one help a person to face the future (which is what good psychiatric practice seeks to do) when he or she is in mortal fear of renewed persecution and possibly violent death?[13] A decision to take one's own life in such circumstances may be a fully rational thing to do

Notes

1. e.g. Letter from P. Wrench of the Immigration and Nationality Division of the Home Office to Antonia Hunt, 8 October, 1990.
2. Copy obtained by courtesy of the Office of the UNHCR.
3. The refugee agencies all wrote to the Home Office to protest that Latchmere House, Richmond, was to be closed as an immigration detention centre and the detainees sent to Haslar which would be far more difficult of access and involve the voluntary agencies in added expense because of the length of the journey. Although all the comments received by the Home Office on this issue were negative, the move went ahead.
4. From May 1987 onwards until October there were frequent press reports on the use of the Earl William, many of them mocking and highly critical of the Home Office, e.g. *Independent* 1 August, *Guardian* 8 August, *Observer* 9 August. A hunger strike in early August highlighted the issue. After the hurricane no further use was made of ferries for detaining asylum seekers.

It may safely be concluded that the Home Office was glad to be rid of a procedure which had become an embarrassment.

5. There was extensive press coverage of this, e.g. *Observer* 8 October 1987, *Independent, Times, Telegraph, Guardian*, 9, 10 October, *Times, Independent* 11 October

6. This case was reported on in the Independent, the asylum seeker being referred to under the pseudonym 'Joseph', on 12 January 1990. He was released from detention on 24 January and granted exceptional leave to remain on 2 April

7. Letter from Kate Collins, Deputy Principal Immigration Officer, 14 August 1990. (The case referred to is *Secretary of State for the Home Department v Thirukumar and others* [1989] Imm AR 402.)

8. e.g. 'The circumstances surrounding the tragic death of Mr Katongole were the subject of an inquest and it would not be appropriate to go into the further in this context. They do not in themselves put into question the decision to refuse My Katongole asylum.' Timothy Renton MP, Minister of State with responsibility for refugees, to Lord Hylton.

9. Copies of the papers in this case, including the immigration officer's notes, were kindly provided by Wilson and Co., Solicitors acting for the relatives of Mr Nsimba Kimpua, and the inquest was monitored for Charter '87 by Messrs. Paul Roberts and Stephen Bailey.

10. United Nations Committee Against Torture, Seventh Session, Summary Record of the 92nd Meeting, p. 5.

11. See Charter '87 for Refugees, Section IV, The Detention of Asylum Seekers. Amnesty International has set out proposed safeguards on detention as follows: * The detention of asylum seekers should be resorted to only for reasons recognised as legitimate by international standards for the protection of refugees, and when other measures short of detention cannot be used. In all cases, the decision to detain an asylum applicant should be the responsibility of a senior Home Office official. * In the event of a decision to detain being taken, the detainee should be provided with a comprehensive written statement of the reasons for his or her detention. The detainee should be held in humane conditions, and should not be accommodated with criminal prisoners unless charged or convicted of a recognisably criminal offence. The detainee should be given adequate opportunity, and the necessary facilities, to contact and to meet with relatives, representatives of relevant non-governmental organisations, and his or her legal representative.

* In all cases, the detainee should be able to effectively challenge the basis for his or her detention at a prompt hearing before an independent, impartial and competent review body. The detainee, and his or her legal representative, should be permitted to attend the deliberations of, and make representations to, the review body at a full, oral hearing. * In reviewing a decision to detain an asylum applicant, the review body should be empowered to consider only whether or not the continued detention of the applicant is both necessary and for reasons recognised as legitimate by international standards; if this cannot be adequately demonstrated by the Home Office, then the detainee should be released immediately. * In the event that the review body authorises continued detention, the detainee should be able to make further challenges to the lawfulness of his or her detention at regular intervals not exceeding 14 days. (Amnesty International British Section, 1992).

12. 'The Bill will make it clear that all those who are turned down in the determination process will be able to appeal while they are in the United Kingdom'. *Hansard* (Lords), 2 July 1991, column 914, The Lord Chancellor speaking. cf. Asylum Bill, 1 November 1991, Asylum Appeals (Procedure) Rules, 5 (1): 'An asylum appeal may be brought only with the leave of a special adjudicator'. (13) I am grateful to Dr Raymond Gardner of Fulbourn Hospital, Cambridge for discussing this issue with me, but responsibility for this paragraph and for its conclusion are entirely mine.

PART THREE

PREVENTION AND SOLUTIONS

INTRODUCTION

Our final group of papers brings together suggestions from Australia and the USA on the prevention of prison suicides and deaths in police custody. In England and Wales, the three years since the conference have seen significant and positive changes in the Prison Service's approach to suicide prevention, at least at the level of policy. The focus has shifted from the individual, medical and psychiatric aspects of the problem to general preventive measures, case conferences, prisoner-led listener schemes and other forms of support, backed up by Samaritan involvement, family contact and wide-ranging training for staff.

There is still no room for complacency, as the material in Part Two so clearly illustrates. Prison health care services, psychologists, officers, managers and other specialist and lay groups can all contribute to the search for effective solutions in what is at last becoming a leading area of inquiry in prisons. As we complete this collection, the prison service is launching a new and compelling 'training and awareness video' on prison suicide called 'Misadventures'. A new and comprehensively re-worked 'self-harm' file for action and guidance in cases of suspected suicide risk is being piloted in establishments around the country. The unhelpful dichotomy between health care and discipline staff over the management of suicide risk is no longer enshrined in policy, and the 1987 Circular Instruction on suicide prevention with its over-emphasis on the medical role will soon be replaced. A new Suicide Awareness Support Unit with three full-time staff collates information and examples of good practice and disseminates these to the field through a magazine called *Life-Support*. The Unit co-ordinates staff training as well as offering support to staff appearing at inquests. Its members spend as much time as they can in establishments talking to staff and prisoners and seeking to translate their concerns into action.

The crucial question, of course, is how far these changes of policy will be translated into practice on the ground. There is still a long way to go, but some establishments can be credited with a real change in ethos and practice and have made progress well beyond the requirements of Circular Instructions. Staff whose own lives have been touched by suicide have often become those most able to transform practice in their own workplaces.

We would like to think that some of these initiatives have been encouraged by the research and experience documented here, as well as by political pressures. In general, as one experienced police researcher has noted, 'The incorporation of research findings into a new body of accepted wisdom is a slow and uneven process in which the intellectual persuasiveness of the research is a great deal less relevant than its political appeal' (Weatheritt, 1986, p.16). Be that as it may, in this context research which we hope is intellectually persuasive does seem to have been incorporated into policy with unusual celerity.

In the time elapsed since the Canterbury Conference, internationally progress on suicide prevention has been moving in a positive direction. Several publications, including a regular Australian paper on Deaths in Custody produced by the Australian Institute of Criminology's Monitoring and Research Program established as one of the Commonwealth Government's responses to the Royal Commission, and a Canadian Issue of their Correctional Service Forum in *Corrections Research Magazine* on Prison Violence and Inmate Suicide and Self-Injury, illustrate the continuing commitment to suicide prevention and the minimisation of custodial deaths observable in many jurisdictions. A detailed report on The Police Role in Dealing with Suicidal Persons and Custody Management was produced by the New South Wales Police Service Research Program in 1991 (Basedow, 1991). No doubt other publications and policy changes have evolved. We hope the publication of these papers stimulates further dissemination of such progress. It has been heartening to see the slow but profitable meeting of policy-makers, academics, penal reformers and practitioners the Conference aimed to encourage.

In this capacity, Joseph Rowan, Correctional Consultant for Juvenile and Criminal Justice International USA has made a welcome and significant contribution to prison service thinking on suicide prevention in England and Wales. During 1992 he was invited to hold a series of training seminars at Newbold Revel Training School, to share his experiences and build upon the changing ethos in the service. His paper demonstrates the message he brought to us first at this conference and then later is his training for staff. In Rowan's view, experience has clearly demonstrated that almost all suicides in police lock-ups, jails and prisons can be averted with the implementation of a prevention program that includes staff training, intake screening, good communication between staff and inmates and a suicide-resistant environment for special management inmates. The key to prevention remains a capable and properly trained staff. They are the backbone ingredient. Such a system, however, will not come to fruition without pro-active administrators who not only maintain an awareness of suicide in custody as a national problem but who take the initiative to prevent such an occurrence in their facilities. Good suicide prevention means good custody, to the extent that this is achievable. Some of our earlier contributions remind us that custodial institutions tend to have the opposite dynamic, without constant effort, evaluation and vigilance.

John Ure from the New South Wales Police Service, Australia discusses 'Police Accountability in Custody Management: Creating the Climate'. He shows how the Royal Commission focused the attention of government agencies, particularly Police and Corrective Services Departments on the manner in which they manage and care for persons who are detained in custody. The underlying theme in custody management is accountability, both at the individual and organisational level. Police officers who are given the task of looking after people in cells at their station will be held accountable if a prisoner suffers death or injury and it is shown that the officer did not discharge an appropriate 'duty of care' - a duty which has become much more onerous in recent times. However, the police service has a duty to create a climate where those officers will accept this accountability and where they will have a genuine concern for the safety and welfare of persons in their cells.

His paper discusses what the New South Wales Police Service has learned about its capacity for custody management and what it is doing to create the 'accountability climate'. In particular it focuses on particular factors such as cell design, station command structures, custody management policies and procedures, assessment and screening procedures, training and the proper investigation of deaths in custody. These are essential components in the search for proper accountability and its acceptance by individual officers. His paper also discusses the notion of moving the Police Force from being a reactive, centrally-controlled organisation where individuals are expected to conform to a rigid set of instructions, to a proactive, locally managed, values-driven service where individual thought and initiative are encouraged and rewarded and where the climate is created for individual officers to willingly accept accountability for their actions.

Lindsay Hayes, the Assistant Director of the National Center on Institutions and Alternatives, Massachusetts, and editor of *Jail Suicides Update* an occasional paper published by the National Center, completed the formal part of the conference proceedings with a paper on 'Jail Suicide Prevention in the USA'. His paper considered both the possible causes of jail suicide and suicide attempts and efforts made to reduce them over the last two decades. He argued that causes could be subsumed under two main categories: the physical/organisational environment of the jail and the way in which inmates are helped to face a crisis situation. He identified effective suicide prevention strategies in the USA which often followed expensive litigation in the courts. He gave details of the strategies successfully adopted by El Paso County, Colorado, which reduced the County Jail's suicide rate to zero. He dramatically illustrated the possibilities of reducing suicide by creating a climate of commitment by prison staff and managers, echoing the sentiments of John Ure's paper on the police. He showed how expensive law suits can be (and in some States have been) replaced by contracts binding establishments to improved standards of care, support for staff and regular reviews of their suicide prevention procedures. Echoes of the welcome introduction of Accredited Standards, Key

Performance Indicators and prisoner and establishment 'compacts' in the wake of the Woolf Report in England and Wales (see Woolf, 1991; Home Office, 1992) come as a great comfort to those who heard the message delivered by these presentations. Hayes also described the Crisis Service Model introduced by jails in New York and the eight step suicide prevention plan adopted by Texas. He concluded with a chilling account of the death in a county jail in New Jersey of Rita Boltax.

Finally, Richard Harding of the Crime Research Centre in Western Australia reviewed the recent history of deaths in custody in Great Britain and Australia. He considered definitions of suicide, attempted suicide, parasuicide and self-inflicted harm. He presented case histories of those who died in custody in Victoria, Australia. They illustrate how staff feel themselves to be manipulated by inmates and how this sense of frustration may mean that important clues to future potential suicidal behaviour are missed. This is particularly significant because of the link between previous self-harm and subsequent suicide which Harding considered with references to recent studies in Australia and Great Britain. Harding's recommendations led to action by the Prison Department including the reduction of 'social crowding' which had been shown to be linked to the number of deaths. These improvements to prison conditions led to a reduction in the number of deaths in subsequent years.

Eleven

Prevention of suicides in custody

Joseph R. Rowan

ADMINISTRATION

The prevention of suicides in custody will be only as effective as the prison and jail administrators understand the suicide issue and actively lead the way in the implementation of a recognised suicide prevention programme, from both a philosophical and policy standpoint.

What does this mean? It means that the administrator:

1. Needs to be aware of what causes suicides. What are the recognised signs and symptoms?
2. Is trained in the principles and techniques of managing suicidal inmates. Otherwise, the *team* approach, direly needed in suicide prevention, will not work effectively. The administrator should be the manager of the suicide prevention team, which represents all of the concerned disciplines, including custody (correctional officers).
3. Must get the resources needed for effective suicide prevention.
4. Must, in his/her day-to-day supervisory role, instill into managers/supervisors under him/her the right philosophy and a strong desire to carry out a recognised duty of care. This is essential training. Effective suicide prevention training starts with the top administrator.

SUPERVISORS

Supervisors must instill in their officers the same desire to be a member of the suicide prevention team that they learned from their 'bosses'/superiors. While skills training in suicide signs and symptoms (s/s/s) and management of suicidal inmates are extremely important, most job learning for officers must come from their day-to-day contact with their supervisors.

THE BACKBONE OF SUICIDE PREVENTION

Administrators and supervisors must instill into officers the fact that *they* (officers) are the backbone of suicide prevention. Officers are the staff:

1. Who monitor suicidal inmates and live with them 24 hours per day.
2. Who generally are the only staff in a position to observe *behavioural changes* (and then report them to their supervisor and/or mental health staff).
3. Who are the only staff to know about new crises situations which can produce *situational depression* and suicide.

THE ROLE OF HEALTH CARE PERSONNEL

Medical and mental health personnel should be the key diagnosticians of suicide, at least in medium and large facilities. In small jails in America, where the *jailer* is the *only one staff* on duty, particularly on the evening and graveyard shifts, s/he is the main assessor of suicide. It is likely that a referral to health care personnel cannot be made until the next morning.

Mental health and medical care personnel are essential support services. They will not be effective if there is not a *Team* approach. Without referrals from officers about new crises and behavioural changes, suicide re-assessment will fail, and suicides will occur. The exception will be where positive-minded and properly trained officers are responsible for the entire suicide prevention process, generally in small jails.

SCREENING FOR SUICIDE POTENTIAL

Receiving screening should be done immediately upon the inmate's arrival at the facility. In America, trained officers do most of the initial health screening, particularly in jails. The

American Medical Association firmly supports the concept of *trained* officers conducting receiving screening.

In large jails and most prisons, screening is done by nurses or emergency medical technicians (EMTs). Medical doctors seldom do any screening, and then only upon referral for a second appraisal.

Psychiatrists, clinical psychologists and social workers generally do follow-up assessments upon referral from custody personnel.

WHY IS SUICIDE MISDIAGNOSED?

In America, professional mental health staff do not always properly diagnose suicide potential. Most often these are part-time *community* mental health personnel who do not recognise the impact of the *custody environment* on suicide. Or, they are not aware of new crises because officers did not relay this crucial information.

Some mental health professionals rely only on their one-to-one session and do not give proper weight to the inmate's past.

Further, diagnoses sometimes are made without the benefit of past health care records, and an inmate bent on suicide may not tell the truth about his current feelings.

The most serious problem, however, is when medical and mental health personnel believe the inmate is 'manipulating' or 'malingering'. Believing this, the 'once-professionals' resort to 'street attitudes', and suicides occur because there is failure to professionally diagnose. There should be no such assessment word as 'manipulation' in the field of suicidology.

NEGATIVE ATTITUDES, BIASES AND PREJUDICES

Some health care and correctional/custody personnel fail to control their negative attitudes, biases and prejudices toward offenders. I learned in police college 44 years ago that 'you can hate the crime, but not the criminal'.

Supervisors play an important role in helping officers resolve and/or control these feelings. Continuing and refresher education plays an important part in preventing health care personnel from resorting to these 'native tendencies'.

Lawsuits against jails and prisons in America all too often find personnel of all levels and disciplines liable for failing to carry out their duty of care because they did not resolve or control their negative attitudes, biases and prejudices. Following the Golden Rule is more likely to effect suicide prevention.

It is commonly agreed by suicide experts in the community, as well as in the custody field, that, if only one person cares or 'gives a damn' and that fact is *perceived* by the suicidal person, a suicide most likely will be prevented. If the booking and cellblock officers and health care personnel are caring people and *show* this, almost all potential suicides which were missed at receiving screening or which developed later will be prevented by this positive attitude.

A professionally firm, fair and consistent philosophy is important not only in preventing suicide, but also for overall operations.

'NOT CLINICALLY DEPRESSED'. 'NOT NOW SUICIDAL'

These diagnostic phrases are often found in health care records. Without a realistic explanation or interpretation, line officers often are mislead by these words into feeling that 'all is OK'. Then tragically, the suicide occurs.

The fact is that few suicides are accompanied by clinical, long-term depression (psychosis). Most are preceded by situational depression. Again, only the housing unit officer generally knows about the 'Dear John' letter, that disturbing phone call, the thrice-postponed court trial or the long sentence just handed down. One hour, one day or a week later, situational depression and suicide occur.

I strongly urge implementation of the recommendation contained in an officers' handbook developed by mental health personnel in New York State: 'If you [officer] believe a detainee is suicidal, you should trust your own judgement. If you believe someone is in danger of suicide, act on your beliefs. Don't let others mislead you into ignoring suicidal signals'.

A GOOD SCREENING INTERVIEW

Some detention/correctional facilities in our country explain the rationale for conducting the receiving screening interview. It is simple and takes only seconds: 'I am going to ask you some questions now which we ask everyone who comes here, because we are interested in your health and welfare'. This statement helps take away the feeling that the interviewee is being picked on and shows care and concern. Additional factors are:

1. Asking questions in a common-sense manner, as privately as possible.
2. Speaking in a normal, quiet, matter-of-fact tone.
3. Using language the inmate can understand, including 'street language'.
4. Not being rushy, abrupt or sarcastic.
5. Repeating slowly and clearly questions not understood.

Many facilities following the above procedures say that over 90 per cent of answers to screening questions are beneficial.

TOTAL HEALTH SCREENING

We strongly recommend total health screening of new admissions to detention and correctional facilities. Unattended medical problems can heighten anxiety and add to suicide stress.

We do the following:

1. Ask detailed questions on the use of alcohol and drugs, to get a handle on possible withdrawal. We have found that the inmate's fear of going through alcohol or drug withdrawal, once he has experienced this, can trigger suicides.
2. We include detailed observations to earmark factors which may indicate potential same-sex rape victims. Attacks or fear of them can trigger suicides. We know the importance of both of these precipitating factors from having asked persons who have attempted suicide, 'Why did you attempt suicide?'
3. We ask and observe *mental* status, because many completed suicides are preceded by a history of mental illness. The same holds true for prior suicide attempts or thoughts of it.
4. We determine if this is the *first* incarceration of an arrestee because over one-third of the suicides are by 'first-timers'.
5. We ask one last question, 'Is there anything special that we should know about you for your welfare or protection?' This very important question often brings forth valuable responses pertaining to AIDS potential, protective custody and health conditions not presented earlier.

Further, asking this question provides legal *liability protection* for the agency.

THE 'DOS AND DON'TS' OF GOOD CUSTODY, DISCIPLINE AND MENTAL HEALTH

The 26 'Dos and Don'ts' of good custody, discipline and mental health provide a proven, solid foundation not only for suicide prevention but for day-to-day custody, inmate management and discipline. With this positive climate, relations between staff and inmates and among inmates mean fewer disturbances, friction and *stress*. As we say, 'You are working in a cooler institution, and even your spouse recognises it!'

Following are the 26 'Dos and Don'ts':

1. Exhibits fairness
2. Shows no favouritism
3. Keeps promises
4. Uses authority and power constructively
5. Admits mistakes
6. No put-downs or is not condescending
7. Does not wash dirty linen - does not criticise other staff
8. Answers questions
9. Asks, does not always order that something be done.
10. Is consistent
11. Talks with inmates
12. Is looked up to by inmates
13. Is a team worker
14. Is self-confident, but not arrogant
15. Demonstrates sincerity and honesty
16. Gives credit when credit is due
17. Accepts constructive criticism: is not defensive
18. Has an open mind
19. Doesn't keep threatening
20. Leaves personal problems at home
21. Does not yell or swear
22. Does more than is expected of him
23. Is patient
24. Doesn't give up easily
25. Doesn't preach
26. Cares

SUICIDE 'BUDDY WATCHERS'/USE OF VOLUNTEERS

In the States we make good use of selected and trained inmates to supplement staff monitoring of suicidal inmates. They usually are not placed in the same cell and have no control over the suicidal inmate. They have demonstrated outstanding service, evidenced by the fact that, so far as is known, there has not been even one lawsuit over their use.

Training and use of other inmates help to break the inmate 'Code of Silence' and encourage general population inmates to inform staff of potential suicide. We know from psychological autopsies/administrative reviews following suicidal deaths that fellow inmates *are often aware* of suicidal signs and symptoms but do NOT tell staff because of the Code of Silence.

Some facilities use volunteers from the community for suicide watch. Members of the well-known Neighbourhood Crime Watch groups are trained in Suicide signs and symptoms (s/s/s/) and are known as Concerned Citizens. As in any volunteer programme, it is simply a case of asking responsible citizens to serve, and they do. Again, the programme will not be any better than the *administration which supports it*.

PROTRUSION-FREE ENVIRONMENT/USE OF ISOLATION

Isolation is the *worst* means of managing a suicidal inmate *unless* the room or cell is suicide-resistant. About three-quarters of our in-custody suicides occur in isolation/single cells or rooms.

We can and do build and retrofit cells to make it impossible for someone to hang. It can be done economically, and at the same time produce a reasonably positive environment that is not de-humanising. In such an environment, it is *not* necessary to strip inmates of their normal clothing. Stripping inmates naked, as a few facilities in our country still do, is not only de-humanising but *worsens* depression. Chapter 16 of our *Training Curriculum on Suicide Detection and Prevention in Jails and Lockups*, 1988, provides details for building and retrofitting sleeping areas for a protrusion - free environment.

SUICIDE PREVENTION REALLY WORKS

For many years, Chicago's Cook County Jail averaged about 15 to 16 suicides (and homicides) per year. After instituting receiving screening and providing special training for its officers, that number abruptly changed to one suicide per year in the late 60s and 70s For nearly two years, with an average daily population of over 6,000 inmates in the mid-80s it did not have a single suicide.

New York State's 62 county jails had 32 suicides in 1984, and *six* in 1990 - an 80 per cent reduction.

Chicago's police lockups used to average *one suicide monthly*. After they instituted receiving screening and gave their officers two days of suicide prevention training (of which I was a part), the suicide rate dropped during the next 18 months from 18 to three - a saving of *15 lives*!

One large jail had no suicides in over 10 years, while across the street, the small police lockup, with one-fiftieth its population, had *six* suicides in less than *two years*. Obviously, the police lockup had no suicide prevention programme.

Many other custody facilities in the USA., have had significant reductions in suicide, making a reality of our brochure title, *Almost All Suicides in Jails and Lockups Can be Prevented If...*

SUMMARY

Suicide prevention in custody is best achieved by positive-minded, properly trained detention/correctional officers, who have learned much about their jobs from good supervisors, who in turn were instilled with a sound philosophy by the top administrator. The facility with the successful suicide prevention programme has in place a suicide *plan* with the following criteria:

1. *Identification* of suicide signs and symptoms observed through receiving/initial health screening.
2. A minimum of eight hours of training for officers, including identification and management of suicidal persons, and the 26 'Dos and Don'ts' of good custody, discipline and mental health.
3. Assessment of suicidal risk level by health care personnel.
4. *Monitoring* procedures defined in writing, based upon risk level.
5. *Housing* procedures, defined in writing, specifying that isolation is not used unless constant observation is maintained. If staffing does not allow this, two or more inmates or a *community volunteer* should supplement staff supervision, which should be at least every 10 to 15 minutes.

6. Referral procedures should be defined in writing, stating that officers and others refer inmates to medical/mental health personnel for an in-depth assessment and advice on management.

7. Procedures for communication between custody and health care personnel should require clear and current information on the status of the inmate.

8. Life-safety intervention.
   Defined procedures should outline proven and acceptable means of handling a suicide in progress, including emphasis on:

   a. Saving a life rather than 'preserving the scene of the crime'.

   b. Letting the officer be the judge in determining whether an inmate is hanging or faking (when only *one* officer is on duty).

   c. Effecting means of *immediately* cutting down a hanging victim.

   d. Emphasise strongly the use of the modified jaw thrust in cardiopulmonary resuscitation instead of the traditional chin up and head back approach.

9. Method of *notification*, involving officials and family/ significant others, concerning potential attempted and completed suicides should be clearly outlined. Officials need to be very sensitive to feelings of loved ones and provide a reasonable explanation of the special incident.

10. *Administrative review / Psychological autopsy*

Procedures should require that, after each attempted and completed suicide, an administrative review be conducted to determine what happened, how and why it happened, and how the next attempt might be prevented.

Equally important, staff feelings/attitudes need to be dealt with and referrals for counselling made where indicated. This is sometimes defined as the psychological autopsy, an essential part of the *Plan*.

Twelve

Police accountability in custody management: creating the climate

John Ure

INTRODUCTION

The key to effective custody management is accountability; police officers must be prepared to be held accountable, both legally and morally, for the manner in which they treat persons who are detained in police cells. This accountability extends to taking all reasonable steps to minimise the trauma which a person may suffer when placed in a cell and, as far as is reasonably possible, identifying behavioural signs which might indicate potential for illness or self-injury.

The New South Wales Police Service has accomplished a great deal in reforming custody management over the past few years. To a certain extent this reform has been driven by the knowledge that the Royal Commission into Aboriginal Deaths in Custody is closely examining our policies and practices. However the reform also reflects a genuine desire by the Police Service to improve the treatment of persons who, for whatever reason, are detained in our cells.

This paper discusses those accomplishments and proposes the notion that it is unreasonable to expect police to accept true accountability unless the police organisation is prepared to provide appropriate physical surroundings, policies, procedures and education. In other words, the police organisation must create the right climate for accountability.

The personal views expressed in this paper are not those of an academic; they are the thoughts of an operational police officer-turned-administrator who is concerned with, and about, the treatment of persons in police custody. Over the past three years I have had the opportunity to examine custody procedures at first hand in all parts of New South Wales, as well as other parts of Australia, and have talked with acknowledged medical experts, particularly in the drug and alcohol fields, and key players in police custody and prison management. The knowledge and experience that I have gained has allowed me to play a part in creating the climate.

NEW SOUTH WALES: AN OVERVIEW

New South Wales - Australia's 'First State' - was named by Captain James Cook on his voyage of discovery in 1770. It lies on the eastern coast of Australia and has an area of 801,000 sq. km (about three times the size of the United Kingdom). There are 1,100 km of coastline to the Pacific Ocean. The narrow, fertile coastal strip is broken by the Great Dividing Range, which runs the full length of the State, from Queensland in the north to Victoria in the south. West of the Great Divide are the western slopes and plains which gradually give way to semi-arid terrain and desert, with temperatures regularly reaching into the mid-forties. Industries in New South Wales include wool and wheat production, coal mining, steel production, timber logging, wine making and tourism.

New South Wales has a population of 5.6 million, which is mainly concentrated in the State capital Sydney (3.4 m.), Newcastle (400,00) and Wollongong (200,000), all of which are coastal cities. The population spread over the remainder of the State is such that, apart from those just mentioned, there are only:

- 6 towns with populations in excess of 25,000
- 24 towns with populations in excess of 10,000 and
- 44 towns with populations in excess of 5,000

These figures are significant when you consider the allocation and management of government resources, including police, to meet the needs of the people in all parts of New South Wales.

The ethnic composition of the New South Wales population is extremely varied, the product of a number of migration policies which have been introduced by various Governments. One fifth of the people of New South Wales (over one million) were born overseas, most of them in Europe (61%) and Asia (22%). Predominant countries of origin were the United Kingdom, New Zealand, Italy, Yugoslavia and Lebanon, however since the end of the Indo-China war in the mid-1970s there has been an increased proportion of Asian immigrants. Over 15% of people in New South Wales (over 740,000) speak a language other than English at home.

There are 59,000 Aborigines in New South Wales, some living in urban areas and others in communities of varying sizes right across the State.

The Government of New South Wales follows the Westminster system. The State Governor represents the Queen and has all the powers and functions of Her Majesty in respect to the State. He is the titular head of Government, performing the formal and ceremonial functions which attach to the Crown. The Government is made up of the Legislative Assembly (the lower house) and the Legislative Council, all members of both houses being chosen at elections where voting is compulsory. The legal system also closely follows the British system.

THE NEW SOUTH WALES POLICE SERVICE

Constitutionally, the Australian States are responsible for law and order, and each State has its own Police Force to carry out the primary roles of protection of life and property, crime prevention and detection and the maintenance of public order. There is a Commonwealth Police Force, which has representation in each State, but its function is limited to dealing with Commonwealth laws and protecting Commonwealth property.

The Police Service is headed by the Commissioner, who is also a member of the Police Board, which provides strategic direction and support to the Minister and the Commissioner. Structurally, the Police Service is divided into four geographical regions and each region is divided into districts and then into patrols. The patrol is becoming the focal point for the delivery of police service, and each patrol has its complement of mobile units and, in some cases, beat police, as well as detectives and traffic enforcement officers (Highway Patrol). The patrol is supported by more specialised units attached to the district or the region, including drug squad police, forensic investigators and specialist investigators in areas such as homicide. The focus on the patrol has clarified lines of command, authority and, most important, accountability. In simple terms, the Patrol Commander is accountable for the effective delivery of police service to his community.

There are 180 patrols in New South Wales. Police numbers in the patrols vary from 12 to 150, depending on the needs of the community. There are in fact some 450 police stations in the State, however most of the smaller stations serve as 'sectors' of the patrol. This is a significant figure when it is realised that until recently each police station had at least one cell operating and was used for the detention of prisoners.

There are just over 13,000 police officers in the New South Wales Police Service, supported by 2,300 administrative officers. Currently the average age of a police officer is 32, although 30 per cent of all police are aged 25 or under and on an age breakdown the largest number are aged 22 years. Since 1984 the minimum educational qualification has been the Higher School Certificate (gained after 6 years at high school) or a recognised trade certificate. State-wide records of detentions are not maintained, however in August 1988 the National Police Custody Survey was conducted (by Mr. David Biles, Consultant Criminologist and Head of Research to the Royal Commission into Aboriginal Deaths in Custody) and during that month 5,582 persons were lodged in police cells in New South Wales. Manual checks were conducted for similar periods at a number of locations and from that it can be inferred that 5,000 to 6,000 incarcerations per month may be a reasonable average. On that basis it can be assumed that at least 60,000 persons are lodged in police cells in New South Wales each year.

THE ROYAL COMMISSION INTO ABORIGINAL DEATHS IN CUSTODY

In October 1987 the Commonwealth and State Governments of Australia announced the Royal Commission into Aboriginal Deaths in Custody, following a disturbing increase in Aboriginal deaths in custody, particularly in police cells, and concerns which had been raised about the circumstances of some of the deaths.

I was appointed as New South Wales Police Liaison Officer to the Royal Commission, and immediately set about gathering data on all deaths which had occurred in police custody since 1st January 1980, which was the period to be examined by the Royal Commission. The data was gathered from police records across the State and those records showed that 44 deaths had occurred in police custody between 1980 and the end of 1987.

The police records showed that of those 44 persons, all of whom were males, who died in police custody:

18 died from 'medical' causes:
   6 were from heart attacks or heart disease
   4 were from drug or alcohol poisoning
   8 were from other causes, including head injuries and choking on vomit or blood
   11 were known to have been affected by alcohol
   15 were detained as Intoxicated Persons (public drunkenness)
   16 were alone in a cell
   3 died within 3 hours of being placed in a cell
   3 were Aborigines

25 died by their own hand:
   24 of those deaths were by hanging
   16 of those hangings involved a cell blanket
   11 were known to have been affected by alcohol
   6 were detained as Intoxicated Persons
   22 were known to have been alone in a cell
   11 were known to have died within 3 hours of being placed in the cell
   5 were Aborigines

The other deceased was a victim of homicide by another occupant of the cell.

The deaths occurred in busy stations and isolated country towns. The ages ranged from 18 to 62 and the length of time in custody from 35 minutes to 2 days. Reasons for detention ranged from Public Intoxication to Armed Robbery.

In other words, there seemed to be no common factors, except perhaps that half were known to have been affected by alcohol.

Aborigines make up just over 1 per cent of the State's population, however the National Police Custody Survey, conducted in August 1988, showed that 14.3 per cent of persons lodged in police cells were Aborigines. This indicates an alarming over-representation in incarceration of Aborigines. However, of the 44 persons who died in police custody in the 8 year period from 1980 to the end of 1987, 18.2 per cent were Aborigines, a little over their rate of representation in police cells. This does not give cause for satisfaction that all is well, it merely points to the fact that death in police custody is not just a phenomenon affecting Aborigines.

The Royal Commission into Aboriginal Deaths in Custody concluded on 31st March 1991. Reports in respect to all Aboriginal deaths in police cells in New South Wales have been published and the reports have been critical of a number of police policies and practices, particularly training, awareness of Police Instructions and policies, and investigations of custody deaths. The National Report, which will canvass general issues which have arisen during the course of the Royal Commission, will be published in the next few months, and I have no doubt that it will be critical of many of the areas which are discussed in this paper.

There have been 13 deaths in police cells in New South Wales since the beginning of 1988.

POLICE CUSTODY MANAGEMENT IN NEW SOUTH WALES: THE WAY IT WAS

In February 1988 a Task Force was established by the Commissioner of Police to assess the suicide resistance of police cells and develop screening methods for persons coming into police custody. Membership of this Task Force included senior operation police, Academy representatives and the police psychologist. The knowledge that the Royal Commission would put the Police Service's capacity for custody management under intense scrutiny, drove the Task Force to undertake a very broad examination of the issue in the short time that the terms of reference allowed.

Policies and instructions for treatment of persons in police custody were examined and found to be largely inadequate. Little advice was given to police who were required to make a judgement on whether a person might attempt suicide or suffer serious illness while in a police cell; consequently, in most cases no such judgement was made.

We found that the approach which had been taken by the vast majority of police to persons in their custody was not unreasonable, it was just based on an almost total ignorance of the factors which might influence a person's behaviour while in a cell.

Traditionally, the police role in dealing with offenders concentrated on the investigation of the crime, arresting and charging the offender and striving for a successful prosecution at court. The custodial aspect was little more than providing a secure place to hold the offender until bailed, taken before a court or transferred to a prison, or, in the case of an intoxicated person, until sober enough to be released.

In other words, police did not look after people in their custody as well as they could and should have, but they were given little guidance or training. On the other hand, instructions were vague and inadequate, for instance:

When practicable, the officer performing station duties or Lockup Keeper will visit prisoners every hour, and, if necessary, more frequently, to prevent risk of their escaping, dying, or committing suicide (Police Instruction 32, para. 6).

On the other hand, some were rigid and unworkable, for instance:

In no instance should prisoners be allowed to remain in exercise yards unless kept continually within view of a member of the Force. A prisoner who has been confined to a cell overnight should be given not more than one hour's exercise in the exercise yard. Such exercise should be taken in one period of one hour or two periods each of half an hour, whichever better suits the requirements of the Station. There is no need to allow a prisoner in the exercise yard unless he has been confined in a cell the previous night and circumstances will prevent his removal from the Lockup during that day. Prisoners should not under any circumstances be allowed to remain in an exercise yard after dark. A prisoner suffering from the effects of alcohol must not be allowed in an exercise yard until sober (Police Instruction 32, para. 5).

Despite the unreasonable restriction that this instruction placed on persons in custody, there was nothing in the instructions which prevented prisoners being left locked in cells at unattended police stations overnight, as was regularly the case. There was little accountability attached to looking after prisoners, and little discretion. When a death did occur in a cell the investigation was generally perfunctory and based on the presumption that the prisoner had either committed suicide or suffered some fatal illness, and endorsed by the Coroner, who was also often inadequately trained. And cells themselves were in such poor condition that police felt incapable of providing any form of comfort or concern for the prisoner.

In respect to the cells, with the assistance of officers from the Physical Evidence Section, every police cell in the State was examined, documented and photographed. 394 police stations were the subject of inspection.

Significant points to emerge from those inspections were:

- 33 per cent of the cells were separate from the police station
- 84 per cent had solid front walls
- 61 per cent had alarm-call systems connected to the cells (although half were not operational when inspected)
- 73 per cent of the cells were assessed as having low resistance to suicide

Many police cells in New South Wales were built last century, or to last century's standards; many are wooden boxes in the yards of the small stations; most have no natural light; there is absolutely nothing in them except a toilet and perhaps a bubbler - prisoners sleep on rubber mattresses on the floor. Many are some distance from police working areas, making it necessary to walk a considerable distance and unlock a couple of doors to inspect the prisoners. Many are underground. They are dark, damp, smelly, de-humanised boxes - but they are all we had.

It is clear that up until about 20 years ago cells were seen as a necessary inconvenience to be included in police station design. I say 20 years ago, because cells built since that time have showed a marked change. They generally have barred, instead of solid fronts. Although natural light is still not a standard feature the quality of lighting has improved significantly. They are generally painted light colours, and the floors are sealed to resist the smell of vomit and urine that pervades most older cells, regardless of how often they are scrubbed. But this had still not gone far enough. Cell complexes were still being built underground and little heed was taken to the opportunities that horizontal bars and exposed plumbing could provide for persons intent on hanging themselves.

POLICE CUSTODY MANAGEMENT: THE WAY IT CAN BE

Faced with a number of inhibiting factors, it was felt that major changes had to be introduced before police could be expected to accept real accountability for the welfare of prisoners. Police cannot be expected to take custody management seriously unless the police organisation clearly demonstrates that it takes the issue seriously.

In short, the Task Force identified a number of areas which were critical to effective custody management and prepared recommendations to overcome the deficiencies. In this paper I also discuss additional matters which must be addressed to create the climate where custody officers will accept true accountability for persons in their charge. I place all of these matters under the following headings:

- Cell design and construction
- Role and status of custody officers
- Custody management policies and procedures
- Assessment/screening procedures
- Training
- Investigation of deaths in custody

Cell design and construction

As a result of the Task Force report, many police stations across the State no longer hold prisoners. Region Commanders have identified those which have a supported need to maintain cells, 'custody stations', and persons who are arrested at other stations are either bailed or transferred to a custody station. This has allowed maintenance funds to be redirected into the upgrading of those custody stations. At all custody stations, an 'observation cell' has been identified and is used for the initial detention of all persons put in the cells, and for the full period of detention of high risk prisoners.

In many cases the observation cell is merely the one closest to the charge room, however its identification allows meagre funds to be directed towards marked improvements to a particular cell rather than spreading them across the whole complex and only getting some of the necessary work completed. This work generally includes the installation of a viewing window into the wall adjacent to the charge room, so that police can have almost constant supervision of the prisoner without having to leave the work area.

Building standards which have now been adopted for police cells include natural lighting and ventilation, a raised bunk for sleeping, barred fronts (except in areas of extreme cold) and piped music. All possible 'hanging points' have been eliminated, and modular stainless steel toilet, bubbler and handbasin suites have been designed. Cell alarm systems are installed in such a way that they are easily accessible for repairs.

Much effort has gone into designing cell layouts so that the best relationship with the working areas of the police station can be achieved. It must be realised that there are only two police stations in the whole of New South Wales which have dedicated staff working in the cell areas; in all other custody stations the management of the cells is the responsibility of police working in the enquiry office or the charge room, depending on the size of the station.

A number of futuristic designs have been discussed and, although at this point the traditional square design is still favoured by the architects it is proposed that a totally new functional layout will be included in a police station to be built in the next few years.

Perhaps the most important new policy in respect to cell design, from a police accountability perspective, is that in every case that a new police station is being designed, the architects consult with the police who are going to occupy the building, and take into account their recommendations and requirements. This has proven to be a remarkably successful method of giving 'ownership' of the cells to those officers who are going to be operating them.

Role and status of custody officers

One of the first steps in accountability in custody management is defining who is to be held accountable if something goes wrong. From a management perspective the Patrol Commander will always carry overall accountability for prisoners and for the actions of police under their command. Individual officers will also be held accountable, both departmentally and at law, for disobeying instructions or failing to properly discharge their duty of care towards prisoners.

At times difficulty has been found in determining just who was responsible for the welfare of prisoners, particularly at the many smaller stations where there are no clearly defined roles and police may perform a number of different, overlapping functions.

Although we have introduced the term 'custody officer' it is a fairly broad definition:

'The term custody officer, or person performing custody duties, when referred to in this instruction includes any police officer having responsibility for the detention and care of persons in custody at a police station.

The custody officer will be responsible for the safe custody and care of all prisoners and their property from the time they are charged or detained at a police station until they are either released or transferred to other custody (Revised Police Instruction 32, para. 32.02).

This at least allows a Patrol Commander to appoint somebody as Custody Officer on each shift and record those duties on the roster. At larger stations, this may be a specific position, however at most stations it will be one of the functions of the station sergeant or station assistant.

At this stage the status of the Custody Officer has not been properly recognised. It is not an 'authorised position', that is it does not have a specific Statement of Duties and Accountabilities and is not included as a specific position, which must be filled, in the establishment strength of the station.

Of course in many small stations the low level of cell occupancy will indicate that a full-time position for a Custody Officer on each shift is clearly not justified, but there is a strong case for having such a full-time position attached to many larger stations. (This is a matter which I will be examining closely while in the United Kingdom). There is also an argument for employing persons other than police, perhaps on a part-time, demand basis, for duty as custody officers. This notion, as well as the possibility of privatising cell security, is currently being examined by the Commander of the Sydney Police District, who has the State's largest cell complex and turnover of prisoners.

Custody management policies and procedures

I have already mentioned that instructions for custody management were inadequate. The title of the Police Instruction reflects its diversity: *Instruction No. 32. Prisoners - Searching, Detention, Release, Property etc.*

The instructions were mainly functional; they told police

what to do in respect to classification of prisoners, searching, recording of property, transfer to prison, provision of and payment for meals, and calculating terms to be served on warrants.

They also contained information about what to do with sick or injured prisoners and prisoners who attempt to commit suicide. In this regard they were specific and practical. However what was missing was any guidance or instruction on how to predict or anticipate that a prisoner might suffer illness or attempt to commit suicide. An example of this is paragraph 14, which stated:

> *Where a prisoner has ever exhibited suicidal tendencies, charges should be disposed of with the least possible delay.*

No guidance was given as to how suicidal tendencies could be identified, nor was there any advice as to what to do with the prisoner until the charges could be disposed of.

It must be said that these instructions were reasonable in the climate that existed at the time that they were written, and they were amended and updated from time to time to reflect a gradual awareness that attitudes of the community and the courts to police custody management were slowly changing. However they were never seriously challenged by the courts, coronial or civil.

Another point to be recognised is that for many years police officers have been required to possess a First Aid certificate prior to joining and regular, but infrequent, first aid and resuscitation training is given. It was therefore accepted, perhaps rather ambitiously, that they had a basic understanding of what to do if a prisoner became ill or required resuscitation.

It was obvious that the instructions had to be reviewed and rewritten. What was also obvious from the information that we had before us, was that there had to be a simple screening process which could be applied to all persons who are to be placed in a cell. Policies must acknowledge the recognised dangers of having unconscious persons in cells and leaving persons in cells at unattended police stations. Policies had to be practical and, while clearly setting out accountabilities for Patrol Commanders and custody officers, have sufficient flexibility to permit proper decisions to be made at a local level. The policies must also be accessible - instructions dealing with persons in police custody could be found in at least a dozen different Police Instructions.

The revised Police Instruction 32 - 'Care, control and safety of persons in police custody' - deals with all aspects of prisoner care and security from the point of arrest or detention to eventual discharge on bail or to the court or prison. It has been written in plain English and includes prohibitions on allowing an unconscious prisoner to be in a cell, regardless of whether the prisoner is insensible from alcohol or any other cause, and on keeping a person in a cell overnight when no police are on duty. It also goes into detail about the frequency and method of inspections of prisoners.

These revised instructions give the Patrol Commander or custody officer discretion on access to the exercise yard by the prisoner, to permit smoking in the cells or visits to the cells by relatives and friends. In other words it is acknowledged that if the Patrol Commander is to be held accountable for the welfare of persons in police cells, then the Patrol Commander is also entitled to make decisions on what prisoners should be allowed to do while in their custody, within the limits of departmental policy.

Coupled with these instructions a 'Prisoner Admission Form' was developed and taken into use from 1st July 1990. This form is completed by the custody officer, with input from the arresting police, every time a person is to be placed in a police cell. Apart from recording management information, such as the frequency of inspections, it also forms the basis of the screening, or assessment, procedure which is applied to every prisoner. At the time of introduction of Prisoner Admission Forms, the 'Police Custody Manual' was issued to all police stations. This manual was also prepared by the task force and provides the advice and guidance on custody management which as previously been missing. It particularly focuses on the screening process and its format is linked to the Prisoner Admission Form.

Assessment / screening procedures

Police are not doctors, they are not psychologists and they are not psychiatrists. This is what you will hear every time you talk to a police officer about assessing a person's capacity to suffer illness or commit suicide in a cell. But experienced police officers are extraordinarily astute in judging people's behaviour. Any good street policeman can tell you when somebody is about to turn nasty or swing a punch. In other words, they may not have the clinical skills but they generally have good powers of observation and judgement.

In developing a screening process for persons in police custody, we built on those attributes. The Prisoner Admission Form is deliberately simple but provides sufficient information to allow the custody officer to make a fairly sound and accurate judgement on the action to be taken, or the level of supervision to be applied, to a prisoner. It provides for a simple subjective opinion by the apprehending officer:

> *Did you detect any medical problems or suicide signs? If yes, describe ...*

This simply puts the police on the street on notice that they have a part to play in the assessment process. Since this screening process has been introduced it is surprising how many police have commented that they have passed on information to the custody officer which they would not have considered important before.

The form then directs the custody officer to look for signs of agitation, depression or illness in the prisoner and then to ask the prisoner a number of questions about medication, previous illness, drug intake, and a direct question to the prisoner:

'Have you ever tried to take your life?'

As I have said, the Prisoner Admission Form is linked to the *Police Custody Manual*. Every question on the form is explained in detail in the manual, and custody officers are advised as to the appropriate course of action to take, based on their assessment. This may include transfer to a public hospital for medical assessment, placement in an observation cell under close supervision or perhaps close observation for the first three or four hours then regular inspections.

It is considered that in some circumstances concern for a person's welfare might over-ride objections to bail, and police have been advised that it is proper to take the person's assessment into account when making a determination on bail.

These procedures have only been in operation for eight months and are about to be reviewed. This is the first time that a screening or assessment process has been used by police in New South Wales and we recognise that there will be room for improvement. It is to be hoped that the evaluation will produce some new thoughts that will make the process more effective.

The screening process is currently being installed onto the computerised charging system at all larger stations. This will provide a menu-driven computer facility for recording all of the assessment information, as well as the records of inspections.

Training

There has been a revolution in training and education in the New South Wales Police Service over the past few years. Recruit training in particular has seen enormous changes and the focus is now turning to field training and executive development.

The head of education for the Service now carries the rank of Assistant Commissioner, on a par with the Region Commanders, the head of Professional Responsibility and the Director of the Drug Enforcement Agency. A position has recently been created, at Superintendent level, to be responsible for field training and that person will be assisted by three Chief Inspectors who will specifically be responsible for quality control and operational reality in field training.

The Police Recruit Education Programme (PREP) requires police recruits to undergo 18 months Academy and field training before they are confirmed as constables. The PREP programme is divided into seven schools - the School of Health, Fitness and Survival; the School of Applied Policing, which deals with the practical, operational aspects of policing; the School of Applied Social Sciences, which deals with how the Police service fits into society and focuses on many of the support and referral services available to the community; the School of Legal Studies, which deals with law, the legal process and the courts; the School of Traffic and Mobile Policing; the School of Management, which explains the Police organisation and prepares students for supervision at the constable level; and the School of Investigation and Intelligence. The teaching staff comprise police and academics, and most of the police lecturers have academic qualifications.

Training in custody management is included in a number of segments of the PREP programme, however it is difficult for young recruits to understand the impact that incarceration can have on a person, particularly as most of them at that stage have never seen a police cell, let alone been inside one. I am currently working with the Dean of Studies at the Academy to develop case studies and discussion papers on the range of reactions that people can have to being arrested and put into a police cell, with a view to creating a greater awareness in young police of the responsibilities which they will shortly bear.

During the last two weeks in the Academy before they begin their twelve month probationary period, the students take part in 'simulated patrols'. The Police Academy becomes a community, 'Northside', with a police station, court, and all the problems which beset an average community. The students are divided into morning and afternoon shifts and they respond to simulated incidents, with other students taking turns as observers and the Academy staff, and invited operational police, evaluating their performance.

The incident could be responding to a street accident, or a domestic violence complaint, or a bag snatching or stabbing, or delivering a death message or investigating a death, or looking for a missing child, or any other real-life problem that police become involved in. And the good guys don't always win. The students are faced with the frustration of not having quite enough evidence or dealing with unco-operative and belligerent members of the public.

Once again, the Dean and I are working on scenarios which involve an incident in a cell at the police station, and we are also working on the idea of selecting a student at random at some time during their Academy training and locking them in the cell overnight. The student's impressions of his or her incarceration could then form the basis of a valuable case study for other students, particularly if this was done on a number of occasions with each intake.

Field training is more difficult. In the past, new instructions and procedures have been published in 'On the Job Training lectures', which were mailed out to Patrol Training Officers across the State. This system just did not work. There was no real control over whether police attended the lectures, and no quality control on the Patrol Training Officers themselves, or their delivery.

Prior to the new custody procedures being introduced last year, a seminar was held and all of the Patrol Training Officers attended. The procedures and the reasoning behind them was comprehensively explained. However it was obvious that some greeted the proposals with scepticism. There is no doubt that this scepticism would have been reflected in their presentations to their patrol police, although there has been no clear evidence of this from any particular patrol. It is to be hoped that the appointment of the senior field training officers will improve the quality and bring uniformity to delivery of field training.

Investigation of deaths in custody

Improved cells, clearly defined roles, effective policies and procedures, and appropriate levels of training should mean that everybody who finds him or herself in a police cell will be treated properly and will have nothing to worry about.

Unfortunately there will always be those police officers who are lazy, or who don't know the procedures, or who don't care, and there will always be the occasion when, despite everything being done correctly by the police concerned with the custody, a person will die or commit suicide in a cell. In either case a thorough, impartial investigation is necessary, and if an officer is found to have acted unlawfully, either through a criminal act or a breach of discipline, then appropriate punitive or remedial action must be taken. On the other hand, if it is found that all police concerned have acted properly, then they must be protected from unfair criticism.

In recent years Coroners, the Ombudsman and now the Royal Commission have been critical of police investigations into deaths in custody. Many of these investigations, particularly into apparent suicides, have been limited to having the scene examined by a police officer from the Physical Evidence Section and short statements being obtained from the police responsible for the custody.

Usually the investigating officer was attached to the station where the death occurred, and on occasions has actually been the officer responsible for the custody. The investigation was 'oversighted' by an officer from the Police Internal Affairs Branch, but in early years this 'oversighting' was often done over the telephone. In 1986 the policy changed and the Internal Affairs officers were required to visit the station where the death occurred, but in many instances there was still on a casual interest in the investigation.

The Coroner, often a clerk attached to the local court, was usually presented with basic information about the circumstances leading to the detention, the processing in the police station and the discovery of the body. A police officer, usually a police prosecutor, assisted the Coroner.

This is not to suggest that sinister inferences should be drawn from the manner of investigation of deaths in custody. The Royal Commission into Aboriginal Deaths in Custody has conducted exhaustive enquiries into deaths in police cells ranging back to 1980 and in no instance has it been found that a police officer was responsible for the death. It was simply that when police found a person dead in a cell, although it was a matter for personal concern and regret, the obvious causes were accepted and presented to the Coroner, who usually endorsed the opinion of the police. It was a natural presumption that if a person was hanging from a cross-bar by a torn cell blanket, then that person must have committed suicide.

There have been a number of significant changes over the last three years. When a death occurs in police custody the Region Commander for that area must appoint an experienced investigator, of or above the rank of sergeant and not attached to the patrol where the death occurred, to investigate the death. The investigation must be conducted on the basis of a possible homicide - the place of death is to be preserved and treated as a crime scene - and should not only include the circumstances of the detention but also the actions of the deceased prior to the behaviour which brought about the detention. Suicide should not be presumed, however if it appears that the death may have been suicide, efforts must be made to gather evidence to support such a state of mind.

A senior investigator from the Police Internal Affairs Branch is appointed to review each custody death. That officer must visit the scene and seize all relevant documentation and follow the investigation through to its conclusion, including attendance at the Coroner's Court. This officer is responsible for ensuring a quality investigation and for providing a quality report on the investigation.

In 1988 the Coroner's Act was amended to provide for the appointment of a State Coroner and a Deputy State Coroner. These officers conduct all inquests into deaths in custody and are assisted by Counsel appointed by the Attorney General. Their coronial enquiries are exhaustive and thorough, and their comments and recommendations have been valuable to the Police Service in improving custody management practices.

Creating the organisational climate for change
The improvements I have outlined demonstrate that over the

past few years the New South Wales Police Service has recognised a pressing need for changes to our custody management policies and procedures.

The timing is not coincidence. During the same period an organisational climate has developed which encourages such changes. The New South Wales Police Service has shifted from being a reactive, centrally controlled, regulation bound organisation where good practice netted little reward, to a proactive, locally managed, values driven Service where individual thought and initiative are encouraged and rewarded, and where the climate is being created for individual officers to accept accountability for their actions.

In simple terms, prior to 1987 all directions came from Police Headquarters. Lines of command were confused and overlapping to the point where it was difficult to identify who was really accountable for any particular action (beyond the basic street level police activity). As I have outlined, policies and instructions were based on performing functions without particular thought to the 'why'.

Upon his appointment as Commissioner in 1984, John Avery commenced a programme of reform. His ideas were simple. One was that if police officers have a set of values to work within, regulations become unnecessary. There will always be a need for guidelines, and in reality there must be clear policy set out with punitive sanctions for disobedience, but his philosophy was that 'in every police activity there must be an ethical component'

To achieve this basic philosophy the Police Force (as it was then known) had to be purged of the corrupt influences which were believed to have penetrated some sections. Commissioner Avery's first task was therefore to rid the police organisation of corruption, a task which he took on relentlessly and unmercifully. Although there will always be individual dishonest police, it can be said with confidence that institutionalised corruption has been eradicated.

The next ingredient in John Avery's recipe for reform was the introduction of Community Based Policing, which is described in our Mission Statement as:

Police and the community working together to establish a safer environment by reducing violence, crime and fear.

Community Based Policing could not hope to get off the ground in an organisation which was totally directed and controlled from Headquarters, so the next step was to provide a structure in which Community Based Policing could operate - regionalisation. This involved dividing the State into four geographical regions, each with its own operational commander, and then pushing authority and accountability down as close as possible to the community itself - to the patrol. This restructuring is now complete and accountability for the delivery of police service sits squarely on the shoulder of the Patrol Commander.

I should also point out that shortly after John Avery became Commissioner, merit-based promotion was introduced, to replace the old seniority system. This means that police who demonstrate that they have the capacity and willingness to accept authority and accountability can reap the rewards of promotion. In fact every Patrol Commander's position in the State has been upgraded to a more senior level, in keeping with the increased accountability which the position demands.

At the same time as the structure was being put in place Commissioner Avery was expanding on the notion of ethical behaviour. The Police Service adopted its 'Statement of Values', which provides a standard of conduct for police:

> *Each member of the Police Service is to act in a manner which:*
>   *Places integrity above all;*
>   *Upholds the rule of law;*
>   *Preserves the rights and freedoms of individuals;*
>   *Seeks to improve quality of life by community involvement in*
>   *policing;*
>   *Strives for citizen and police personal satisfaction;*
>   *Capitalises on the wealth of human resources;*
>   *Makes efficient and economical use of public resources; and,*
>   *Ensures that authority is exercised responsibly.*

It does not automatically follow that because we now have this set of values that the conduct of very police officer will be beyond reproach, nor does it mean that mistakes, either honest or careless, will not be made, however it provides a yardstick to measure conduct and performance against. It is also a 'statement of intent' to the community - these are the values that the Police Service is striving to achieve.

Police policies, procedures, education and training are underpinned with the Statement of Values. Accountability then follows as a consequence of adherence to those values.

CONCLUSION

My subject is accountability - holding police officers responsible for the manner in which they treat persons in their custody. The theme is that for accountability to be accepted at the individual level, it must also be accepted at the corporate level.

There are ample provisions within police regulations, legislation and common law to deal with police officers, and others, who do not properly discharge their duty of care towards prisoners. The question is though, have these sanctions, as persuasive as they may be, been sufficient to instil a willingness on the part of police to effectively care for the persons in their charge? I think not.

The only way that we will ever get police to look after people in their custody properly is by voluntary compliance. Sanctions are certainly necessary, and as I indicated, sanctions in themselves are very persuasive. But if we are to have police willingly accept their accountability for prisoner care, police administrations must do their utmost to create the right climate. What I have spoken about is what we in New South Wales see as necessary to create that climate.

Former Commissioner John Avery has said that there must be an ethical component in every police activity. That, together with legality and morality, provides the basis for a style of policing which is acceptable to the government and the community, and rewarding to the police themselves. Every action of a police officer must be ethical, moral and legal. In respect to the care of prisoners I would add two other ingredients - it must be thoughtful and it must embody a basic, unequivocal respect for the rights and humanity, of the individual.

We are not there yet; we still have a long way to go in improving our cells, developing the best policies and procedures, and educating our police. We are not yet at the point where all police are prepared to accept that high level of accountability.

I submit, however, that over the past few years we have made significant progress towards achieving the level of accountability, at both organisational and individual level, which will satisfy the community and our critics.

As John Avery also once said: 'You may not be able to see the end of the road ahead of you, but look over your shoulder and see how far you've come'.

Thirteen

Jail suicide prevention in the United States: An overview of yesterday, today and tomorrow

Lindsay M. Hayes

Suicide is the leading cause of death in jails within the United States. By definition, jails include holding facilities (which normally detain persons for less than 48 hours) and detention facilities (which normally detain persons or house committed/ sentenced offenders for more than 48 hours, but less than two years). Experts project that the rate of suicide in jails is approximately nine times greater than that of the general population. These suicides have created publicity, increased public awareness, and ultimately, litigation against jail facilities, city governments and county commissioners. Correctional experts also believe, however, that increased awareness of jail personnel to the potential of suicide is critical to prevention. Certain signs and symptoms of suicidal behaviour exhibited by the inmate often foretell a possible suicide and, if detected, could prevent such an incident. What an individual says and how they behave while being arrested, transported to the jail, and at booking or in the housing unit, are vital in detecting suicidal behaviour. Properly trained personnel, who have a basic understanding of the problem, should be in a position to assess suicide potential at various stages of an inmate's incarceration and to thwart most suicides.

Jail suicides, however, have not always been associated with increased awareness by correctional personnel. Zebulon B. Brockway was considered an eminent penologist in the early 1900s. As warden of Elmira Reformatory (often described as the original model from which progressive penology evolved), Brockway attributed prison suicide 'to instinctive imitation, craving curiosity, mischievous desire to elicit alarm, an attempt to create sympathy for favours, and a certain abnormality induced by pernicious practices'.

Fortunately, our current understanding of the causes for suicidal behaviour within jails has survived Warden Brockway's questionable wisdom. My experience has been that there are two major causes for jail suicide - first, jail environments are conducive to suicidal behaviour, and second, the inmate is facing a crisis situation. From the inmate's perspective, there are certain unique characteristics of the jail environment which enhance suicidal behaviour, including, fear of the unknown, authoritarian environment, no apparent control over the future, isolation from family and significant others, shame of incarceration, and the dehumanising aspect of that incarceration. In addition, an inmate facing a crisis situation resulting in a suicide attempt often experiences various pre-disposing factors, including a prior attempt, recent excessive drinking and/or use of drugs, recent loss of stabilising resources, severe guilt or shame over the alleged offence, current mental illness, poor physical health or terminal illness, and approaching emotional breaking point.

The road to a better understanding of jail suicide behaviour, as well as implementing steps toward prevention, has been bumpy and uneven in the United States. In 1977, the American Medical Association (AMA) developed health standards for local jails. In the preface to a later edition of the standards, the AMA noted that - 'Studies show that the most frequent cause of death in jails is suicide, frequently alcohol and/or drug-related, and secondly, withdrawal from alcohol and drugs independent of medical supervision'. The standards recommended the use of receiving screening, to be administered immediately upon an inmate's entry into a jail facility. 'Most jails following this approach', the AMA boasted, 'coupled with the training of all jailers regarding mental health and chemical dependency aspects, are able to prevent all or most suicides'.

Until recently and despite concern about the severity and apparent prevalence of suicide in jails, few large scale comprehensive research projects had been conducted. As one researcher noted in 1974 - 'Even in this late date in American penology, very little substantial research has been conducted to explain why so many - or so few - prisoners kill or mutilate themselves. As with other distasteful aspects of incarceration, the problem by and large continues to receive only cursory, postmortem treatment'.

In 1980, I served as project director for the National Centre on Institutions and Alternatives' *And Darkness Closes In... A National Study of Jail Suicides,* the first in-depth look at the problem. Through a US Justice Department grant, we documented 419 suicides occurring in jails through the United States during 1979, and collected data on 344 of these deaths. Data revealed three strong characteristics of jail suicide - intoxication, length of incarceration, and isolation. In 1986, we replicated the prior research and collected data on jail suicides occurring during 1986. Data revealed, in part, that:

1. 75% of the victims were detained on non-violent charges, with 27% detained on alcohol/drug-related charges;
2. 60% of the victims were intoxicated at the time of their incarceration;
3. 94% of the suicides were by hanging, and 48% of the victims used their bedding;
4. two out of three victims were held in isolation;
5. 51% of the suicides occurred within the first 24 hours of incarceration; 29% occurred within the first three hours;
6. 78% of the victims who were intoxicated died within the first 24 hours of incarceration; 48% died within the first three hours; and
7. 89% of all victims were not screened for potentially suicidal behaviour at booking; 97% of holding facility victims were not screened for potentially suicidal behaviour at booking.

Our research has indicated, both in the not too distant past (1979 and 1986) and from the present, that suicide remains the leading cause of death in jails throughout the United States. Unfortunately, despite the widespread distribution of this data as well as increased awareness of the problem, suicides continue to prevail within our jails while prevention efforts remain uneven. My experience in the field has borne frustration and impatience; perhaps because I see the problem and its solution within arms' length. When suicide prevention does occur within our jails, I find that its presence is piecemeal and often following initiation of litigation. As such and perhaps unlike most countries, jail suicide litigation has become an important to prevention efforts in the United States. Ten years ago, it was unusual for a jail to be sued for negligence following a suicide. Today, it is unusual if a suit is not filed. Further, at the same time that both state and federal courts are making it increasingly difficult to hold public officials, jail administrators and their personnel liable for a jail suicide, these same courts are requiring a higher standard for operating a proper jail facility.

Perhaps the one piece of litigation that best exemplifies jail suicide prevention is *Garcia v. Board of County Commissioners of the County of El Paso (Colorado)*. Vincent Garcia had been arrested for suspicion of drunk driving in Colorado Springs, Colorado on 26 March 1982. He was transferred to the El Paso County Jail and placed in an isolation cell where he was found hanged approximately seven hours later. It marked the third suicide at the facility in less than a year. A lawsuit, filed by the victim's family, culminated in a Consent Judgement by both parties on 4 January 1985. In addition to a $10,000 settlement to the victim's estate and payment of attorney fees, El Paso County agreed to:

1. provide intensive supervision of all recently admitted inmates during the first 24 hours of incarceration;
2. replace the doors on all of the existing holding cells in the booking area with 'Lexan' glass doors;
3. modify the existing light fixtures, ventilator covers and other protrusions in all holding cells;
4. create and maintain a special ward for mentally ill inmates;
5. provide intensive and recurring suicide prevention training to all staff;
6. provide intensive screening of all inmates at the time of booking for risk of suicide;
7. contract for licensed mental health staff to be on call 24 hours a day; and
8. close isolation cells.

During the past year, I have had the opportunity to travel throughout the United States and evaluate model jail suicide prevention programmes for inclusion into our Jail Suicide Update newsletter. My journey recently took me to Colorado Springs and the El Paso County Jail. Walking past Vincent Garcia's isolation cell more than nine years after his death, I noticed that the door was still sealed by a padlock. A sign on the door read - 'Do not open by order of the Sheriff'. It was an eerie feeling and in retrospect perhaps that sign symbolised the County's commitment to avoiding such tragedy then, now and in the future. Not surprisingly, the El Paso County Jail has not experienced a suicide since Vincent Garcia's 1982 death and, in my opinion, best exemplifies suicide prevention programming in the United States.

Several other county jails are also worthy of praise for their suicide prevention efforts. My visits to the Oneida County (New York) Correctional Facility, Mobile County (Alabama) Jail, Champaign County (Illinois) Correctional Center, and Laramie County (Wyoming) Detention Center all resulted in the impression that each has embarked upon and maintained pro-active approaches to suicide prevention. These five facilities (including El Paso County Jail) have combined to experience only one suicide despite housing over 152,000 inmates since 1985. In contrast, the preceding five-year period resulted in 10 suicides in those five facilities combined. As one sheriff told me, 'We learned an important lesson through those deaths ... and will not tolerate it any more'.

As I have previously stated, efforts to prevent jail suicides in the United States have been disjointed at best. There are indications, however, that we are beginning to see meaningful progress, albeit not as quickly as one would like. In 1986, our research indicated that the states of New York and Texas were responsible for 71 jail suicides in the United States - almost 20% of the total. Cognisant of the problem, the state of New York embarked upon an ambitious and comprehensive jail suicide prevention programme in the Fall of 1974. Through the combined efforts of the various state and county agencies, the Local Forensic Suicide Prevention Crisis Service model was developed and field tested in five counties during 1985 and made available to over 300 jail and lockup facilities from 1986 to 1988.

The model, designed to establish administrative and direct service linkages among county jails, police lockups and local mental health programmes while clearly defining roles and responsibilities for each agency in the identification and management of suicidal inmates, contained four major components:

1. Policy and Procedural Guidelines for county, police lockup, and mental health personnel. The policies and procedures

outline administrative and direct service actions which will enable staff to identify, manage and serve high risk mentally ill and suicidal inmates.

2. Suicide Prevention Intake Screening Guidelines that can be administered by jail and lockup officers during intake to identify high risk inmates.

3. Eight-hour Training programme for jail and lockup officers in suicide prevention, including a trainer's manual and videotape.

4. *Mental Health Practitioner's Manual* designed to provide basic information to staff furnishing clinical care at jails and lockups.

To date, the results are most impressive. During a three-year period of 1986 to 1988, the total number of jail suicides across the state of New York declined from 25 in 1986 to 8 in 1988, the fewest in over 10 years. This decline is even more dramatic when viewed in the context of the inmate population size. During a five-year period ending 1989, the state's average daily population grew from 19,503 to 31,809. Suicide prevention efforts have also been felt in the state prison system. In 1989, New York state prisons experienced 11 suicides. Utilising the Crisis Service Model, however, the system experienced only two suicides during 1990.

The state of Texas has always had a significant problem with jail suicides - it led the country in 1986 with 46 such deaths. Beginning in 1987, I conducted training seminars for personnel representing over 240 county jails in the state. The general premise of these seminars was that most jail suicides can be prevented through increased awareness of the problem. Training remains on-going and resulted in the Texas Commission on Jail Standards' subsequent awareness of the problem and dedication to dramatically reducing the number of jail suicides across the state. In November, 1990, the Commission (a government body mandated by state law to establish minimum standards of custody, care and treatment of inmates) unanimously approved a recommendation to require all county jails to develop an 8-step suicide prevention plan. The essential elements of the plan are:

1. Training: provisions for staff training on the procedures for recognition, supervision, documentation, and handling of potentially suicidal inmates and all elements of the

suicide prevention plan.
2. Identification: procedures for intake screening to identify potentially suicidal inmates, and procedures for referrals to available mental health officials.
3. Communication: procedures for communication of information relating to potentially suicidal inmates between staff members.
4. Housing: procedures for the assignment of potentially suicidal inmates to appropriate housing.
5. Supervision: provisions for adequate supervision of potentially suicidal inmates and procedures for documenting supervision.
6. Intervention: procedures for staff intervention prior to the occurrence of a suicide and during the progress of a suicide.
7. Reporting: procedures for reporting of potential, attempted, and completed suicides to appropriate outside authorities and victim family members.
8. Follow-Up/Review: procedures for follow-up and review by the sheriff (or his designee), mental health, and medical officials of all potential, attempted and completed suicides.

The Texas Commission on Jail Standards' new requirements for suicide prevention are the most comprehensive I have seen in any state that utilises jail standards. Once operational in county jails (police lockups are not required to adopt to standards), I am confident that Texas will see a dramatic reduction in jail suicides. In fact, through on-going training and increased awareness, the state has begun to see a reduction. In 1990, for example, there were 32 suicides in Texas jails - a drop from the 46 reported in our 1986 study.

In conclusion, if the United States is to experience a dramatic reduction in jail suicides, which I firmly believe it can, a comprehensive approach and commitment similar to that shown by the states of New York and Texas will have to be made. And on a more personal note, people often ask me how I ever became involved in the field of jail suicide. Like most people who can point to an event that focused their career choice, I too remember a particular incident. While leafing through a pile of newspaper clippings one day, each carrying a story of a jail suicide somewhere in the United States, I stopped to read an account of Risa Boltax's death on 31 August 1981. For the most part, hers was a typical suicide - a young detainee arrested for a minor offence and held in isolation at the Union County (New Jersey) Jail. The facility had two suicides and over 50 attempts that year. But what was unique about Risa's story were her words, chilling even today, and scratched on a piece of paper that was found in her cell:

today
the pain of the clang of steel
reaches the depths of my soul
and I cry
tears of frustration...
and the new life I began
is dashed-shattered in pieces
of blue sky around my feet.
the dull puke-green bars and
yellow-white walls depress the spirit
and the sun doesn't shine for me
in this place of empty space
only darkness reigns
and the memory that I once found a friend
buried in the depths of a mental hospital...
but nothing much matters anymore -
in an eight by eight by four foot cage
I am an animal in a cage
and the darkness is closing in...
help me, please...

blackness, death and dopefiend wishes
screaming pain from insanity
deep inside, the child
has given up...
no hope, no choice -
no desire to live
among the trash and rejected reality
this jail is.
a sheet for the bed, tied to bars...
jump from the bed on to air -
feel neck snap, as the Final Rush during which
the mind sees life, death, birth -
and blackness of peaceful sleep at last.

I will never forget those words. We should never forget Risa Boltax.

Fourteen

What can we learn from suicide and self-injury?

Richard Harding

RECENT HISTORY: AUSTRALIA AND GREAT BRITAIN

Let me begin by saying how privileged I am to be sandwiched in this programme between His Honour Judge Stephen Tumim and Ms. Helen Grindrod QC, the two people who in England have between then done so much to put the question of deaths in prison custody onto the correctional agenda at last. I say 'at last', because to the eyes of an outsider the Home Office, despite having picked the issue in the mid-Eighties as potentially an important one, was unacceptably tardy in responding to the evident crisis which blew up in the English prison system during the late Eighties.

This impression arose as follows. In September 1989 the Howard League released the Grindrod report (Grindrod and Black, 1989) relating to the deaths of five young prisoners in Leeds Prison. I recall, reading it in November of that year, being flabbergasted at the arrogance of the authorities: for example, the refusal of access to Leeds Prison itself; the denial of co-operation from prison or medical authorities; and the refusal of the Leeds Coroners' Court to make available transcripts of the inquests relating to the deaths of the five young men on the impertinent basis that the Howard League were not 'properly interested persons'.

Later that same month I visited the Prison Service of the Home Office to discuss emerging trends in prison suicide patterns with a view, perhaps, to learning something useful for the enquiry I myself was about to commence in the State of Victoria. I have to say that, just as Judge Tumim has characterised Circular Instruction 20/1989 as 'a defensive mechanism' (Tumim, 1990b, para.2.34), so also I gained the impression that the quite extensive record-keeping was likewise carried out for defensive purposes rather than for pro-active analysis and change.

To illustrate: although it was already well understood from research in other jurisdictions that the young, first-time inmates, ethnic minorities, violent offenders and remand prisoners might be particularly vulnerable, it quickly emerged that not even the most cursory analysis had then been carried out to identify any such trends. The case histories themselves were in the filing cabinets; comprehensive but essentially meaningless lists could thus be recited in answer to parliamentary questions (see *Weekly Hansard*, issue number 1475, pp.834-839); but the process of *learning from the available data* had not yet commenced. If there were arrogance in dealing with turbulent ginger-groups, such as the Howard League, there was a certain lack of imagination, even complacency, back home in Cleland House.

The contrast with the Australian situation could hardly, at that time, have been more marked. As early as 1984, after the emerging problem of deaths, particularly suicides, in prison custody had been identified, Correctional Administrators of the States commissioned a research project by the Australian Institute of Criminology. They opened up their records for the necessary scrutiny, and authorised the publication of the excellent research report which resulted (Hatty and Walker, 1986). (At that time, however, police authorities were not receptive to the idea that the Institute should undertake a parallel exercise in relation to lock-ups).

Unfortunately, the findings of that research report were not put into operation within prisons with the degree of commitment which they deserved. Thus the trends continued, then markedly deteriorated. Accordingly, by 1987 more rigorous scrutiny was being brought to bear, first within the print media, then at the political level, finally with the establishment of the Royal Commission into Aboriginal Deaths in Custody. Seldom in the history of police and prison administration can any problem have been so minutely examined as has been the case in Australia in the subsequent four years.

Whilst this process has been continuing, most States have

simultaneously set up enquiries of their own into the prevention of custodial deaths and have progressively implemented many of the ensuing recommendations. Such an approach had been recommended by the Royal Commissioner, Justice Jim Muirhead (press reports, 20 November 1987) on the basis that there was an urgent need to ameliorate the situation which could not await the long-term analysis and findings. This process has pre-eminently been a public undertaking, with the full co-operation naturally of the relevant authorities and public availability of the respective reports. That was how I myself became involved in this matter - reviewing first from 1988 to 1990 the policies and practices of the Northern Territory with regard to deaths in police custody, protective custody in sobering-up shelters, and prison custody; and then in Victoria from 1989 to 1990 with regard only to prison custody (Harding, 1988; 1990a; 1990b).

Coming to this international conference, then, from a country which recognised its problems before they were acute, even so failed to address them adequately, but subsequently has exposed them to greater scrutiny and implemented more changes than any other country in the western world, I find it particularly gratifying that the host country has at last started to give this problem the attention it requires. This is not only due to the efforts, previously described, of the Howard League and Mrs. Grindrod QC but, evenly more notably, of His Honour Judge Tumim, whose December 1990 report on 'Suicide and Self-harm in Prison Service Establishments in England and Wales' (Tumim, 1990b) has moved the debate about policies and practices to a new plateau not only of understanding but also of likely action.

Rather as in Australia, as I mentioned earlier, a good deal of work had already been done in the mid-1980s: see, for example, A Thematic Review of Suicides in Prison (HM Inspectorate of Prisons, 1984); Report of the Working Group on Suicide Prevention, (HM Prison Service, 1986); and the Report of the Review of Suicide Precautions at HM Detention Centre and HM Young Offenders Institution, Glenochil, (Chiswick, 1985). But, again rather as in Australia, full strategic and operational advantage had not been taken of these reports.

However, in the last year or so, the work of Lloyd (1990), Dooley (1990) and NACRO (1990) have each contributed to the process of putting this issue on the political agenda. Also, Judge Tumim's report on the conditions in Brixton Prison, though not concerned with suicide as such, has inevitably kicked the issue along simply because of the fact that Brixton is, from the point of view of suicide rates and most other things, one of England's very worst gaols (Tumim, 1990a).

SUICIDE, ATTEMPTED SUICIDE AND SELF-HARM:
DEFINING THE SCOPE OF THE PROBLEM

In the Glenochil Report (Chiswick, 1985) the Working Group, charged with the task of looking at suicide events from the point of view of recommending precautions, adopted a wide-ranging definition of suicide. Their definition included not only all self-inflicted deaths but non-fatal acts of self-poisoning or self-injury. The Report (para 2.3.1.) stated:

Such behaviour is now described as 'para-suicide'. This avoids the assumption implicit in the old fashioned term, 'attempted suicide', that the individual actually intended to die. An act of para-suicide may occur for various reasons: sometimes it is indeed a failed suicide; more often the person is indifferent as to whether or not he survives; in most cases it happens because an individual wishes to relieve tension in the way that others may do by loss of temper or by getting drunk; it frequently occurs as a means of signalling distress, especially if other methods of communication have failed or are not available.

The Report thus 'looked at current episodes of para-suicide and the self-inflicted deaths that have occurred in relation to the 'total institution'.' Of course, in that fact - that prisons are total institutions - lies the justification, if one is needed, for adopting an extended definition.

The Australian Royal Commission was confined, by its specific terms of reference, to examining cases of *actual death*, and only *of Aborigines*. Of course, such deaths were not limited to suicides or even self-inflicted deaths in the broader sense, but included natural deaths, accidents and homicides. However, in considering its overview position, i.e. in relation to suicide prevention, the Commission has taken a broader approach, very much akin to that of the Glenochil Report.

The Criminology Research Unit of the Commission has likewise adopted wide-ranging definitions. In Research Paper no. 7 (Biles et al., 1989) it is stated that the 'term 'suicide' is used in this paper with the meaning used by social scientists and that of everyday speech ..., namely covering all self-inflicted deaths regardless of whether or not the person had formed a definite intention of dying by his or her own hand'. Similarly, in Research Report No. 16 (Fleming et al., 1990) it was stated that 'the terms 'attempted suicide' and 'self-inflicted harm' are ... used interchangeably in this paper'. The conduct discussed encompasses 'any action which is potentially suicidal or self-destructive, regardless of whether or not it is believed to be a genuine attempt at suicide'.

By contrast, Circular Instruction 20/1989 evidently contemplates that it is possible reliably to identify a clear difference between genuinely suicidal behaviours and other incidents involving self-harm: see para. 39. English data are consequently presented according to this rigid behavioural classification: see, for example, *Weekly Hansard*, issue no. 1475, page 504, relating to 'suicides' and 'attempted suicides' in various English prisons; the Tumim Report on Brixton Prison, para. 4.30, where a category of 'serious attempts' is set out; and the Prison Officers' Association figures (Grindrod Report, p.16) relating to 'self-inflicted injuries', on the one hand, and 'attempted suicides', on the other, occurring in Leeds Prison between 1 January 1989 and 13 July 1989.

The Grindrod Report treated the distinction, derived from the presumed intent of the person, as a significant one, whilst conceding that it could not always be reliably made. It accepted that these categorisations would 'provide very relevant information to another establishment if a prisoner returns to custody in the future'.

However, it may be doubted whether such a distinction is a useful one, either from the point of view of individual suicide prevention or in the context of wider issues of prison management - equally important matters when one is seeking to learn management lessons from self-harm incidents. I will return to this point later; but let me first explore why it is that prison authorities have often been somewhat dismissive of all but the most serious instances of self-harm.

TWO CASE HISTORIES:
MANIPULATIVE PRISONERS AND STRETCHED RESOURCES

In the state of Victoria, semi-independent Suicide Audit Reports are made following any such death. Here are extracts from two of them:

Prisoner R

In October 1985 he attempted to escape from 'A' Division with another prisoner - they were apprehended... In March 1986 he was involved with two prisoners in possession of Molotov cocktails in 'B' Division. On 3 April 1986 he stated 'he has many problems at the moment and requests sedation'. On 24 April 19086 he lacerated the insides of both elbows with cuts two to three inches long, and was seen by forensic psychiatry staff. He stated that he had cut himself because he was distressed over his father's illness (who was apparently dying), because he had not been visited by his girlfriend and son, and because he had no property in K Division. He reportedly wrote on the wall in blood 'I'm down here for shit'. *He admitted that he hoped to be transferred to St. Vincent's Hospital, where he felt he would be able to get daily visits more easily* (emphasis added). He did not want to die. He was referred again to psychiatric staff and Welfare. A psychiatric note on 16th May 1986 records: 'No follow up necessary. No psychiatric problems ...' In June 1986 he complained of headaches and insomnia: *a manipulative element was suspected.* (Emphasis added). However, he was noted to see the optometrist. .... In April 1987 he was assaulted by an unknown prisoner, receiving large lacerations to the chest requiring 20 sutures ... Dr. X (of the Prison Medical Service) felt that none of these recorded instances of self-harm showed any determined attempt to actually kill himself'.

Several months after this diagnosis he hanged himself in Pentridge.

Prisoner T

This prisoner made at least one major attempt on his own life in 1980, during an earlier period of imprisonment. In 1985 he commenced a sentence of six years minimum for armed robbery at Pentridge Prison. After various incidents of a self-delusional nature, but not involving on this occasion self-harm, he was recommended by a prison doctor for transfer to 'G' Division [the area which specialises in housing psychiatrically abnormal prisoners]. A second opinion was requested by the Classification Committee from the prison psychiatrist. Dr. Y reported in part:

> *Dr. Z's formulation was of an obsessive compulsive neurosis, and later she was concerned that his odd beliefs about his ears and his hair might be delusional and the possibility existed*

that he might have a schizophrenic illness.

Informal discussion with Corrections staff indicated there were reservations about adopting this course of action, [i.e. moving him to 'G' Division]. **It was put to me that the prisoner might be using this in a manipulative way** *(emphasis added).*

On 16th February the Assistant Supervisor of Classification wrote to me [raising] this concern that **there might be other possible motives for wanting placement in 'G' division as he had also made application for the Drug Treatment Unit at the same time as he was assessed as being psychiatrically ill ...** *(**emphasis** added). Last evening he toyed with the idea of hanging himself, and he has on the right side of his neck a burn mark supporting this story. ... I would recommend transfer elsewhere in the first instance.* **'G' Division has a waiting list of openly psychotic people awaiting transfer in** *(emphasis added).*

Within three months of this assessment, Prisoner T had hanged himself.

What each of these case histories show is the *universal, sub-cultural obsession of prison staff that frequently they are being manipulated by prisoners.* Generally, this feeling is most marked amongst uniformed staff; but it spreads also, as they become institutionalised themselves, to professional and medical staff. Thus there arises at best a reluctance and at worst a positive refusal to make proper use an important clue as to possible future suicidal behaviour.

Also, as the second case history shows and as abundantly emerges from the Grindrod Report and the report of Judge Tumim on Brixton Prison, resources and facilities are generally so stretched that staff are constantly tempted to fudge their judgements, diminishing their characterisation of the problem and thus leaving what specialist services there are available for other prisoners.

RESEARCH FINDINGS:
LINKS BETWEEN PREVIOUS SELF-HARM AND SUBSEQUENT SUICIDE

Not all prisoners who commit suicide have previously harmed themselves whilst in custody; and not all those who harm themselves subsequently commit suicide. But the available research evidence does indicate an association, as well as an imprecise correlation, between such events.

The Tumim Report (1990b) cited a NACRO study (NACRO, 1990) which suggested that, for all prison suicides between 1972 and 1987, 43 per cent had a past record of some kind of deliberate self-harm and 22% had injured themselves during the month immediately preceding the suicide. Other research has suggested that between 30 per cent and 50 per cent of those prisoners committing suicide had a history of previous self-harm (Topp, 1979, regarding the UK; Novick and Remmlinger, 1987, regarding New York City; and Clark, 1989, regarding New South Wales). Conversely, a follow-up study of a sample of self-harming prisoners suggested that more than 1 per cent of them would die by suicide within the next 12 months (Wool and Dooley, 1987).

There is nothing at all surprising about this kind of association. However, data collection in this area has tended to be neglected in the past, so that it is not easy to be confident about the strength of the association. Judge Tumim's report documents the fact that 'by no means all incidents of self-harm are recorded'. One of the principal reasons for this is that 'many are dismissed as attention-seeking gestures' (Tumim, 1990b, paras.2.31-2.32). Apparently, the relevant form (F220) had previously left a degree of discretion to prison authorities in this regard. However, the 1990 addendum to Circular Instruction 20/1989 has now made it unambiguously clear that all acts of deliberate self-injury are henceforth to be recorded. Judge Tumim states: 'Once proper records are taken, management must develop a robust programme for dealing with such incidents. There must be a positive response in respect of the individual ...' (ibid, para.2.31).

Similarly, in Australia inadequate attention was initially given to such incidents. However, in the Northern Territory, my own July 1988 recommendation (Harding, 1988) that report forms should be developed was implemented *within two days* - an excellent indicator of the desire and determination of authorities to address this problem in the new climate of awareness which followed the establishment of the Royal Commission. It has, I understand, already proved a useful tool for individual suicide prevention management, enabling better track to be kept of emerging crises, so that for example in several cases prisoners have been moved to a secure psychiatric facility for observation and stabilisation by medical and nursing staff. (Personal communication from the Secretary of the Department of Corrective Services, 8th March 1991). the implication is that such cases may not have been picked up in the past. Indeed, some previous Northern Territory cases of prison suicides had involved prior self-harm; but there has only been one suicide, of a man with no previous history of self-harm, within the system since this new procedure commenced.

Likewise, record-keeping in Victoria has been improved so as to ensure that more detailed incident reports will henceforth be made. And the Royal Commission Criminology Research Unit, as previously mentioned, has carried out a six-month survey of all such recorded incidents in Australian prisons and police lock-ups (Fleming et al., 1990).

Self-harm is thus progressively being recognised and used as a clue, albeit an inexact one, that suicide may be part of the particular prisoner's future agenda.

THE BROADER SIGNIFICANCE OF SELF-HARM INCIDENTS

Whilst it is certainly useful from the point of view of individual suicide prevention to collect individual information on self-harm, too much reliance should not be placed upon this procedure. Self-harm is a symptom of distress; thus, the causes of distress must themselves be mitigated even if they cannot be removed; and these causes are frequently some aspect of the prison experience or prison conditions themselves. From this point of view, self-harm incidents are almost invariably symptomatic of morale within the particular prison or prison system.

Actually, from my own experience over the years in reviewing a wide range of imprisonment issues - suicide, self-harm, treatment of mentally ill and intellectually disabled offenders, prison officer training, and educational and development programmes for prisoners - it has become apparent to me that, whatever knife one uses to cut into prison regimes, one is likely to uncover the same maggoty interior. Every facet reflects the same message. However, of all the analytical knives available, suicide and self-harm is the sharpest. Let me illustrate this from my experience in Victoria.

In the course of my Review of Suicide and Suicide Attempts by Prisoners in the Victoria Prison System (Harding, 1990b), I naturally visited a great number prisons. Most people at this conference, I feel sure, will have had the experience of going to a particular prison and almost immediately having a strong sensation that all is not right - indeed all is very wrong - in that particular institution. It is often an intuitive feeling, but invariably fortified by more tangible incidents of one kind or another.

My visit to the principal Women's Prison in Victoria soon turned into such an experience. The very first files I wanted to see were not there, and manifold contradictory excuses were offered for this. The reception process quickly revealed itself as having some obvious defects, mainly related to the time at which the prisoner was being received. But, more significantly, there was a general air of demoralisation amongst the staff.

This manifested itself in two quite remarkable ways. First, when I explained to a senior female officer what my mission was - namely to see if procedures could be put in place with regard to the problem of 'slashing-up' - her response was to ask whether I was referring to a procedure whereby sharper knives could be made available; and, second, when I asked why a particular prisoner was in the management (i.e. punishment) cell, I was told that it was because she had attacked a (named) female officer and that it was a pity she hadn't made a better job of it. In each case, these remarks were treated as somewhat amusing by some more senior staff present, rather than attracting the rebukes or discipline that they seemed to demand.

To refer to the self-harm incidents themselves, in a prison whose daily average muster over the 2 year period May 1988 to May 1990 was about 70, there were 138 recorded incidents of self-harm, mainly slashings-up. These involved 50 distinct persons, with 27 having been involved in multiple incidents.

As I have said, staff morale was extraordinarily low at that prison; so too was prisoner morale. The mix of prisoners encompassed the heavy criminals such as murderers and drug pushers, first-timers, remand prisoners, social security fraud offenders, fine defaulters - the whole gamut. They were mixed into six-person living units, not exactly randomly but in a way which inevitably reflected the overall characteristics of the intake. The few work programmes available were humiliating, the most enthralling task being that of packing nails into plastic bags. The prison regime was run down and depressed;

and, as it turned out, the very best formal indicator of this was the extraordinary rate of self-harm incidents - the factor which had taken me to the prison in the first place.

Although it was no part of my official brief, I immediately consulted with the Director-General of the Department and informed him that I believed he should take prompt steps to review the organisation and operations of the prison and the treatment of women prisoners generally. As luck would have it, a report which had earlier been commissioned on the conditions and treatment of female prisoners had just been presented, in terms which were highly critical. My own comments were thus made at just the moment when the Director-General, understandably perplexed by the alarmist tone of the earlier report, was considering how best to handle it.

Accordingly, a taskforce was now set up to bring forward an action plan with regard to that prison. Decisions were rapidly made to reduce the number of inmates to a maximum of 50, and to use the prison as a reception/orientation prison for sentenced offenders, a holding prison for first offenders whose crimes did not require them to be held in maximum security, and a unit for managing mothers with young children. Serious offenders and major recidivists were moved out. At the same time a standing advisory committee on women's prisons, drawing upon external as well as departmental persons, was established.

The 9 month period since May 1990, there have been only 18 incidents of self-harm at the prison - *a fact which is an enormously important symptom of the management reality that morale has improved markedly.* Nor has the phenomenon simply been displaced to other prisons as prisoners have been moved; the slash-up rate at the other women's prisons has also markedly fallen.

So my point is this: in examining and analysing self-harm incidents and trends, one can learn not only crucially important matters about individual prisoner management, but also fundamental lessons about the current nature of any given custodial regime, either generally or in relation to a particular prison. Amongst all the available warning signs that the general morale and sense of purpose in a prison may have deteriorated to an unacceptable point, self-harm incidents are the most graphic. For those correctional administrators, if there still are any, who see such incidents as having no significance beyond that of a prisoner's own bizarre attempt to manipulate the system, I would say that it is in his or her own self-interest to listen intently to the messages which such incidents convey.

COMPLETED SUICIDES AND PRISON MANAGEMENT

Of course, equally cogent lessons may be learned about the general nature of the custodial regime from completed suicides. Judge Tumim has, in each of the reports to which I have referred, put the question of suicide prevention firmly in the area of humane, just, purposeful, efficient, hygienic, and productive detention. He has stressed that it is not simply a medical matter, for medical interventions cannot be separated out from the general nature of the prison regime. Ms. Grindrod, for her part, has put the issue into the context of the use of imprisonment for young remandees generally, but also has related it to overcrowding.

In this context, it is relevant to refer to the work of an American Scholar, Paul B. Paulus (1988, pp.48-52). Paulus has convincingly documented a direct relationship between what he calls 'social crowding' (as opposed to merely spatial crowding) and the death rate from all causes within prisons. In particular, suicide rates appeared to increase almost exponentially with overcrowding, as also did disciplinary infractions and psychiatric commitments.

Crowding is just one aspect, though an extremely significant one, of prisoner stress. If we think of prisoner health holistically, then we will see the issue of suicides and self-harm within the broader context of general prison conditions. Self-harm, I have attempted to argue, is a particularly graphic indicator that something is going seriously wrong. As a phenomenon, such incidents provide valuable information not only about individual prisoner treatment and needs, but also about the suitability of the correctional regime generally. This, in turn, bears upon broad patterns of suicide within institutions.

We shall never succeed in altogether eliminating completed suicides and self-harm incidents in prisons. But if we use all available information, including that relating to self-harm, we can certainly do a lot better than has been the case in the recent past.

Fifteen

Minimising the risk of suicide in custody

Rod Morgan

BACKGROUND

I know of no one who has ever had any connection with prisons that does not find prisoner suicide a deeply disturbing issue and I do not subscribe to the view that we should set aside whatever emotions are stirred within us by contemplation of the topic. There was no moment more poignant during the conference of which this text is the product than when Deborah Coles and Tony Ward from Inquest introduced the parents of two youths who recently committed suicide in prison. Their inarticulate grief and spontaneous anger at the perceived heartlessness of Prison Service procedures following the death of their children galvanised the attention of the audience at Canterbury. Whatever our individual reactions to their implicit appeal that more care be taken, there was thereafter no room for complacency. And rightly so. Whatever horrors prisoners may individually have perpetrated, they remain human beings vulnerable to the might of the state behind closed walls. The corollary of our deprivation of their liberty is our moral and legal duty for their care. If we deny that then we deny the fundamental tenets of that which we call civilisation. The reason why any suicide in any coercive context should bring us up short is because the event may - not necessarily, but may - indicate that collectively we have failed the ultimate test of a civilised society.

I have been in and out of custodial institutions talking to their inhabitants for many years. Since this experience frames my approach to suicide in prison I had better briefly explain it.

For almost a decade I was a member of a board of visitors for a remand centre infamous for its impoverished regime and low staff morale. The institution was also the scene of a good deal of self-destructive behaviour. In April 1990, several years after I resigned from the board, the prisoners, many observers thought not before time, laid waste the institution in a night of almost exultant destruction. A few days later I surveyed the rubble as a member of the Woolf Inquiry team, appointed to consider the riots at Strangeways Prison, Manchester and elsewhere. Prior to this investigation I spent several years collecting data on the custodial repercussions of the Police and Criminal Evidence Act 1984 (PACE). This led to my being asked to monitor the implementation of an initiative - lay visiting to police stations - recommended by Lord Scarman in his seminal report on the inner city riots of April 1981. Both the custodial provisions of PACE and the introduction of lay visitors were designed to safeguard the position of suspects held in police stations and to make police procedures more transparent and thus accountable. It was necessary not least because several deaths in police custody had given rise to public doubts about the propriety of what was occasionally happening in the then the hidden terrain of police detention areas (Home Affairs Committee, 1980; Kemp and Morgan, 1989). I currently spend a good deal of my time undertaking investigatory missions into custodial conditions generally - in police stations, immigration centres, prisons, mental hospitals and youth custody centres - in many countries. I advise the Council of Europe Committee for the Prevention of Torture or Inhuman or Degrading Treatment or Punishment (CPT). I also advise Amnesty International. I have seen a lot of institutions all over the world.

Suicide, and deaths from other causes, in custody is not a peculiarly British preoccupation. It is a universal phenomenon which, when it involves indigenous minority communities, as it did in Australia in the 1980s, may be perceived as the final stages of cultural genocide (Graham, 1989). In these circumstances the issue may cause sufficient controversy for the government to decide that a Royal Commission be instituted (see Biles, this volume). To the extent that it is found that high death rates in police stations and prisons are associated with differential and high incarceration rates, and with high mortality rates in the community, then much wider questions of social as well as criminal justice are posed. When custody involves locking someone alone in a cell resembling a tomb, and that person decides to respond accordingly, then we should ask ourselves what it was that we intended.

ANALYTICAL TRAPS

Those engaging in research on suicide in prison, or who have a policy responsibility for the context within which it takes place, face certain analytical dilemmas which, if responded to in certain ways, can become traps. Each trap results from de-contextualising the issue of death in custody.

Definitional stops

Several of the papers in this volume have rightly been concerned with questions of definition. How many deaths in custody really comprise suicides? When is an attempted suicide genuinely an attempted suicide? What is to count as an act of self-harm? Unless we define precisely what we mean how can we know whether one group of prisoners is more vulnerable than another, or whether a particular locale generates more of a problem than another? Indeed, given that the best-regulated and most caring environment will be the site of occasional self-destructive acts beyond the preventive capacity of anyone, how many incidents do there have to be before we decide that there is a problem that needs to be addressed? We have to know what it is that we are counting. We have to enlist definitions.

I accept all of this. But in developing 'counting' conventions we should not lose sight of the meaning, insofar as we can know it, which acts of self-harm have for perpetrators, nor of the wide variety of forms that deliberate self-harm can take. Liebling wisely suggests that we should see 'suicide - both in action and intent - as a continuum along which one step may prove to be the first stage of a pathway to despair' (Liebling, 1992, p.67). I concur. Moreover, I suggest that self-harm - whether interpreted as 'attention-seeking', 'a cry for help' or as a suicide 'attempt' - should be defined more broadly than cutting up arms or swallowing glass. For example, a high proportion of prisoners exhibit signs of stress in custody, certainly a much higher proportion of prisoners than, according to the requirements of PACE, are considered by the police to warrant the presence of an 'appropriate adult' (see Irving and McKenzie, 1989; compared to Brown, 1988: and Brown et al., 1992). Further, anyone acquainted with custodial environments knows that there are a variety of acts in which prisoners engage which will have disastrous consequences and which reflect despair. I recently undertook for the Home Office a study of prison disciplinary proceedings. Though it was not part of the study (Jones and Morgan, 1991), what struck me from the files inspected and the adjudications observed was how many offences against the disciplinary code are literally desperate acts - smashing up, assaults committed in the certain knowledge that the consequences will be far more injurious than anything dished out, absconsions or escape attempts during which no attempt is made to elude detection and recapture is accepted with fatalistic indifference, and so on. Such events are often the social equivalent of slashing one's wrists. Moreover, though prisoners engage in such events as rooftop protests for a variety of reasons, in many instances they amount to intimations of death. One of the young prisoners who remained longest on the roof at Strangeways in April 1990 committed suicide in a punishment block a few weeks later. When Michael Hickey, serving a sentence of life imprisonment for the murder of Carl Bridgewater, spent 89 days alone in freezing weather on the roof at Gartree Prison in 1984 to protest his innocence (Foot, 1986, pp.242-45), it brought him close to death, he was subsequently sentenced to two months in solitary confinement and at the time of writing he has been transferred to a special hospital because of his deteriorating mental condition.

It is a complex matter to bring such disparate acts together within a single analytical frame. But any assessment of deaths in custody worthy of the name will place suicide in the broader context of stress and despair, acts of self-destruction and strategies for self-preservation and survival (Cohen and Taylor, 1972).

Statistical fallacies

As O'Mahony has impressively demonstrated (this volume), a good many comparisons which have been made in the literature between the risk of suicide in prison among prisoner groups, or between prison and other locations, are flawed because of the naive manner in which the relative risks have been calculated. Time-at-risk has often been unequally measured. At least three misconceptions, with important policy implications, are worthy of attention. First, it is not the case that most suicides occur within a few hours or days of reception such that, if custodial staff concentrate their preventive efforts during this early period, the majority of suicides might be prevented. Second, if time in custody is held constant, it is not the case that sentenced prisoners are as much at risk as those on remand: there is a substantially higher risk that remand prisoners will commit suicide. Third, when calculating the relative risk of death in custody (from whatever cause) of a particular prisoner group, as in the Australian context with regard to Aboriginal prisoners, one must take into account not merely the proportion of the average daily population made up by that group, but also their representation by legal category (remands being at greater risk than sentenced prisoners), the average duration of their custody (Aboriginal prisoners in Australia are in custody for typically much shorter periods than whites) *and* their repeated career experience of custody. As Broadhurst and Maller (1990) have shown vis-a-vis Aboriginal prisoners, if one takes these longitudinal factors into account then the risk of death in custody may be substantially higher than for the prison population generally.

It may, in the light of what I have argued above, seem callously technical to engage in such statistically esoteric debates. However, unless we read the evidence correctly then we run the risk of becoming dangerously complacent about the low level of risk involved on the one hand or of creating unfair and possibly inappropriate expectations as to what can or should be done by way of prevention on the other. It may be, as Biles has argued (this volume), that for some categories of very high risk prisoners, the likelihood of death is actually reduced by incarceration.

Over-emphasising the totality of institutions

The sociology of prisons literature points to the existence of a prison culture in which both prisoners and prison officers have roles. There has been a longstanding debate as to whether this culture, to the extent that it exists, is of primarily indigenous or imported origin. The problem with indigenous accounts (see, for example, Sykes, 1958; Goffman, 1968) is that they fail to provide a satisfactory explanation of change and they over-emphasise the 'transformation of the self' wrought by institutions. They understate the cultural baggage that prisoners bring with them into prison (see Irwin, 1970) as well as the changing uses to which prisons are put and the manner in which prison life is impacted by changing currents in the world beyond the walls (Jacobs, 1977). Most contemporary accounts recognise that the prison culture is a product of indigenous *and* imported factors, and both perspectives need to be acknowledged in the analysis of deaths in custody. The nature of the prison population is changing and it follows, therefore, that what it means to be sent to prison is changing also.

In most jurisdictions a declining proportion of suspects and convicted offenders are being imprisoned and there is progressive bifurcation of serious as opposed to run-of-the-mill offenders (Bottoms, 1977; Muncie and Sparks, 1991). The consequence is that the average duration of imprisonment has tended in many countries to increase and prisons may now be housing categories of offenders at greater risk of self-harm. In Britain, for example, prisons now contain many prisoners who are mentally disturbed but are relatively unamendable to treatment (Gunn et al., 1989; Dell et al., 1991), an increasing proportion of the prison population comprises sex offenders regarded by their fellow prisoners as pariahs (Prison Reform Trust, 1990) and, because of the manner in which bail decisions are now made, more and more remand prisoners probably comprise suspects lacking any real community ties (see Morgan and Jones, 1992). The character of the prison population in England and Wales has until recently not been well surveyed, but the data now available suggest that many prisoners are tragically marginal socially and economically. A high proportion of prisoners have experienced local authority care during childhood or adolescence and many suffer from a legacy of fractured familial relationships prior to their incarceration (Walmsley et al., 1992). It may be analytically useful to think of prisons as 'total institutions' but prisons are subtly permeated by a multitude of climatical changes which are likely to effect the way in which prisoners think about themselves and respond to their predicament.

Failing to see the wood for the trees

For custodial staff a death in custody is at the very least a bureaucratic nightmare and at worst an horrific shock. It will lead to many questions being asked. It is an event against which all custodial staff want their backs to be well protected. Police officers take little persuading that a doctor should be called if a suspect is looking physically vulnerable (Morgan et al., 1989) and prison officers are relatively amenable to the idea that prisoners should be screened to reduce the risk of suicide. The policy-making corollary of this grass-roots practitioner concern is that a good deal of data-analytical effort has been devoted to isolating person, event and situation-related factors which might enable staff to predict suicide attempts and thereby prevent their occurrence. This effort is understandable and for the most part laudable. However, all the evidence indicates that our capacity to predict suicide is poor - it results in too many 'false positives' being identified and too many 'false negatives' being ignored (Lloyd, 1990) - not least because there are almost certainly complicated interaction effects between person, event and situation-related factors. Interestingly, efforts at identifying and predicting 'troublesome' prisoners have also borne little fruit (see Williams and Longley, 1987; and a critical review by King and McDermott, 1990). Moreover, the methodological individualism which prediction studies in both these areas involve, and some of the preventive practices that they encourage, have been profoundly damaging.

There are at least three lessons that we can draw from the research on both prison disorder and suicide. First, the removal of 'disruptive' prisoners or the isolation of 'suicidal' prisoners seldom prevents the 'trouble' that staff are keen to avoid. Though there are a few prisoners whose response to imprisonment is so disruptive or aggressive that they must for a time be segregated, the removal of 'disruptive' prisoners seldom prevents trouble. Such prisoners are labelled and often go on to live up to their labels (Jimmy Boyle's autobiographical accounts (1977 and 1984) are object lessons in this process). Further, the situation within which their disorderly behaviour was identified typically generates further disorder (Hay and Sparks, 1991). The administrative identification of 'suicidal' prisoners has in the past been no less calamitous and inhumane. Prisoners already despairing were too often placed in conditions almost designed to drive them over the edge: they were routinely placed in isolation 'strip' cells, without proper clothing and deprived of human contact other than a cold observing eye through a spyhole every fifteen minutes (HMCIP, 1984). Moreover, though accommodated in an environment designed to make suicide almost physically impossible, some prisoners nevertheless managed to take their lives, such was their state of despair.

Whenever, as a member of a board of visitors, I saw a prisoner placed in such conditions it struck me as obscene as the death watch mounted in days gone by for prisoners awaiting execution, the function of which was explicitly to prevent the prisoner from 'cheating the gallows'. When in Australia in 1991 I was shown some newly-erected cells which the police described, I was uncertain with what degree of irony, as 'Muirhead cells' after the first Commissioner of the Royal Commission into the Deaths of Aboriginals in Custody whose final report had recently been published (1991). These cells had been specially designed to make it well-nigh impossible for prisoners to hang themselves: they were devoid of protrusions, window-frames and the like. I was relieved to see that in many police stations these grim unstimulating 'safe' cells were vacant while traditional communal accommodation, which most Aboriginal prisoners reportedly prefer, continued to be used. My conclusion, therefore, is that to prevent both most suicides and disorder we have primarily to address the *situations* and *procedures* which generate the problem.

The second lesson, which follows from our relative incapacity to predict, is that it is the regime experienced by the 'mainstream' prison population to which we have to turn our attention. It is within mainstream situations that most disorder arises and most suicides occur. It is true that a disproportionate number of prison suicides occur in special locations such as hospitals or segregation units (see Wool and Ilbert, this volume), but *most* suicides take place in mainstream accommodation, including a significant number in shared accommodation though not necessarily shared at the moment of suicide - see Prison Service, 1992b, para 21. By the same token the lesson from the English prison disturbances of 1986 and 1990 must be that disorder can occur in any type of establishment and that once the touchpaper is lit almost any type of prisoner may take part (Home Office, 1987, 1990d). It is insulting and trivialising to use the nursery language of 'copycat' when talking of series of riots or suicides: prisons, like any social environment, develop a climate within which collective streams of consciousness are generated. It is on this general climate that preventive work must largely be focused.

Third, following closely on the second lesson, the quality of life in prison depends largely on the nature of relationships between prisoners and basic grade prison officers. This suggests, to take the crime preventive analogy adopted by Hay and Sparks (1991), that what is required is a 'social' rather a 'situational' strategy to minimise the likelihood of both suicide and disorder. Rather than relying on segregation, technological surveillance and so on, we should develop what Dunbar (1985) has termed 'dynamic security' - devising 'active' regimes in which prison staff can become positively involved *with* prisoners through humanising and purposeful activity. Let us term this strategy 'dynamic prevention' and consider briefly what it involves.

DYNAMIC PREVENTION

One principle should underpin everything that follows. Suicide prevention, whatever practical form it takes, should be based on life enhancement not life restriction. The object should be to lift the cloud of despair giving rise to the impulse to end life. It should employ human agency to emphasise the intrinsic worth and potential of the person in despair.

Perhaps the best way of illustrating this principle is to point to its antithesis. It might be possible to design a prison which was almost escape, disorder and suicide-proof. Prisoners *could* be kept naked in strict isolation in reinforced cells with rubberised walls with cardboard furniture and paper plates. It is worth setting out this horrific prospect because we have in England come very close to resorting to just such a regimen for a minority of prisoners in the very recent past, and possibly still today. I have personally repeatedly witnessed the use of such measures. In 1984 I submitted, on behalf of the Association of Members of Boards of Visitors (AMBOV), written evidence to the Inspectorate of Prisons arguing that life enhancing measures should be adopted instead of physically preventive measures. I stressed that this should be done '*even if that were to mean that the physical risk of suicide being accomplished were marginally increased'* (quoted in Home Office, 1984, p.12). An escape, disorder or suicide-proof prison would be an inhumane and unacceptable prison within which to either live or work (one should never underestimate the alienating impact on staff, who on average spend much longer in prisons than do prisoners, of dehumanising prison regimes). It follows that even in the best regulated, most humane and civilised prison there will always be the physical risk of suicide and suicides will occasionally occur for which, arguably, no one should feel guilty. Suicide is ultimately an individual's right. We should do everything that can humanly be done within the framework of the fact of imprisonment to persuade prisoners that their lives have value, but we should not restrict them to the point that we make that choice impossible. That is not a tolerable remedy.

I should not wish to be misunderstood on this point. I fully support discreet attempts to identify high suicide risks and the adoption of discreet physical precautions designed to make suicide physically less likely. Indeed such measures, on the lines now commended within the Prison Service, are vital (see Circular Instruction 20/89, and Prison Service 1992a; see also Council of Europe, 1993). But these precautions should be life enhancing and that principle should always dictate the choice between alternative precautions and the primacy given to certain measures over others. Thus, for example, the Chief Inspector of Prisons favours the more widespread use of CCTV, but he is careful to stipulate that 'CCTV should not be a substitute for nurse/inmate face to face communication' (HMCIP, 1990, para.7.13). Moreover, and the Prison Service's current policy statement endorses (1992a), the Chief Inspector's thematic report on suicide emphasises, suicide prevention is not essentially a specialist question (traditionally a medical question) involving expertise applied to a screened-out minority of identified prisoners. Rather, it is about the quality of life *generally* within the institution. It is about relationships between ordinary prison officers and the generality of prisoners on mainstream location. That is the essence of the Chief Inspector's report on suicide as it is of the Woolf Report (of which the Chief Inspector was co-author) on the 1990 disturbances. This is why the parallel between these two treatises on the prevention of suicide and the prevention of disorder (Home Office, 1990d, 1990e) - both seen as acts of desperation with their genesis in structural forces - is apposite.

It would not be appropriate, and there is not space, to give an account of the Woolf/Tumim analysis and reform agenda. However, it may be worth sketching the core of the argument. Neither Woolf nor Tumim provide a coherent account or critique of the ongoing debate about the purpose of imprisonment as it has developed in recent years. The decline of 'treatment and training' and the loss of faith in the 'rehabilitative ideal' is not discussed and the debate as to whether the 'humane containment' or 'positive custody' formulae devised in the late 1970s adequately served to fill the gap left by that decline, is not gone into (see Bottoms, 1990; and Morgan, 1993b; for a discussion). However, though Woolf commends the Prison Service current Statement of Purpose he enters two vital caveats. First, he is critical of the absence of any reference to justice and, second, he considers inadequate the provisions for unconvicted and unsentenced prisoners (Home Office, 1990d, paras.10.16-10.64). It is Woolf's insistence on making justice central to the organisation of prisons which is his notable contribution to the philosophical debate and from which all his and the Chief Inspector's practical recommendations flow.

The argument is this. The Prison Service serves the public by keeping in custody those suspects or offenders committed to prison by the courts and by furthering the broader purpose of the criminal justice system, namely, by preventing crime. That means, according to Woolf, minimising the negative effects of imprisonment, safeguarding prisoners' civil rights, ensuring that standards of life in prison are as close to life beyond the walls as possible, requiring the prisoner to take responsibility for his or her offences and positively preparing the prisoner for release. The corollary is that to the extent that prisons are inhumane, or serve to embitter or disaffect prisoners, then they are acting contrary to their mandate and the purposes of the criminal justice system. For:

> *If the Prison Service contains (the) prisoner in conditions which are inhumane or degrading .. then a punishment of imprisonment which was justly imposed will result in injustice ... it is the Prison Service's duty to look after prisoners with humanity. If it fulfils this duty, the Prison Service is partly achieving what the Court must be taken to have intended when it passed a sentence of imprisonment (ibid, para.10.19).*

Woolf argues that the dynamics of prison life comprise three elements, 'security, control and justice', and that all three are important and must be balanced (ibid, para.9.21). It is apparent that in both Woolf's and Tumim's view - and the Chief Inspector has had the opportunity repeatedly and implicitly to reiterate this view in his inspection reports on particular establishments - that the Prison Service has over-emphasised security, given insufficient weight to justice and often adopted inappropriate control measures which, far from promoting order, have often led to the reverse. According to this analysis, trouble - by which I mean, on the lines sketched out above, various acts of desperation including some suicides and self-harm - has been the product of what we may term a 'disorder amplification spiral'. The injustices of much prison life (the absence of due process in decision-making, the failure to meet reasonable prisoner expectations, the insecurity of much prison life and the degradation represented by many prisoner conditions) serve to alienate, embitter, disaffect, frighten and depress prisoners. Trouble - disorder on the one hand and self-harm on the other - is often the result. The incidence of trouble makes both prisoners and staff feel even more insecure. The insecurity of prisoners serves to bolster the power of the strong and make even more vulnerable the position of weak or marginal prisoners. The same response is apparent among staff ranks. They also are alienated and adopt defensive tactics. They become excessively reliant on 'control and restraint' techniques and the 'alternative' or 'underground' disciplinary system which is always at their disposal (Prison Officers' Association, 1985). As a result justice is further undermined. Therefore alienation increases, disorder is amplified, security is threatened and the anxiety which prisoners individually suffer is heightened.

The riot at Strangeways in April 1990 represented the ultimate nightmare in such a spiral. The Woolf Inquiry heard accounts from prisoners whose terror at the height of the incident was so great that some attempted to take their own lives. This should serve to demonstrate, if further demonstration is needed, that suicide prevention is fundamentally about creating humane prison conditions within which *all* prisoners and *all* prison officers can feel secure and within which they can forge positive relationships. It follows that the Woolf and Tumim reformist agendas, which on the face of it often appear to be far removed from the practicalities of suicide prevention, are in fact fundamental to it. The provision of decent physical standards, the enhancement of staff job-satisfaction and professionalism, the promotion of community prisons, the pursuit of active regimes, the inculcation of prisoner responsibility, and the creation of small physically secure accommodation units - these are not abstract ideals. They concern day to day practicalities. It may be worthwhile making one final connection between these issues and the subject of this book.

The View from Strasbourg.

In August 1990 The Council of Europe Committee for the Prevention of Torture visited the United Kingdom for the first time (for an account of the constitution and *modus operandi* of the CPT see Evans and Morgan, 1992). The Committee was favourably impressed with much that they saw. The delegation visited five police stations including Paddington Green, where prisoners detained under the Prevention of Terrorism Act in the capital are often held, and Brixton in London and Chapeltown in Leeds, both of which are in areas that were the site of serious public disturbances in the 1980s. The delegation:

> *... found no evidence of ... ill-treatment ... (no detainees) had any complaints about the manner in which they had been treated ... (they were) impressed by the high degree of professionalism displayed by the police officers... particularly in their dealings with the detainees. The business of the police stations was conducted in an efficient but humane manner ... the result was ... a rather relaxed atmosphere (Council of Europe, 1991, paras.206-7).*

Further, having summarised the safeguards and procedures regarding detention in the police station under the Police and Criminal Evidence Act 1984 (PACE) - including suspects' rights not to be held incommunicado, access to legal advice, the stipulation that detainees may be examined by a doctor of their own choice, and provisions for the calling of 'appropriate adults' for vulnerable prisoners such as juveniles and the mentally disordered - the Committee concluded that:

> *... the legislation and subsidiary rules concerning the detention, treatment and questioning of persons held by the police ... add*

up to an impressive level of legal protection against the ill-treatment of detainees (ibid, para.216).

The fact that the CPT reached these conclusions about the conditions in English police stations and the legal safeguards for suspects, should not lead us to be complacent about the use of police custody. There is no shortage of critics who judge the provisions of PACE to be inadequate (see, for example, Sanders and Bridges, 1990). Nevertheless there is a striking difference between what the CPT, a Committee whose international experience and professional standing is considerable (see Morgan and Evans, 1994), had to say about English police stations and what they had to say about some of the English prisons they visited.

The Committee visited five prisons in August 1990, two of which were for women and which attracted either praise (Holloway) or moderate criticism only (Bullwood Hall). However, conditions in the three prisons for men that were visited resulted in the most critical report that the Council of Europe had then published (though an equally critical report on some French prisons has since been published, see Council of Europe 1993). In the CPT's judgement conditions at Brixton, Wandsworth and Leeds amounted to 'inhuman and degrading' treatment, a phrase taken from and a practice prohibited by Article 3 of the European Convention of Fundamental Human Rights and which the Committee would not have used lightly. The Committee adopted a cumulative view in order to reach this conclusion. Thus conditions that might in themselves not be inhuman and degrading become so when combined with others. The building blocks for the judgement were: overcrowding (of which the worst case was three prisoners occupying cells designed for single accommodation); lack of integral sanitation (prisoners having to defecate and urinate in plastic pots without privacy in front of cell mates); and lack of out-of-cell activities (some prisoners were locked in their cells for 22 and a half hours per day). These were the conditions in which the mainstream population on ordinary locations in the three prisons inhabited, a high proportion of them prisoners awaiting trial (at Brixton and Leeds) or recently sentenced and awaiting allocation (almost all at Wandsworth) - that is, precisely those prisoners most likely to be suffering stress and to harm themselves. Part of the CPT indictment was more focused still, however.

In Brixton's F Wing 200 cells were set aside for prisoners, both unconvicted and convicted, in need of psychiatric care or observation. Here most prisoners had cells to themselves but again were left in them alone without sanitation for most of the day 'subject to intermittent observation by a hospital officer' (ibid, para.159). There was virtually no association, no group therapy, no individualised treatment programmes, not even rooms within which the prison doctors could discuss matters with patients. Further:

> *A severely mentally disturbed and violent patient would be placed in a 'special medical room' ... (a) bare cell equipped only with a mattress on the floor ... (with) poor natural light ... scarcely different from those (cells) to which a recalcitrant prisoner placed in the Segregation Unit would be subject (ibid, para.163).*

These were in effect strip cells by another name, cells that have no place in a facility for disturbed prisoners. The delegation, which included three acknowledged international experts in psychiatry or institutional medicine, came to the conclusion that 'such an environment (F Wing generally) could easily exacerbate rather than improve the state of a mentally disordered person'. The delegation cannot have been surprised to learn of the serious history of suicides and self-harm at Brixton and Leeds. Indeed a prisoner fatally hanged himself while they were visiting Leeds (ibid, para.170).

POSTSCRIPT

The function of Brixton's F Wing has changed and the strip cells have literally been removed (personal communication from the governor). Further, neither Brixton, Wandsworth or Leeds, or indeed any other local prison, is at the time of writing (June 1993) as overcrowded as in 1990. Placing prisoners three to a cell has been virtually eliminated from the English prison system (see Prison Service, 1993a p.6) and a serious attempt is being made to enhance regimes for local prisons, in particular for prisoners on remand (Prison Service, 1992b). Whether this progress continues depends crucially on the future size and shape of the prison population, however, and the signs are ominous. The latest Home Office projections suggest that the prison population will rise from approximately 44,000 at present to 50,700 by the year 2000 (Prison Service, 1993b, Figure 4), in which case prison overcrowding will continue into the 21st century unless a further building programme is initiated. Most depressingly it appears that even when improvements appear generally to be taking place, the Chief Inspector of Prisons goes on coming up with reports on establishments where apparently nothing has changed. In May 1993, to take the latest example, he reported on Cardiff, a local prison and remand centre. He pronounced that the conditions at Cardiff when he inspected it in October 1992 'were as bad as have been found in any prison inspected by the Inspectorate ... the treatment of prisoners at Cardiff was a disgrace' (Home Office, 1993 and press release). His report goes on to describe squalid conditions and an inactive regime which have become painfully familiar to English penal observers over the years.

There were two prisoner suicides in Cardiff in 1991 and in 1992, according to the Inspectorate, 'unfurnished rooms' were still being used for 'potentially suicidal' prisoners 'with intermittent observation' (ibid, para.6.64), a practice contrary to correct Prison Service policy (see Prison Service, 1992b, para.40). No reader should be in any doubt about the continued need for this book.

References

American Correctional Association (1989) *Certification Standards for Health Care Programs*. Laurel, Maryland: ACA.

American Medical Association (1978) *Training of Jailers in Receiving Screening and Health Education*. Chicago: AMA.

Amnesty International (1980) *Amnesty International's Work on Prison Conditions of Persons Suspected or Convicted of Politically Motivated Crime in the Federal Republic of Germany: Isolation and Solitary Confinement*. London: Amnesty.

Amnesty International (1983) *Rapport au sujet des allégations de mauvais traitements infligés à des prisoniers du pénitencier Archambault au Québec (Canada)*. London: Amnesty.

Amnesty International British Section (1990) *United Kingdom: Deficient Policy and Practice for the Protection of Asylum Seekers*. London: Amnesty.

Amnesty International British Section (1992) *Towards a Credible Asylum Process: A Model for Fair and Practicable Procedures*. London: Amnesty.

Anderson, O. (1987) *Suicide in Victorian and Edwardian England*. Oxford: Clarendon Press.

Australian Office of Corrections (1985) *Suicide and Other Deaths in Prison Including Victorian Results from the National Deaths in Corrections Study*. Unpublished Report. Victoria, Australia: Research Unite, Office of Corrections.

Backett, S. (1987) Suicides in Scottish Prisons. *British Journal of Psychiatry, 151*, pp.218-21.

Backett, S. (1988) Suicide and stress in prison. In S. Backett, J. McNeil & A. Yellowlees (Eds.), *Imprisonment Today*. Basingstoke: Macmillan.

Barraclough, B.M. & Hughes, J. (1987) *Suicide: Clinical and Epidemiological Studies*. London: Croom Helm.

Basedow, M.K. (1991) *A Report on the police role in dealing with suicidal persons and custody management*. NSW: New South Wales Police Service Research Programme.

Benn, M. & Worpole, K. (1986) *Death in the City: A Study of Police-Related Deaths in London*. London: Canary Press.

Bernheim, J.-C. & Lorain, L. (1980) *Les Complices*. Montréal: Québec/Amérique.

Bottoms, A.E. (1977) Reflections on the renaissance of dangerousness. *Howard Journal, 16*, pp.70-96.

Bottoms, A.E. (1990) The aims of imprisonment. In Centre for Theology and Public Issues (Ed.), *Justice, Guilt and Forgiveness in the Penal System*. Edinburgh: Edinburgh University.

References

Boulter, R. (1990) *Probation in Prisons*. Leeds: Regional Staff Development Office.

Bowker, K.H. (1980) *Prison Victimization*. New York: Elsevier.

Boyle, J. (1977) *A Sense of Freedom*. Edinburgh: Canongate.

Boyle, J. (1984) *The Pain of Confinement: Prison Diaries*. Edinburgh: Canongate.

Bracken, P. & Gorst-Unsworth, C. (1991) The mental state of detained asylum seekers. *Psychiatric Bulletin, 15*, pp.657-59.

British Medical Association (1990) *Working Party Report on the Health Care of Remand Prisoners*. London: BMA.

Broadhurst, R. & Maller, R.A. (1990) *White Man's Magic Makes Black Deaths in Custody Disappear*.

Brown, D., Ellis, T. & Larcombe, K. (1992) *Changing the Code: Police Detention Under the Revised PACE Codes of Practice*. (Home Office Research Studies, No. 129.) London: HMSO.

Brownlie, D. (Ed.) (1983) *Basic Documents in Human Rights* (3rd ed.). Oxford: Clarendon Press.

Bulthe, B. & Janssen, C. (1984) *Les prisons et la contestation collective*. Brussels: Bruylant.

Bundred, S. (1982) Accountability and the Metropolitan Police. In D. Cowell, T. Jones & J. Young (Eds.), *Policing the Riots*. London: Junction Books.

Burke, H. (1990) *Examination of Inquests into Deaths of Mental Patients*. London: Brunel University Socio-Legal Working Papers.

Burtch, B.E. & Ericson, R.V. (1979) *The Silent System: An Inquiry into Prisoners Who Suicide*. Toronto: Centre for Criminology, University of Toronto.

Carot, E., Paraire, J., Charlin, A. & Bachet, M. (1949) Les réactions psychopathologiques de captivité. *Annales Médico-psychologiques, 7(4)*, pp.369-401.

Castel, R. (1988) *The Regulation of Madness*. Cambridge: Polity Press.

Chappell, D. & Graham, L.F. (1987) *Police Use of Deadly Force: Canadian Perspectives*. Toronto: Centre of Criminology, University of Toronto.

Clemmer, D. (1940) *The Prison Community*. Boston: Christopher.

Coggan, G. & Walker, M. (1982) *Frightened For My Life: An Account of Deaths in British Prisons*. London: Fontana.

Cohen, R. & Goulbourne, S. (1987) *The Detention of Asylum Seekers in the UK: Report Commissioned by the British Refugee Council from the Centre for Research in Ethnic Relations*. Coventry: University of Warwick.

Cohen, S. & Taylor, L. (1972) *Psychological Survival*. Harmondsworth: Penguin.

Colin, M., Gonin, D. & Ducottet, F. (1975) La suicide en prison. *Instantanés Crim., 25*, pp.3-12.

Cooper, H.H.A. (1974) The all-pervading depression and violence of prison life. *International Journal of Offender Therapy and Comparative Criminology, 18(3)*, pp.217-26.

Cormier, B. (1957) Types of regression determined by deprivation of liberty and their implications in rehabilitation. *Proceedings of Canadian*

Congress of Corrections, pp.137-49.

Cormier, B. (1971) *Evaluation of the special correction unit: preliminary report to the Solicitor-General of Canada*. Unpublished.

Cormier, B. & Williams, P. (1966) La privation excessive de la liberté. *Canadian Psychiatric Association Journal, 11(6)*, pp.470-84.

Correctional Service Canada (1981) *Self-Inflicted Injuries and Suicides*. Ottawa: Bureau of Management Consulting.

Cosyns, P. & Wilmotte, J. (1973) *Suicide et criminologie*. Louvain: Ecole de Criminologie, Université Catholique de Louvain.

Council of Europe (1991) *Report to the United Kingdom Government on the Visit to the United Kingdom carried out by the European Committee for the Prevention of Torture and Inhuman or Degrading Treatment or Punishment from 29 June 1990 to 10 August 1990*. Strasbourg: Council of Europe.

Council of Europe (1993) *Rapport au Gouvernement de la République Française relatif à la visite effectuée par la CPT en France du 27 octobre au 8 novembre 1991*. Strasbourg: Council of Europe.

Crelenstein, R.D. (1981) *The study of the effect of isolation in the laboratory and in the prison*. Université de Montreal, Centre internationale de criminologie comparée, mimeo.

Cullen, M.J. (1975) *The Statistical Movement in Early Victorian England*. Hassocks, Sussex: Harvester.

David, R. & Brierly, J.E.C. (1985) *Major Legal Systems in the World Today* (3rd ed.). London: Stevens.

Dell, S., Grounds, A., James, K. & Robertson, G. (1991) *Mentally Disordered Remand Prisoners: Report to the Home Office*. Cambridge: University of Cambridge.

Diekstra, R.F.W. (1987) Renée: chronicle of a misspent life, and Renée or the complex dynamics of adolescent suicide. In R.F.W. Diekstra & K. Hawton (Eds.), *Suicide in Adolescence*, pp.25-77. Dordrecht: Martinus Nijhoff.

Dooley, E. (1990a) Non-natural deaths in prison. *British Journal of Criminology, 30(2)*, pp.229-34.

Dooley, E. (1990b) Prison suicide in England and Wales. *British Journal of Psychiatry, 30(2)*, pp.40-45.

Dooley, E. (1990c) *Seminar given at the Institute of Criminology, Cambridge*. February 1990.

Dorlhac de Borne, H. (1984) *Changer la prison*. Paris: Plon.

Douglas, J.D. (1967) *The Social Meanings of Suicide*. Princeton, NJ: Princeton University Press.

Dunbar, I. (1985) *A Sense of Direction*. London: Prison Service.

Durkheim, E. (1952 [1897]) *Suicide*. London: Routledge & Kegan Paul.

Eichenberger, G. (1978) Les médicaments en prison préventive. *Information Pénitentiaire Suisses., 102(2)*, pp.106-16.

Eldrid, J. (1988) *Caring for the Suicidal*. London: Constable.

Evans, M. & Morgan, R. (1992) The European Convention for the Prevention of Torture: operational practice. *International and Comparative Law Quarterly, 41*, pp.590-614.

Eyler, J.M. (1979) *Victorian Social Medicine: The Ideas and Methods of William Farr*. Baltimore: Johns Hopkins University Press.

Favard, J. (1984) *La labyrinthe pénitentiare*. Paris: Le Centurion.

Fawcett, J. & Mars, B. (1973) Suicide in the county jail. In B.L. Danto (Ed.), *Jail House Blues*. Michigan: Epic Publications.

Fitzgerald, M. (1977) *Prisoners in Revolt*. Harmondsworth: Penguin.

Fitzgerald, M. & Sim, J. (1979) *British Prisons*. Oxford: Blackwell.

Flaherty, M.G. (1983) *The National Incidence of Juvenile Suicide in Adult Jails and Juvenile Detention Centers*. Urbana-Champaign: University of Illinois.

Foot, P. (1986) *Murder at the Farm: Who Killed Carl Bridgewater?* Harmondsworth: Penguin.

Forbes, T.R. (1977) Crowner's quest. *Transactions of the American Philosophical Society, 68,* p.33.

Forbes, T.R. (1978) Coroners' inquisitions on the deaths of prisoners in the hulks at Portsmouth, 1817-27. *Journal of the History of Medicine and Allied Sciences, 33,* pp.296-309.

Foucault, M. (1977) *Discipline and Punish: The Birth of the Prison*. Harmondsworth: Penguin.

Garland, D. (1985) *Punishment and Welfare*. Aldershot: Gower.

Gayda, M. & Vacola, G. (1984) Les suicides en prison. *Psychol. médicale, 16(5),* pp.831-3.

Genders, E. & Player, E. (1987) Women in prison: the treatment, the control and the experience. In P. Carlen & A. Worrall (Eds.), *Gender, Crime and Justice*. Milton Keynes: Open University Press.

Goffman, E. (1968) *Asylums*. Harmondsworth: Penguin.

Gover, R.M. (1879) Report of the Superintending Medical Officer. In Board of Prison Commissioners, *Third Annual Report*, pp. (1878-79) xxxiv, 1.

Graham, D. (1989) *Dying Inside*. Sydney: Allen & Unwin.

Grindrod, H. & Black, G. (1989) *Suicides at Leeds Prison: An Enquiry into the Deaths of Five Teenagers During 1988/89*. London: Howard League.

Guignet, A. (1981) *Étude descriptive d'une population à haute risque: les suicidants à la prison préventive de Champ-Dollon du 1er octobre 1977 au 31 mars 1979*. Thesis no. 3892, Faculty of Medicine, University of Geneva.

Gunn, J., Madden, A. & Swinton, M. (1991) *Mentally Disordered Prisoners*. London: Institute of Psychiatry.

Gunn, J., Robertson, G., Dell, S. & Way, C. (1978) *Psychiatric Aspects of Imprisonment*. London: Academic Press.

Hacking, I. (1990) *The Taming of Chance*. Cambridge: Cambridge University Press.

Hall, S., Critcher, S., Jefferson, T., Clarke, J. & Roberts, B. (1978) *Policing the Crisis*. Basingstoke: Macmillan.

Harding, R. (1988) *Aboriginal Deaths in Custody: The Response of the Northern Territory Government*. Canberra: Report to the Northern Territory Government in records of the Royal Commission into Aboriginal Deaths in Custody.

Harding, R. (1990a) *Evidence on Overview Issues*. Canberra: Records of the Royal Commission on Aboriginal Deaths in Custody.

Harding, R. (1990b) *Review of Suicide and Suicide Attempts by Prisoners in the Custody of the Office of Corrections, Victoria*. South Melbourne: Office of Corrections.

Harding, T.W. (1984) Dépression en milieu carcéral. *Psychol. médicale, 16(5)*, pp.835-39.

Hatty, S.E. & Walker, J. R. (1986) *A National Study of Deaths in Australian Prisons*. Canberra: Australian Centre of Criminology.

Hawkins, G. (1976) *The Prison*. Chicago: University of Chicago Press.

Hay, W. & Sparks, R. (1991) Maintaining order in the English dispersal system. In *Special Units for Difficult Prisoners*. Hull: University of Hull Centre for Criminology and Criminal Justice.

Hayes, L.M. (1983) And darkness closes in... A national study of jail suicides. *Criminal Justice and Behaviour, 10(4)*, pp.461-84.

Hayes, L.M. & Rowan, J.R. (1988) *National Study of Jail Suicides: Seven Years Later*. Alexandria, Virginia: National Center on Institutions and Alternatives.

Hill, M.D. (1857) *Suggestions for the Repression of Crime*. London: Parker & Son.

Hivert, P.E. (1970) Le suicidant, la prison et le médicin. *Revue pénitentiare et du droit pénale, 94(3)*, pp.369-74.

HMSO (1992) *Report of the Committee of Inquiry into Complaints about Ashworth Hospital*. London: HMSO (Cm. 2028 I and II).

Hobhouse, M.A. & Brockway, A.F. (1922) *English Prisons Today*. London: Longman, Green & Co.

Hogan, R., Hogg, R. & Brown, D. (Eds.) (1988) *Death in the Hands of the State*. Redfern, NSW: Redfern Legal Centre.

Home Office (1984) *Suicide in Prisons: A Report by HM Chief Inspector of Prisons*. London: Home Office.

Home Office (1986) *Report of the Working Group on Suicide Prevention*. London: Home Office.

Home Office (1987) *Report of an Inquiry by HM Chief Inspector of Prisons into the Disturbances in Prison Service Establishments in England and Wales between 29 April - 2 May 1986*. HC 42, London: HMSO.

Home Office (1988a) *HM Prison Hull: Report by HM Chief Inspector of Prisons*. London: Home Office.

Home Office (1988b) *Report on the Work of the Prison Service 1987-88*. London: HMSO.

Home Office (1990a) *HM Prison Brixton: Report by HM Chief Inspector of Prisons*. London: Home Office.

Home Office (1990b) *HM Prison Haslar: Report by HM Chief Inspector of Prisons*. London: Home Office.

Home Office (1990c) *HM Prison, Leeds: Report by HM Chief Inspector of Prisons*. London: Home Office.

Home Office (1990d) *Prison Disturbances, June 1990*. London: HMSO.

Home Office (1990e) *Report of a Review by HM Chief Inspector of Prisons of Suicide and Self-Harm in Prison Service Establishments in England and Wales*. London: HMSO.

Home Office (1990f) *Report of the Work of the Prison Service 1988-89*. London: HMSO.

Home Office (1992a) *Custody, Care and Justice*. London: HMSO.

Home Office (1992b) *HM Prison Styal: Report by HM Chief Inspector of Prisons*. London: Home Office.

Home Office (1992c) *HM Prison Winson Green: Report by HM Chief Inspector of Prisons*. London: Home Office.

Home Office (1993a) *HM Prison and Remand Centre Cardiff: Report by HM Chief Inspector of Prisons*. London: Home Office.

Home Office (1993b) *HM Prison Swansea: Report by HM Chief Inspector of Prisons*. London: Home Office.

House of Commons (1980) *Third Report from the Home Affairs Committee: Deaths in Police Custody*. HC 632, London: HMSO.

Howard League (1993) *Suicides in Feltham*. London: Howard League.

Hudson, B. (1987) *Justice Through Punishment: A Critique of the 'Justice' Model of Corrections*. Basingstoke: Macmillan.

Ignatieff, M. (1981) State, civil society and total institutions. In M. Tonry & N. Morris (Eds.), *Crime and Justice: An Annual Review of Research*. Chicago: University of Chicago Press.

Independent Committee of Inquiry (1980) *The Death of Blair Peach*. London: NCCL.

Independent Committee of Inquiry (1988) *Policing in Hackney, 1945-1985* (2nd ed.). London: Karia Press.

INQUEST (1983) *Annual Report 1982-83*. London: INQUEST.

INQUEST (1989) *Annual Report 1988-89*. London: INQUEST.

INQUEST (1990) *Suicides in Prison: Submission to HM Chief Inspector of Prisons*. London: INQUEST.

Institute of Race Relations (1991) *Deadly Silence*. London: IRR.

Irving, B. & McKenzie, I. (1989) *Police Interrogation: The Effects of the Police and Criminal Evidence Act 1984*. London: Police Foundation.

Irwin, J. (1970) *The Felon*. Englewood Cliffs, NJ: Prentice Hall.

Jackson, M. (1983) *Prisoners of Isolation: Solitary Confinement in Canada*. Toronto: University of Toronto Press.

Jacobs, J.B. (1977) *Stateville: The Penitentiary in Mass Society*. Chicago: University of Chicago Press.

JCWI (1990-91) *Annual Report*. London: Joint Council for the Welfare of Immigrants.

Jepson, N. & Elliott, K. (1985) *Shared Working between Prison and Probation Officers*. London: HMSO.

John Howard Society of Saskatchewan (1975) *Report on Suicides Occurring at Saskatchewan Penitentiary Nov. 18 1972 - June 16, 1973*. Regina: John Howard Society.

Johnson, E. (1973) Felon self-mutilation: correlates of stress in prison. In B.L. Danto (Ed.), *Jail House Blues*. Michigan: Epic Publications.

Johnson, R. (1978) Youth in crisis: dimensions of self-destructive conduct among adolescent prisoners. *Adolescence, 13 (51)*, pp.461-82.

Johnson, R. & Toch, H. (Eds.) (1982) *The Pains of Imprisonment*. Beverly Hills: Sage.

Joly, D. & Nettleton, C. (1990) *Refugees in Europe*. London: Minority Rights Group.

Jones, H. & Morgan, R. (1991) *Report of an Experiment in 13 Prisons Using Magistrates' Court Clerks for Boards of Visitors' Adjudications*. London: Prison Service.

King, R. & McDermott, C. (1990) 'My geranium is subversive': some notes on the management of trouble in British prisons. *British Journal of Sociology, 41(4)*, pp.445-71.

Klare, H.M. (1973) *People in Prison*. London: Pitman.

Korn, R.R. (nd) *Summary of Testimony in the Case of McCann v. The Queen*. Berkeley: Centre for the Study of Criminal Justice.

Kreitman, N., Carstairs, V. & Duffy, J. (1991) Association of age and social class with suicide among men in Great Britain. *Journal of Epidemiology and Community Health, 45*, pp.195-202.

Lester, D. (1987) Suicide and homicide in USA prisons. *Psychological Reports, 61*, p.126.

Liebling, A. (1992) *Suicides in Prison*. London: Routledge.

Liebling, A. (1994) Suicides amongst women prisoners. *Howard Journal, 33(1)*, pp.1-9.

Liebling, A. & Krarup, A. (1993) *Suicide Attempts in Male Prisons*. Report submitted to the Home Office, London.

Little, M. & Bullock, R. (1990) *Young Men in Prison: The Influence of Criminal Identity on Patterns of Offending Behaviour*. Unpublished Paper.

Lloyd, C. (1990) *Suicide and Self Injury on Prison: A Literature Review*. (Home Office Research Studies, No. 115.) London: HMSO.

Lucas, W.E. (1976) Solitary confinement: isolation as coercion to conform. *Aust & NZ Jnl. of Criminology, 9*, pp.153-67.

MacGuigan, M. et al. (1977) *Rapport à la chambre du sous-comité sur le régime d'institutions pénitentiare au Canada*. Ottawa: Ministry of Supplies and Services.

Maltaverne, S. (1982) La suicide en prison. In J. Vedrine, O. Quénard & D. Weber (Eds.), *Suicides et conduites suicidaires* (pp. 179-85). Paris: Masson.

Mausner, J.S. & Kramer, S. (1985) *Epidemiology: An Introductory Text*. Philadelphia: WB Saunders.

McCann et al. v The Queen (1976) 29 CCC, 337-336.

McClure, G.M.G. (1984) Recent trends in suicide amongst the young. *British Journal of Psychiatry, 144*, pp.134-38.

McClure, G.M.G. (1987) Suicide in England and Wales, 1975-1984. *British Journal of Psychiatry, 150*, pp.309-14.

McDowell, D. (1989) *The Alevi Kurds*. London: Minority Rights Group.

McFadyean, M. (1993, July 28) Death in cell 22. *Guardian*, pp.12-13.

McGurk, B.J. & McDougal, C. (1981) The *Prevention of Bullying Among*

Incarcerated Delinquents. DPS Report, Series II No. 114 (restricted circulation). London: Home Office.

McHugh, M. (1989) *Personal communication on suicides at Leeds prison*.

McIntosh, J.L. (1985) *Research on Suicide: A Bibliography*. Westport, Conn.: Greenwood Press.

Medical Foundation for the Care of Victims of Torture (1992) *Protection of Torture Victims by the European Community: The Medical Foundation's Concerns*. London: Medical Foundation.

Morgan, R. (1993a) An awkward anomaly: remand prisoners. In E. Player & M. Jenkins (Eds.), *Prisons After Woolf*. London: Routledge.

Morgan, R. (1993b) Imprisonment. In M. Maguire, R. Morgan & R. Reiner (Eds.), *The Oxford Handbook of Criminology*. Oxford: Oxford University Press.

Morgan, R. & Evans, M. (1994) Inspecting prisons:. *British Journal of Criminology*, *34*, pp.141-59.

Morgan, R. & Jones, S. (1992) Bail or jail? In E. Stockdale & S. Casale (Eds.), *Criminal Justice Under Stress*. London: Blackstone.

Morgan, R., McKenzie, I. & Reiner, R. (1989) *Police Powers and the Police: A Study of the Work of Custody Officers*. Report to the Economic and Social Research Council, Unpublished.

Morris, P. & Morris, T. (1963) *Pentonville: A Sociological Study of an English Prison*. London: Routledge & Kegan Paul.

Muncie, J. & Sparks, R. (1991) Expansion and contraction in European prison systems. In J. Muncie & R. Sparks (Eds.), *Imprisonment: European Perspectives*. London: Harvester Wheatsheaf.

NACRO (1990) *Suicide in Prison*. (Briefing Papers, No. 103.) London: NACRO.

National Commission on Correctional Health Care (1987) *Standards for Health Services in Jails*. Chicago: NCCHC.

Netherlands (1991) *Jaarsverlag 1990 van het bureau van de Geneeskundige Inspectie*. Den Haag: Ministerie van Justitie.

Netherlands (1992) *Gevangenisstatistiek 1990*. Voorburg-Heerlen: CBS.

New York (1972) *Report on Prison Suicides and Urgent Recommendations for Action*. New York: NY City Board of Corrections.

New York State Commission of Corrections, State Office of Mental Health, & Ulster County Community Mental Health Service (1986) *The Officers' Handbook*. Albany, NY: Authors.

Novick, L.F. & Remlinger, E. (1978) A study of 128 deaths in New York city correctional facilities (1971-1976). *Medical Care*, *16(a)*, pp.745-56.

OPCS (1990) *Morbidity Statistics*. London: HMSO.

Paulus, P. (1988) *Prison Crowding: A Psychological Perspective*. New York: Springer-Verlag.

Phillips, M. (1986) *A Study of Suicides and Attempted Suicides at HMP Brixton 1973-83*. (Department of Psychological Services Reports, Series 1, No. 24.) London: Home Office.

Power, K.G. & Spencer, A.P. (1987) Parasuicidal behaviour of detained Scottish young offenders. *International Journal of Offender Therapy and*

Comparative Criminology, 31(3), pp.227-35.

Priestley, P. (1985) *Victorian Prison Lives*. London: Methuen.

Prior, L. (1989) *The Social Organization of Death*. Basingstoke: Macmillan.

Prison Officers' Association (1985) *The Prison Disciplinary System: Submissions to the Home Office Departmental Committee on the Prison Disciplinary System*. London: POA.

Prison Reform Trust (1987) *Arrangements for the Prevention of Suicide in Prison*. Submission to HM Chief Inspector of Prisons.

Prison Reform Trust (1990) *Sex Offenders in Prison*. London: PRT.

Prison Reform Trust (1991) *The Identikit Prisoner*. London: PRT.

Prison Service (1992a) *Caring for Prisoners at Risk of Suicide and Self-Injury: The Way Forward*. London: Home Office.

Prison Service (1992b) *Model Regime for Local Prisons and Remand Centres*. London: Home Office.

Prison Service (1993a) *Business Plan 1993-94*. London: Prison Service.

Prison Service (1993b) *Corporate Plan 1993-96*. London: Prison Service.

Reynolds, D.K. & Farberow, N. L. (1976) *Suicide: Inside and Out*. Berkeley: University of California Press.

Richmond, G. (1975) *Prison Doctor*. Vancouver: Antonson Publishing.

Rowan, J.R. (1984) *Almost All Suicides in Jails and Lockups can be Prevented If....* Roseville, Minnesota: Juvenile and Criminal Justice International, Inc.

Rowan, J.R. (1989a) Health care providers with 'street attitudes' incur lawsuits. In *Corhealth*. Dayton, Ohio: American Correctional Health Services, Inc.

Rowan, J.R. (1989b) Jail/correctional officers with 'street attitudes' incur lawsuits. In *American Jails*. Hagerstown, Maryland: .

Rowan, J.R. & Hayes, L.M. (1988) *Training Curriculum on Suicide Detection and Prevention in Jails and Lockups*. Alexandra, Maryland: National Center on Institutions and Alternatives.

Royal Commission into Aboriginal Deaths in Custody (1991) *National Report* (Vol. 1-3). Canberra: Australian Government Publishing Service.

Royal Commission on Penal Servitude (1878) *Minutes of Evidence*. pp. (1878-9) xxxvii, 1.

Ryan, M. (1978) *The Acceptable Pressure Group: Inequality in the Penal Lobby - A Comparative Study of the Howard League and RAP*. Farnborough: Gower.

Ryan, M. & Ward, T. (1989) *Privatization and the Penal System: The American Experience and the Debate in Britain*. Milton Keynes: Open University Press.

Samaritans (1990) *Who Cares if ι Live or Die? Suicide in Great Britain*. London: The Samaritans.

Samaritans (1992) *Annual Report*. London: The Samaritans.

Sanders, A. & Bridges, L. (1990) Access to legal advice and police malpractice. *Criminal Law Review*, p.494.

Schaub, S. et al. (1971) Conduites suicidaires, libre arbitre et d'ontologie médicale. *Med. lég. et dommage corp.*, *4*, pp.225-28.

References

Schaub-Landau, S. (1972) Réflections sur les limites du rôle de l'équipe médico-psychologique en milieu pénitentiare à propos de candidates suicidaires ou de refus d'aliments. *Revue pénitentiaire et du droit pénale, 96(1)*, pp.41-48.

Schmidt, M. (1989) *Drunkenness Offenders: The State of the Nation*. London: Out of Court.

Scott-Denoon, K. (1983) *B.C. Corrections: A Study of Suicide, 1970-1980*. Victoria: Ministry of the Attorney General.

Scottish Home and Health Department (1985) *Report of the Review of Suicide Precautions at HM Detention Centre and HM Young Offenders' Institution, Glenochil*. Edinburgh: HMSO.

Scraton, P. & Chadwick, K. (1985) Glenochil: the experiment that went wrong. *The Abolitionist, 20*, pp.28-33.

Scraton, P. & Chadwick, K. (1986) Speaking ill of the dead: institutionalised responses to deaths in custody. *Journal of Law and Society, 13(1)*, pp.93-115.

Scraton, P. & Chadwick, K. (1987) *In the Arms of the Law: Coroners' Inquests and Deaths in Custody*. London: Pluto.

Scraton, P., Sim, J. & Skidmore, P. (1991) *Prisons under Protest*. Buckingham: Open University Press.

Sherman, L.W. & Langworthy, R.H. (1979) Measuring homicide by police officers. *Journal of Criminal Law and Criminology, 70*, pp.456-60.

SHHD (1985) See Scottish Home and Health Department (1985).

Shine, J., Wilson, P. & Hammond, D. (1990) Understanding and controlling violence in a long-term young offender institution. In N.L. Fludger & I.P. Simmons (Eds.), *DPS Reports, Series 1: 34. Proceedings from Psychologists' Conference 1989,* pp. 115-32. London: Directorate of Psychological Services.

Sim, J. (1990) *Medical Power in Prisons*. Buckingham: Open University Press.

Sim, J. & Ward, T. (Forthcoming) The magistrate of the poor? Coroners and deaths in custody in nineteenth-century England. In M.J. Clark & C. Crawford (Eds.), *Legal Medicine in History*. Cambridge: Cambridge University Press.

Smith, R. (1991) 'Taken from this place and hanged by the neck...'. *British Medical Journal, 302*, pp.64-65.

Stewart, R.L. et al. (1984) *Rapport sur les allegations de mauvais traitement de détenues à l'établissement Archambault après les incidents du 25 juillet 1982*. Ottawa: Enquêteur correctionel.

Suedfeld, P. (1978) Solitary confinement as a rehabilitative technique: reply to Lucas. *Aust. & N.Z. Jnl. of Criminology, 11*, pp.106-12.

Swackhammer, J. W. et al. (1972) *Rapport de la commission d'enquête sur la soulèvement survenu du pénitencier de Kingston, en avril 1971*. Ottawa: Information Canada.

Sykes, G. (1958) *The Society of Captives*. Princeton, N.J.: Princeton University Press.

Takagi, P. (1974) A garrison state in 'democratic' society. *Crime and Social*

Justice, 1, pp.27-33.

Taylor, S. (1982) *Durkheim and the Study of Suicide*. Macmillan: Basingstoke.

Thorburn, K. M. (1984) Self-mutilation and self-induced illness in prison. *Journal of Prison and Jail Health, 4(1)*, pp.40-51.

Thornton, D. (1990) Depression, self-injury and attempted suicide amongst the YOI population. In N.L. Fludger & I.P. Simmons (Eds.), *Proceedings from Psychologists' Conference 1989. DPS Report Series 1 no. 34*, pp.47-55. London: Directorate of Psychological Services.

Toch, H. (1975) *Men in Crisis: Human Breakdowns in Prison*. New York: Aldine.

Topp, D.O. (1979) Suicide in British prisons. *British Journal of Psychiatry, 134*, p.2427.

Tournier, P. & Chemitte, P. (1979) *Contribution statistique à étude des conduites suicidaires en milieu carcéral 1975-1978*, Vol. 1 & 2. Paris: Ministère de la justice.

Tweedie, J. & Ward, T. (1989) The Gibraltar shootings and the politics of inquests. *Journal of Law and Society, 16(4)*, pp.464-76.

van den Brûle, I. (1989) Sterfgevallen in handen van justitie en politie. In *Crimineel Jaarboek 87/88*. Breda: Coornhert-Liga.

van der Vijver, C.D. (1987) Bijlage II: Vuurwapengebruik door de politie. In Commissie bezinning op het geweldgebruik door die politie (Ed.), *Geweldgebruik door de politie*. Den Haag: Ministerie van Justitie.

van Koot, H.G. (1988) Schieten ter aanhouding. *Tijdschrift voor Politie, 2*.

Waddington, P.A.J. (1977) *The Occupational Socialisation of Prison Governor Grades*. Unpublished PhD Thesis, Leeds University.

Walker, H. & Beaumont, B. (1981) *Probation Work*. Oxford: Blackwell.

Walker, H. & Beaumont, B. (1985) *Working with Offenders*. Basingstoke: Macmillan.

Walmsley, R., Howard, L. & White, S. (1992) *The National Prison Survey 1991: Main Findings*. (Home Office Research Study No. 128.) London: HMSO.

Warwick Inquest Group (1985) The inquest as a theatre for police tragedy: the Davey case. *Journal of Law and Society, 12*, pp.35-56.

Weatheritt, M. (1986) *Innovations in Policing*. London: Croom Helm.

Williams, M. & Longley, D. (1987) Identifying control-problem prisoners in dispersal prisons. In A.E. Bottoms & R. Light (Eds.), *Problems of Long-Term Imprisonment*. Farnborough: Gower.

Willis, P. (1988) *Learning to Labour: How Working-Class Kids Get Working-Class Jobs*. Aldershot: Gower.

Wilson, J.G. & Prescor, M.J. (1939) *Problems in Prison Psychiatry*. Caldwell, Idaho: Canton Printers.

Wool, R. & Dooley, E. (1987) A study of attempted suicides in prisons. *Medicine, Science and the Law, 27(4)*, pp.297-301.

Zamble, E. & Porporino, F.J. (1988) *Coping, Behaviour and Adaptation in Prison Inmates*. New York: Springer-Verlag.

Index

Participants in the ISTD Conference March 1991

* Indicates a contributor to this book

Gordon ADDISON Senior Probation Officer, HM Prison Channings Wood, UK
Nicola AMATO Director General, Penal Administration, Italy
Leena ARPO Ministry of Justice, Finland
Simon BACKETT Consultant Psychiatrist, Bangour Village Hospital, West Lothian, UK
Susan BAILEY Consultant Adolescent Forensic Psychiatrist to the Home Office and NW
    Regional Health Authority, UK
Cipriano BAPTISTE Assistant Commissioner of Prisons, Trinidad and Tobago
Grenvil BARNARD Prison Governor, HM Prison Thorpe Arch, UK
Colin BARTON Medical Officer, Home Office, UK
Margaret BENEDICT Chair, Board of Visitors, HM Prison Cardiff, UK
C. BERKLEY Broadmoor Hospital, UK
*Jean Claude BERNHEIM Professor of Criminology, Universities of Ottawa and Montréal
Kristel BEYENS Researcher, Free University, Brussels, Belgium
Kathy BIGGAR Co-National Outreach Co-ordinator, Prisons, Samaritans, UK
*David BILES Deputy Director, Australian Institute of Criminology, formerly Consultant
    Criminologist and Head of Research, Royal Commission into Aboriginal Deaths in
    Custody, Australia
William BLOOMER Principal Officer Tutor, HM Prison Service College, Millisle, UK
Keith BOTTOMLEY Professor of Criminology, Dept. of Social Policy and Professional
    Studies, Hull University, UK.
Gail BRADLEY Probation Officer, UK
Roy BURROWS Senior Medical Officer, HM Prison Wandsworth, UK
Ian BYNOE Legal Officer, MIND, UK
Leonard CARRION Governmental Adviser on Human Rights, Ministry of Government,
    Quito, Ecuador
Muhammad Masud CHOHAN Medical Practitioner; Senior Medical Officer, Liverpool, UK
Dot CLARKE Senior Probation Officer, Cambridgeshire Probation Service, UK
Keith COCKMAN Social Worker, Hertfordshire, UK
*Deborah COLES Co-Director, Inquest, UK
Dee COOMBES Criminal Justice Student, London, UK
John Nigel COURT Head of Inmate Activities; Chair of Suicide Prevention Committee,
    HM Prison Wandsworth UK
Frances CROOK Director, Howard League, UK
Luigi DAGA Director, Penal Institutions, Ministry of Justice, Italy
Arthur DANIELS Probation Officer, Lincolnshire Probation Service, UK
*Gerard DE JONGE Senior Lecturer in Criminal Law, University of Limburg, Holland
*Enda DOOLEY Director, Prison Medical Services, Dublin, Eire
Stephen DOUTHWAITE Prison Officer, Leicester, UK
Richard EVANS Prison Medical Officer, HM Prison Leeds, UK
Martin FARRELL Director, ISTD, UK
The Hon. Sir Henry FISHER President, Howard League, UK

Conference Participants

Lady FISHER

John FREEMAN Director of Criminological Studies, King's College London; Chair ISTD, UK

Patricia FRENCH Senior Lecturer, Kingston Polytechnic, UK

Jill FRICKER Alternative to Custody Development Officer, Brent Employment Training, UK

Irene FROST Administrator, ISTD, UK

R.G. GAINES Prison Officer, HM Prison Brixton, UK

Jeff GARDNER Chief Inspector, Metropolitan Police, UK

Rozalinda GHITA Legal Officer, Ministry of Justice, Bucharest, Rumania

Halta GOWAN Researcher, Amnesty International, UK

Helen GRINDROD QC Co-author, *Suicides at Leeds Prison*, UK

John HALL Senior Medical Officer, Prison Medical Service, HM Prison Winson Green, UK

Tony HAMMERTON Senior Probation Officer, HM Prison Magilligan, N Ireland UK

*Richard HARDING Professor, Crime Research Centre, University of Western Australia

Tim HARDING Chargé de Cours, Institute of Legal Medicine, Geneva, Switzerland

David HARKNESS Senior Medical Officer, HM Prison Lincoln, UK

Patrick HARMAN Prison Service, HM Prison Blantyre House, UK

Derek HARRISON Governor, Nursing Service, HM Prison Wandsworth, UK

Richard HARRISON Hospital Principal Officer, HM Prison, Brixton, UK

John HATCHARD Law School, University of Buckingham, UK

*Lindsay HAYES Assistant Director, National Centre on Institutions and Alternatives, Massachusetts, USA

Philip HESSELDEN Former Inmate, HM Prison Leeds, UK

James HEYES Governor, HM Prison Swansea, UK

Peter HODGSON Principal Officer, HM Prison Service, UK

Mr and Mrs HOOK

Jean HOWROYD Barrister, UK

Kevin HUNTER Hospital Senior Officer, HM Prison Armley, UK

*Robin ILBERT Senior Medical Officer, Prison Medical Service, UK

William JACKSON Senior Probation Officer, HM Remand Centre, Hindley, UK

Francis KEMP Probation Officer, HMYOI and Remand Centre, Glen Parva, UK

Henk KERSTING Lawyer, Amsterdam, Netherlands

Irene KEW Administrative Officer, Medical Directorate, Prison Service, UK

Yasmin KHAN Legal Administration Officer, Commission for Racial Equality, UK

John KIRBY Hospital Senior Officer, HM Prison Wormwood Scrubs, UK

John KLAUS Director of Operations, Correctional Services, Canada

*Roel KLEINJAN Head, Dept of Policy and Planning, Prison Service, Netherlands

Helen KRARUP Research Associate, Institute of Criminology, Cambridge, UK

Luigi LAURIOLA Diplomatic Advisor, Ministry of Justice, Italy

Michael LENEGHAN Clinical Psychologist, Adolescent Psychology Unit, Belfast, Northern Ireland, UK

*Alison LIEBLING Research Associate, Institute of Criminology, Cambridge, UK

Ronny LIHAWA Chief of Secretariat of National Criminal Bureau/Interpol, Indonesia

Charles LLOYD Senior Research Officer, Home Office Research and Planning Unit, UK

W.J. MACGOWAN Governor, HM Prison Lincoln, UK

Horace MAYNARD Hospital Senior Officer, HM Prison Brixton, UK

Bryan MCCALLEY Head of Activities and Services, HMYOI Huntercombe, UK

Charles MCILWRICK MBE Member, Joint Central Committee, Police Federation, UK

Prasert MEKNAMEE Deputy General, Department of Corrections, Bangkok, Thailand

David MILLS

Margaret MILLS

Robert MITCHELL Prison Medical Officer, HM Prison Frankland, UK

Doughlas MOON Civil Servant (Prison Department) HM Prison Wormwood Scrubs, UK

*Rod MORGAN Professor of Criminal Justice, University of Bristol, UK

Ronald MORGAN College Co-ordinator, Scottish Prison Service College, Falkirk, UK

David NEAL Civil Servant, Home Office Prison Department, UK

Tim NEWELL Governor, HM Prison Winchester, UK

William NEWELL Principal Officer Tutor, Prison Service College, Millisle, UK

Bryan O'BRIEN Civil Servant, Prisons Division, Department of Justice, Dublin, Eire

*Paul O'MAHONY Research Psychologist, Dept. of Justice, Dublin, Eire

Lily OJO Director, Prison Service, Ministry of Internal Affairs, Nigeria

*Simon PAGE Acting Senior Probation Officer, West Yorkshire Probation Service UK

Alexander PEDEN Scottish Prison Service College, Falkirk, UK

*Louise PIROUET Co-ordinator, Charter '87, UK

David REYNOLDS Senior Prison Officer, HM Prison Manchester, UK

Bron ROBERTS Probation Officer, National Association of Probation Officers Campaigning Committee, UK

William ROBERTSON Hospital Prison Officer, HM Prison Dartmoor, UK

*Joseph ROWAN Correctional Consultant, Juvenile and Criminal Justice International, USA

Angela RUMBOLD Minister of State, Home Office, UK

Georgette SCHALLER Institute of Legal Medicine, Geneva, Switzerland

Patric SCRIVEN Governor (Prison Governor's Association), HMYOI Onley, UK

David SEED Suicide Prevention Officer, Prison Service College Newbold Revel, UK

Judith SERRARENS Netherlands

K. SHAW Probation Officer, HM Prison Manchester, UK

Graham SMITH Governor (Trainer) Prison Service College Wakefield, UK

Helen SMITH Senior Probation Officer, HM Prison Armley, UK

John SMITH Medical Officer, HM Prison Lewes, UK

Julian SMITH Medical Officer, HM Prison Lewes, UK

Patrick SMYTH Priest, Irish Commission for Prisoners Overseas

Veerapra Fillia SOMASUNDARAM Senior Prison Medical Officer, HM Prison Brixton, UK

Alex TATE Senior Probation Officer, Southwark Crown Court, UK

George TAYLOR Governor, HM Prison Dumfries, UK

Remi TOMASZEWSKI Prison Department, Fresnes, France

*Stephen TUMIM HM Chief Inspector of Prisons, UK

*John URE Director, Programme Development Branch, New South Wales Police Service, Australia

Rikki VAFIDIS Clerk, Penal Affairs Committee, Quaker Department of Social Responsibility, UK

Margaret WALL Vice-Chair, Board of Visitors, HM Prison Wandsworth, UK

*Tony WARD Ex-Director, Inquest; Researcher, Leicester Polytechnic, UK

Jack WILLIAMS Prisons Consultant, Group 4, UK

Stephen WHITTLE Manchester, UK

*Rosemary WOOL Director, Prison Medical Service, UK

Lyton ZGAMBO MPhil Student, York University; Lecturer at UNZA, Zambia